D1255980

The Obsolete Necessity

America in Utopian Writings, 1888-1900

by Kenneth M. Roemer

THE KENT STATE UNIVERSITY PRESS

ISBN 0-87338-178-5

Library of Congress Catalog Card Number 75-17279

Manufactured in the United States of America

Designed by Harold M. Stevens

Library of Congress Cataloging in Publication Data

Roemer, Kenneth M, 1945-

  The obsolete necessity.

  Bibliography: p.

  Includes index.

  1. Utopias. 2. Utopias in literature. 3. American fiction—History and criticism.
I. Title.

HX806.R56   335'.02   75-17279
ISBN 0-87338-178-5

Dedicated to My Best Teachers

Including My Parents, My Wife, and My Children

Contents

List of Tables and Illustrations

Tables

Plates

Preface

Misshelved, yellowed with bent and broken corners, lost—but most of all forgotten. Why disturb them? Why exhume an outpouring of American utopian visions over a half-century old?

To answer these questions I shall try to define the nature of this book. It is not a literary study. True, I stress the importance of certain settings, character types, plot elements, conventions, and images, but those interested in literary analyses should turn to Part 2 of J.O. Bailey's *Pilgrims Through Space and Time* or to several of the dissertations described in the secondary source listings for more detailed literary surveys. Nor is this book a social history of actual utopian communities. By the late nineteenth century the golden era of American utopian settlements had passed; most idealists were writing or organizing, not settling. Of course, utopian communes still existed, and studies of these experiments are valuable. But the utopian writings, especially popular works such as Edward Bellamy's *Looking Backward,* had a greater impact on the late nineteenth and twentieth centuries. Furthermore, the utopian authors were not restrained by the nagging, day-to-day problems of founding communities. Therefore they could let their imaginations roam beyond the limits of present realities where they often revealed their most fundamental hopes and fears about the past, present, and future.

Neither a literary nor a social history, *The Obsolete Necessity* is primarily an attempt to examine 160 American fictional and nonfictional utopian, anti-utopian, and partially utopian works with three goals in mind. First, I want to make the utopian authors' ideas and attitudes more accessible to scholars and nonscholars whose interests include utopian speculation. This is the major function of the annotated bibliographies, the content analyses, and the summaries of plots and proposals. The increase in seminars, conferences, courses, dissertations, and articles on utopian literature, the tremendous popularity of science fiction and the activities of the newly established Science Fiction Research Association, the Arno Press reprints of 41 American utopian works, and the general tendency towards a re-evaluation of American ideals all suggest the need for greater accessibility to this relatively untilled field of Americana.

My second goal is to evaluate the relevancy of specific utopian reforms and utopian speculation in general. The utopian authors advocated numerous reforms relating to problems all too familiar to us—problems such as economic slumps, technological unemployment, social inequality, pollution, sex discrimination (both male and female), corruption in government, and the apparent irrelevancy of school curricula and religious creeds. Possibly some of the authors' solutions to these problems may be helpful to us. And this possibility leads to other broader questions. Can utopian speculation serve any useful purpose today? Or does it simply foster unrealistic expectations, or worse, lead us down the paths imagined by Orwell and Huxley?

My third and primary goal is to see what the utopian works can tell us about American culture, past and present. Most of the authors came from an important socio-economic group—the middle and upper-middle classes. Hence their utopias may reflect how this group reacted to the rapidly changing world of late nineteenth-century America, which of course means that we would also gain insights into that turbulent era. A second advantage to studying American utopian works published between 1888 and 1900 is that often their visions of ideality were closely tied to present realities. Thus analyses of these parallel presents, especially attempts to delineate which parts of the present were kept and which discarded, offer provocative hints about which elements of American culture were most cherished during the late nineteenth century. Another interesting characteristic of this literature is suggested by the many Nationalist Clubs inspired by Bellamy's immensely popular *Looking Backward* and the fact that many of the utopian authors were political activists or reform journalists. This demonstrates that the outburst of utopian works was more than a literary vogue. It spilled over into concrete reform activities. Therefore, the utopian proposals may illuminate the nature of American reform movements in general. Finally, since utopianism has been such a persistent mode of self-definition in America and since utopian fiction forces authors to examine multitudes of topics ranging from abstract principles to the minutiae of daily living, the utopian works may help us to understand the American Dream or Experience or Character or Style—the exact term depending upon which student of American culture is trying to answer Crèvecoeur's old question, "What is an American?" Or at least the utopias envisioned may suggest the limits of our ability to answer this question.

"May reflect," "may illuminate," "may help," "may suggest"—certainly I cannot claim that one collection of books published during a twelve-year period will reveal all there is to know about the middle and upper-middle classes during the late nineteenth century, American reform movements, and the American Character. The brief discussion of methodological problems in Chapter 1 should make this clear. Nevertheless, the utopian works examined represent more than the ravings of wild-eyed dreamers or the boring sermons of amateur economists. If handled carefully, they offer insights into the hopes and fears of past and present Americans, since many of the attitudes expressed by the authors were shared by their contemporaries and are still with us today.

A few words about terminology and organization may further clarify the nature of this book. Utopia, outopos, eutopos, dystopia, kakotopia, utopians, utopists, utopographers—the study of imaginary ideal societies is burdened with enough strange-sounding names to convince an interloper to take a course in Greek cognates. I have tried to keep my terms as simple as possible: utopia—hypothetical community, society, or world reflecting a more perfect, alternative way of life; utopians—beings (usually humans) who live in utopia; a utopian work—a piece of literature depicting a particular utopia; a utopian author—a person who writes a utopian work. In the first chapter these definitions will be refined and adapted to late nineteenth-century American utopian literature. Besides simplifying the terminology, I have attempted to organize the study in a logical manner. Chapter 1 suggests the possibilities and limitations of my subject by briefly justifying the periodization and by defining the sample, the authors' backgrounds, and several methodological problems. Chapters 2 through 4 examine the authors' basic assumptions about how America might be transformed into utopia. These prophets were especially concerned with three questions: when will The Change occur?; where will it occur?; and is it possible to change human nature? Chapters 5 through 8 analyze the results of the transformation. I adopt the role of an anthropologist visiting a foreign country: the most frequently discussed cultural areas are surveyed roughly in order of their importance to the authors, and Chapter 8 on the utopian city serves as an overview of the utopian culture. The final chapter expands upon central ideas presented in Chapters 1 through 8; it deals primarily with my second and third goals.

A preface is incomplete unless the author attempts to reveal his or her biases. My views on several recent issues, directly related to problems examined by the utopian authors, should be quite obvious and need not be enumerated here. My belief that an important element in the American temperament is a fundamental ambivalence towards change should also be obvious. But my feelings about utopian speculation may not be as clear. Much of this book is a critique of the limitations of American visions of utopia. These are frightening limitations because they have survived and still influence American beliefs and behavior. My criticisms of the utopian authors should not, however, be interpreted as attacks on utopianism per se. Humane, careful speculation about ideal futures is crucial. Indeed the rate of change in the twentieth century and the accompanying temptation simply to let change determine its destiny have made dreaming about America as utopia more than an idle luxury; it is a necessity.

Many people aided me in the preparation of this book. First I would like to thank Professors Hennig Cohen, Michael Zuckerman, and Wallace E. Davies who supervised my dissertation on utopian literature at the University of Pennsylvania. These same professors offered valuable suggestions for revision for book publication as did the readers and editors of Kent State University Press. Next I would like to thank Professors Murray G. Murphey and Anthony N. B. Garvan, also from Penn, who introduced me to new ways of studying American culture, and Professor Stephan Thernstrom, whose course at Harvard first interested me in American utopianism. Clayton L. Eichelberger and Glenn Negley offered their expert advice about the bibliographies, and my search for obscure utopian works was aided by the library staffs of Duke University, the Library of Congress, the New York Public Library, the University of Pennsylvania, SUNY at Oneonta, and UT Arlington. UT Arlington also awarded me grants to cover the cost of typing the manuscript. Finally, I would like to thank my wife, Micki, for hours of proofreading and valuable criticism.

Several editors of journals listed in the secondary source bibliography have kindly granted permission to reprint revised versions of my articles as sections of this book. Yale University Press allowed me to quote from Roger B. Salomon's *Twain and the Image of History*; McGraw-Hill permitted me to make a long quote from the second edition of Richard Gerber's *Utopian Fantasy*; and the authors or the graduate schools of the dissertations described in the bibliographies have permitted me to make brief quotes or paraphrases.

1

Utopias and Utopian Authors:
Possibilities and Limits

What a conjunction, big with universal blessings: the greatest race, the greatest civilization, the greatest numbers, the greatest wealth, the greatest physical basis for empire!
—the Rev. Josiah Strong, The New Era *(1893)*

We are today confronted by portentous indications in the conditions of American industry, society and politics that this great experiment [America], on which the last hopes of the race depends, is to prove, like all former experiments, a disastrous failure. Let us bear in mind that, if it be a failure, it will be a final failure. There can be no more new worlds to be discovered, no fresh continents to offer virgin fields for new ventures.
—Edward Bellamy, "Letter to the People's Party," The New Nation *(1892)*

"The United States has seldom been realistically evaluated; it has either been fantastically exalted or extravagantly condemned."[1] Early English explorers spun yarns about a new Paradise. Or was it a howling wilderness? John Winthrop had visions of a glorious "City upon a Hill" but warned that the New World might "shame the faces of many of God's worthy servants." Even today we boast of our Great Society and our worldwide moral leadership while bemoaning the failure of our social programs, the spectres of Vietnam and Watergate, and gloomy economic forecasts.

Similar ambivalent attitudes have permeated much of our religious and political rhetoric, our economic expectations, our imaginative literature, the justifications for our utopian settlements, and even our paintings and songs. Recently scholars, notably Michael Kammen, have examined several aspects of this contradictory mode of self-definition, but one fascinating offshoot of our penchant for paradox has not received the attention it deserves.[2]

Between 1888, the publication date of Edward Bellamy's *Looking Backward,* and 1900 there was a tremendous outpouring of utopian literature in America. Like most ancient and modern utopian works, these utopian novels and treatises were built around implicit and explicit contrasts and contradictions: contrasts between what America had been, was, and would be; contradictions between the "good" and "evil" in the present. Thus, glimpses of ideal civilizations were juxtaposed with nightmarish visions of poverty, revolution, and wasteland skylines. (See Plates 2 and 3.) This characteristic makes the utopian works excellent sources for a case study in the nature and causes of the ambivalent outlooks that pervade American attempts at self-definition.

Two other characteristics that make these utopian works attractive as indices to American attitudes are their popularity and their explicitness. Bellamy's *Looking Backward* was one of the biggest best sellers of the nineteenth century. According to Frank Luther Mott, it was a slow starter; but after inexpensive editions were printed, sales soared. Within the first year 60,000 copies were sold. After another year the figures rose to 213,988; sometimes over 1,000 copies were bought on a single day. By March 1890 *The Nationalist,* a magazine inspired by the novel, advertised that 310,000 copies of *Looking Backward* were in print. *The Nationalist* itself boasted a circulation of 69,000 as early as December 1889.[3] The entire June 1890 issue of *Overland Monthly* was devoted to responses to Bellamy, and one unpublished study estimates that 11 magazines besides *The Nationalist* and *The New Nation* (edited by Bellamy) were reactions to *Looking Backward.*[4] Another impressive, though seldom noted, indication of the novel's popularity is a survey of "all the important libraries in the United States" described by the critic Hamilton W. Mabie in 1893. Each library was asked to compile a list of the 150 "most popular works of fiction" in circulation. As early as 1893 *Looking Backward* was included on 44% of the lists and was ranked 44th in a cumulative listing of 173 popular works. Although this ranking placed it behind Dickens's *David Copperfield* and Scott's *Ivanhoe,* in only five years since its publication, *Looking Backward* had surpassed works such as *The Swiss Family Robinson, A Tale of Two Cities, Pilgrim's Progress,* and *Aesop's Fables* in library circulation.[5] During the twentieth century the sales have soared into the millions; it is no wonder that as late as 1935 John Dewey, the philosopher, Charles Beard, the historian, and Edward Weeks, the editor of *Atlantic,* felt that of the books published since 1885 only Marx's *Das Kapital* had done more to shape the thought and action of the world.[6] But *Looking Backward* was not the only popular late nineteenth-century utopian work. Mott includes the utopian, anti-utopian *A Connecticut Yankee in King Arthur's Court* (1889) as a "better seller"; and by 1965 Alice Payne Hackett estimated that the partially utopian *In His Steps* (1897) had reached the 8,065,398 sales mark.[7] Furthermore, the sheer numbers of utopian, anti-utopian, and partially utopian works published from 1888 to 1900 add to the evidence of their popularity. One critic has called this publishing phenomenon "the largest single body of utopian writings in history";[8] a minimum of 160 were published, probably many more. Considering this outburst of literary utopianism and the popularity of Bellamy, it may not be an exaggeration to say that "for a decade the utopian novel was perhaps the most widely read type of literature in America."[9]

This tremendous popularity invites speculation about beliefs shared by the authors and their contemporaries, and it also insured that readers' reactions would be preserved for posterity. Many reviews appeared in "radical" and "reform" journals such as *The Nationalist, The New Nation, Arena,* and *Forum* as well as in "respectable" magazines such as *Atlantic* and the Boston *Literary World.* Moreover, several works inspired readers to establish actual communities or to organize reform groups—for example, Majority Rule Clubs, the New Era Union, and, of course, the Nationalist Clubs. Everett Mac Nair estimates that by the early 1890s, over 160 Nationalist Clubs spanned America from New York to California. This movement was short lived; but it did push legislation in several states, especially Massachusetts, and it influenced both the Populists and the Democrats.[10]

Almost as important as this record of popularity and influence left to students of American civilization is the painful explicitness of most of the utopian works. Numerous prefaces, afterwords, and articles (e.g., Bellamy's "How I Came to Write 'Looking Backward'" essays) stressed that the fictional form was only a sugarcoating for the authors' realistic blueprints for the future. In part, this practical utopianism was a reflection of the traditional American assumption that serious literature should be didactic—an expression of the authors' faith in the power of the written word to change behavior. (*Looking Backward* and *Uncle Tom's Cabin* were often used to support this faith.) The inexperience of most of the authors as novelists also may explain the literal-mindedness of the books. In any case, this characteristic seems to make the problem of using utopian works as indices simpler than the difficulties facing scholars attempting to use complex novels such as *Moby-Dick* to gain insights into American culture.

Nevertheless, there are obvious limitations to using late nineteenth-century utopian works as indices to American attitudes. When the questions anthropologists, social scientists, and historians are supposed to ask about their data are applied to these "cultural artifacts," they reveal that this seemingly safe and provocative undertaking is plagued by at least four problems: What are the justifications for the periodization? How is the sample defined? How representative are the opinions expressed by the authors? How does one weigh the evidence? Such questions rarely inspire the liveliest reading material, so I will make my answers as brief as possible. But in spite of their brevity, attempts to respond to these four methodological problems are crucial to an understanding of this book and most other genre or "formula" fiction studies; they will also help to delineate who wrote utopian works, why they wrote them when they did, and why they were received so enthusiastically.[11]

Utopian literature has been written during all periods of American history, from John Winthrop's colonial city upon a hill to the inner cities of consciousness envisioned by Charles Reich. Vernon Louis Parrington, Jr. lists 20 utopian works published before 1714, Joel Nydahl notes 17 between 1715 and 1865, Robert L. Shurter surveys 14 between 1866 and 1887, Charles J. Rooney, Jr. utilized Lisle A. Rose's bibliographies to uncover 33 between 1901 and 1917, Parrington, Jr. mentions 11 between 1918 and 1947, and Frederick Earl Pratter defines a large body of modern "social science fiction," though he admits that utopian fiction declined after the turn of the century.[12] These figures demonstrate that the period 1888 to 1900 had no monopoly on American utopian literature; it is especially evident that the decline since 1900 was gradual. Nevertheless, there is general agreement that this twelve-year period represents the heyday of American utopian novels and treatises; their popularity, numbers, and influence attest to that.

Still, the statistics raise more questions than they answer. Why the sudden upsurge of literary utopianism during the late nineteenth century? Why 1888? Why did most of the authors prefer novels or romances to treatises? Why the decline in utopian speculation during the twentieth century?

As Lewis Mumford, Joyce Hertzler, and almost every student of utopian thought agree, utopian literature thrives during turbulent transition periods; and most historians, including Henry Steele Commager, describe the late nineteenth century as such a period in American history. Millions of Americans were confused and distressed by the panic of 1873, the ups and downs of the 1880s, and the crash of 1893. The numerous strikes and the confrontations at Haymarket Square, Pullman, and Homestead terrified workers and employers. The unequal distribution of wealth (by 1896 seven-eighths of the wealth was owned by one-eighth of the population, and 1% of that one-eighth owned more than the other 99%) heightened tensions between the haves and the have-nots.[13] White, native Americans feared the influx of blacks from the South and the shiploads of immigrants from southeastern Europe. The disappearance of accessible, cheap, fertile land accompanied by rapid urbanization and increased technological advancements threatened frontier and agrarian world views and perplexed Americans with the phenomenon of "progress and poverty." Even the most sacred retreats, religion and the family, were assailed. John Fiske's popular lectures, the sermons of devout but troubled ministers, and articles in *Arena, Forum, Atlantic, Harper's,* and *Century* were exposing apparent conflicts between religion and science; and divorce rates were rising, which to many signaled the collapse of civilization. Given this cluster of circumstances, it is more than probable that many late nineteenth-century Americans suffered from "future shock" long before Alvin Toffler popularized the term, and it is not surprising that recent scholarship has rediscovered the neurotic woman and uptight businessman of the seventies, eighties, and "Gay Nineties." At certain periods of their lives many of these Americans, like Bellamy's narrator Julian West, must have felt that they had been thrown suddenly and violently into a new and confusing world where

> all had broken loose, habits of feelings, associations of thought, ideas of persons and things, all had dissolved and lost coherence and were seething together in apparently irretrievable chaos. There were no rallying points, nothing was left stable.[14]

During such periods of cultural crisis, authors might be expected to turn to a form of expression that not only offered escape but also supplied reassuring guidelines for adapting to the future, guidelines that the traditional sources of socialization—parents, school teachers, and ministers—might not be able to provide. Therefore, most students of American utopianism routinely point to the turmoil of the late nineteenth century as the primary explanation for the explosion of utopian writing. This theory is logical, but it obscures the ambivalent nature of the utopian authors' reaction to their era. If they were only disturbed by the late nineteenth century, why weren't their utopias purely escapist prophesies? Why were their visions so closely tied to the present they despised?

The answer is found in their ambivalent attitude towards their times. Yes, they were distraught, but they were also enthralled by their Age of Energy and Age of Reform, to borrow Howard Mumford Jones's and Richard Hofstadter's terms. Machines threatened the agrarian world view and chained children to factory life, but they also held the promise of less drudgery and more inexpensive goods for farmhand and factory worker alike. Cities were dirty and crime-ridden, but they were also exciting—fortunes could be made in the city and a whole world of music, art, and theater were close at hand. Furthermore, there were indications that many old and new reform battalions were preparing for a full-scale onslaught against the evils of the era. Municipal leagues and grass-roots Populists were gaining momentum; purity crusaders attacked prostitution; powerful temperance groups assailed the triumvirate of alcohol manufacturer, saloon keeper, and politician: it seemed as if there were a cleanup campaign raging against every speck of dastardliness in sight. If only some unifying vision could unite these diverse elements, then the dynamic, idealistic spirit of the age would thrive while the chaos and evil would wither and die.

This was precisely the function the utopian authors hoped their works would perform. Utopian projections or formulas necessitate an overall view of an alternate culture. Moreover, utopian speculation also allows an author to preserve what he likes about the present—thus offering a sense of continuity—while discarding what confuses or frightens him—thus offering a hopeful introduction to a new world. Therefore, in the best of all worlds, the utopian author could have his cake and eat it. Yet one of the most striking characteristics of late nineteenth-century American utopian literature is that the utopias envisioned often represent schizoid clashes between fears and hopes rather than true resolutions. These utopian works were mirrors, not cures: they reflected more than they solved.

The pessimistic optimism of the late nineteenth century helps to explain why utopian literature flourished during this period, but it doesn't explain why the outpouring began in 1888, nor the preference for fiction. Both the date and the form of expression, however, are understandable. 1888 was the year *Looking Backward* was published. Its popularity inspired numerous utopian and anti-utopian novels; authors even borrowed Bellamy's title, setting, and characters as indicated by such titles as *Looking Ahead, Looking Beyond, Looking Within, Looking Forward, Looking Further Forward, Looking Further Backward, A.D. 2000, One of "Berrian's" Novels,* and *Young West.* Other reformers, like Archibald McCowan, simply dedicated their novels to "THE AUTHOR OF 'LOOKING BACKWARD.'" Still, the preference for novels and romances was not entirely the result of *Looking Backward*'s popularity. As Barbara C. Quissell, Virgil L. Lokke, and Jean Pfaelzer have pointed out, the utopian works were influenced by the literary traditions of the domestic, sentimental romance, the popular, sentimental reform novel and the "oral conventions of the pulpit, the lecture platform, and the stage."[15] The sentimental utopian novel packed with sermons, speeches, and dialogues seemed to be the ideal means of reaching a large audience since it "enabled readers to experience what would otherwise be strange and incomprehensible social, political, and economic theories in a context that was familiar and reassuring."[16]

But the familiar can become too familiar. As early as 1890 a reviewer for *The Literary World* complained that "books on the twentieth or twenty-first century are getting to be so numerous that the whole subject will soon be a deadly bore." This solo complaint grew into a chorus of criticism during the 1890s and helps to explain the gradual but decisive decline of utopian works by the turn of the century.[17] Fragmentation and absorption also robbed the utopian literary-reform movement of its momentum. For example, it wasn't long before feuds erupted between the theoretical and activist factions of the Boston Nationalist Clubs. Such divisions soon plagued Bellamy and Nationalist Clubs across the country; and Bellamy's decision to start an activist magazine, *The New Nation,* instead of supporting the more theoretical *Nationalist,* made the fragmentation of his movement painfully clear. Later, what was left of the Nationalists suffered the fate of the Populists. In *The New Nation* Bellamy advocated Populist reforms, and representatives from Nationalist Clubs attended Populist conventions where, according to Mac Nair, they exercised some influence.[18] But the Nationalist reforms were eventually absorbed and overshadowed by Populist concerns, which were in turn obscured by the Free Silver panacea that dominated Bryan's Populist-Democratic campaign, which in turn failed. Bryan's defeat and the return of relative prosperity during the closing years of the century offer a final explanation for the decline of literary utopianism. Like John Winthrop's vision of a city on a hill, the authors' utopias were predictive: if Americans behaved the way the authors advised, America would become utopia; if they didn't, there would be a catastrophic plunge back into the Dark Ages. Well, Nationalism collapsed, McKinley was elected, the rich got richer, and no lightning bolts fell. Instead prosperity returned, we had a "glorious little war," and the Progressives ignored the utopian authors' concept of multidimensional change in favor of piecemeal reform. In other words, the utopian authors made themselves vulnerable by making explicit, short-range predictions. Initially these predictions helped them gain a reading audience. But when the short-range prophesies were deemed inaccurate, the utopian authors suffered a dual setback: their predictions were ridiculed and their long-range ideals were ignored.

As the twentieth century has progressed, the outlook of the nineteenth-century utopian authors seems to have been disproved in another, more terrifying way. Because they hoped to bring order out of chaos, these reformers often advocated centralized governments and economies supported by advanced technologies. Nazism and Stalinism have demonstrated the horrible potentialities of this combination when carried to extremes.

Therefore, the popular form of future gazing became the anti-utopia as popularized by George Orwell and Aldous Huxley. Even the modern social science fiction and the inner utopian visions of Herbert Marcuse, Norman O. Brown, and Charles Reich are in part negative reactions to the nineteenth-century concept of utopia. Much of this criticism is unfair since it is usually based on misunderstandings and oversimplifications of late nineteenth-century American utopias. But few writers or readers have the time, interest, or patience to read the scores of utopian works published between 1888 and 1900. Hence the utopian authors will probably continue to be strawmen for modern writers, and it is unlikely that we will witness another golden era of old-fashioned utopian fiction in the near future.

Determining golden eras and the probable reasons for their existence are important first steps in studies of particular types of writing, painting, music, or even political and religious styles. But these steps don't necessarily solve the problem of which examples to survey, especially when dealing with vague categories such as "utopian" literature. Since most of the bibliographies published before my own listed about fifty works published between 1888 and 1900, initially it seemed possible to read "all" the utopian material.[19] Then too, the sample could be held to a manageable size by focusing on fictional works offering detailed descriptions of ideal American societies. But sticking religiously to these boundaries would have meant the exclusion of anti-utopian novels and treatises that often contained sophisticated criticisms of specific utopian ideas and implied alternative visions of ideality. Popular semi-utopian novels, such as Charles M. Sheldon's *In His Steps,* that dramatize the growing acceptance of utopian principles but not their ultimate fruition, would also have to be omitted as would complex novels such as Mark Twain's *A Connecticut Yankee in King Arthur's Court,* which is utopian and anti-utopian. Finally, what about the nonfiction, book-length utopian works? Since even the authors admitted that fictional elements were often mere trappings, it seems quite arbitrary to exclude nonfictional forecasts. A sample that excluded these various types of utopian expression would be clearly defined and manageable. But would it be a true reflection of late nineteenth-century American utopianism? It is very doubtful. Therefore, I decided not to omit anti-utopian, partially utopian, and nonfictional utopian works. Such works, along with several short stories, are, however, marked appropriately in the annotated bibliography.

Unfortunately, this decision led to another problem. It wasn't long before the list swelled to over 150 titles, almost three times the length of previously published bibliographies for 1888 to 1900. But considering the hundreds of social, political, economic, religious, and science-fiction novels published during this period and the numerous short utopian pieces appearing in the periodicals, it is clear that the sample is not complete and probably never will be.

Still, despite the diversity and the assumed incompleteness of the sample, the primary sample of 160 works (related novels and tracts are mentioned in the annotations; the overall total is over 200 titles) constitutes a definable group, since most of the books suggest a concept of a utopian work that might best be formulated as a book that predicts a drastic improvement that (1) grows out of a dynamic but potentially catastrophic present and (2) profoundly affects the individual's total environment.

Attempting to uncover the backgrounds and biases of the 154 authors is another major problem facing the student of late nineteenth-century utopian literature. A few well-known individuals did contribute to the genre, for example, Mark Twain, William Dean Howells, Edward Bellamy, Harold Frederic, Joaquin Miller, the Reverend Charles M. Sheldon, the economist Laurence Gronlund, "the Kansas fire eater" Mary Elizabeth Lease, John Jacob Astor, and King Camp Gillette of safety-razor fame. But most of the authors were unknowns who sometimes courted obscurity by using pseudonyms such as Anon Moore, Myself and Another, Two Women of the West, Untrammeled Free-thinker, and Omen Nemo. One reaction to the problem of sketching a profile of these forgotten writers has been simply to assume that they were "average" Americans; another concedes that "information is too incomplete to make any sweeping generalities."[20] Although the second opinion is much closer to the truth, a careful examination of nineteenth- and twentieth-century biographical reference works, comparisons with 1890 census reports, and a random sample of 100 late nineteenth-century American authors taken from a listing of 26,000 writers reveal some definite trends that should help to determine how representative the utopian authors were.[21]

In two respects the utopian authors were representative. Except for Southern writers, Table 1 demonstrates that their geographical distribution was a much closer approximation of the population distribution in 1890 than was the distribution of the "typical" author as defined by the random sample.[22] The other representative characteristic that the authors' lives reflected was the migration from the country to the city. Of the 65 authors for whom relevant information is available, 52 (80%) moved from rural or small town environments to large urban centers such as New York, Boston, or Chicago. The locations of the authors when they wrote their utopian works were available for 35 more writers; 29 (83%) lived in large cities. Thus, even though the evidence is incomplete, the move to the city is obvious.

The geographical distribution and flight from the country support Jay Martin's contention that "in some senses, the utopian novel became for a

TABLE 1

	Utopian Authors	Random Sample	Population 1890
Northeast & Mid-Atlantic	48%	74%	30%
Midwest	34%	13%	34%
South	5%	9%	24%
West	13%	4%	12%

brief period the true National Novel."[23] An occupational survey also reveals that the utopian authors were more representative than the authors from the random sample. For instance, their occupational backgrounds were more diversified than the occupational backgrounds of the random sample, which were more heavily weighted towards traditional professions (*random sample*: clergy, 18%; lawyers, 13%; physicians, 15%; teachers, 13%; *utopian authors*: clergy, about 13%; lawyers, about 5%; physicians, about 4%; teachers, about 4%). By contrast the utopian authors included many who either modified traditional professions and became social-gospel ministers and reform lawyers, or they chose "newer" professions: about 15% were businessmen, inventors, engineers, or scientists; about 14% described themselves as political reformers; and at least 25%, the largest concentration, were journalists (*random sample*: about 7%, 5%, and 5%, respectively).[24]

The utopian authors, moreover, included some occupational black sheep as well as examples of the economic extremes of progress and poverty. Chauncey Thomas was a carriage builder, Milton Ramsey was a carpenter, and Walter McDougall was a cartoonist. But according to a contemporary rival from Boston, Thomas was not only very "successful," he was "the one man in the business whom we all acknowledged to be our superior." He also registered twenty patented improvements on carriages and wrote an article on the development of the American carriage industry for Chauncey Depew's *One Hundred Years of American Commerce*. Ramsey was a Minnesota carpenter who wrote several adventure and science-fiction novels; and McDougall was not just a cartoonist, according to *The* [Washington] *Evening Star,* he was the "Dean of American Cartoonists." He was also an experienced writer and a personal friend of Theodore Roosevelt. As for the extremes of the economic spectrum: John Jacob Astor, who wrote a quasi-utopian, science-fiction novel, was one of the wealthiest men in the world; Mary Elizabeth Lease of "raise less corn and more hell" fame knew what it was to be "dirt poor"; and Bradford Peck, a successful Maine department store owner, could have been created by Horatio Alger.[25]

But despite the trend away from traditional professions, the occupational and economic diversity, and evidence that as many as one-half of the authors experienced some financial difficulties during their lives, available occupational information suggests that a clear majority of the utopian authors were middle- and upper-middle-class professionals. Educational and family data reflect a similar profile. During the academic year of 1891–1892, less than 1% of the population were attending college, and estimates indicate that only 28% of the business elite and 29% of the national leaders had college degrees.[26] By comparison, about 72% of the utopian authors went to college, and at least 18 authors held advanced degrees.[27] Since college degrees usually meant "good" homes, it is not surprising to find that most of the authors were the scions of respected families whose ancestors often helped found their home towns. For instance, John Bachelder and Benjamin O. Flower were descended from the founding fathers of their hometowns in New York and Illinois. Ralph Albertson's ancestors were among the first Dutch settlers in New Amsterdam; Mary Agnes Tinckner's ancestors came over on the Mayflower; and Will N. Harben could claim kinship with Daniel Boone!

The religions, nationalities, races, sexes, and ages of the authors also suggest how unrepresentative they were of the diversity of late nineteenth-century America. With few exceptions they were Protestant, native American, white, male, and middle-aged (about fifty-years old in 1894). Even some of the exceptions were not quite exceptional. The well-known Populist Ignatius Donnelly, for instance, was born a Catholic, but he was not devout and drifted towards spiritualism in later life.[28] The only truly notable exceptions were three successful Jewish immigrants—Rabbi Solomon Schindler, Rabbi Henry Pereira Mendes, and David Lubin—one respected black minister, Dr. Sutton E. Griggs, and a handful of women (14).

Thus it would be foolish to assume that the opinions expressed by the utopian authors represented the beliefs of the "average" American. But ironically, this limitation may make the study of late nineteenth-century utopian literature particularly revealing for two reasons. First, for the past two decades scholars such as Richard Hofstadter, Samuel P. Hays, and Robert Wiebe have been uncovering the importance of middle- and upper-middle-class professionals and businessmen to the Populist, Progressive, and New Deal reform activities. Since the utopian authors seem to fit into this category including both "overshadowed" professionals, to borrow Hofstadter's term, and the ones who were doing the overshadowing, an analysis of the utopian attitudes may offer new insights into the ideas and motivations of this important socio-economic group of reformers. Second, the biographical backgrounds of the authors almost dictate a body of literature saturated with tensions and contradictions. Here we have a group of writers whose reform activities and willingness to be associated with a "radical" form of expression (which had been branded by reviewers as "lunatic" literature and "rose-water mush"),[29] suggest that they were sincerely concerned about the lower classes and sincerely believed fundamental changes were necessary. And yet, most of the utopian authors were born and raised before the Civil War and were thoroughly confused, even frightened, by the changes of the late nineteenth century. Could such a group create a truly dynamic vision of an ideal America that would satisfy or even realistically include immigrants, blacks, Indians, and other people outside their heritage? Whatever the answer to this question is, one thing is clear: the tensions and contradictions inherent in the lives and attitudes of the utopian authors should make their works excellent sources for the study of ambivalent attitudes about America's past, present, and future.

The problems of periodization, sampling, and determining the authors' biases are complex, but the most frustrating difficulty facing the student of late nineteenth-century utopian literature is weighing the evidence. One approach is to arbitrarily assign each book equal weight. Then content analyses can be used to reveal the frequencies of different attitudes on specific issues and values. Indeed, in an unpublished dissertation, Charles J. Rooney, Jr. has done this with a clearly defined sample of 106 utopian works published between 1865 and 1917.[30] But in spite of the satisfying concrete results such studies yield, when they are used as the sole means of analyzing a body of literature as diverse as the utopian works, their value is highly debatable. Several novels were very popular; some were poor sellers. Many were ponderous fictionalized treatises; a few were lighthearted satires. The majority were explicit, but several important works were ambiguous and complex. This diversity suggests that it is misleading to assign an equal value to each book since the different intents and talents of the authors and the varying popularity of the works may give the same words, arguments, and concepts very different meanings, differences that most content analyses will obscure.

Possibly a better approach is to emphasize the popular works in the sample, an attractive alternative since it invites speculation about attitudes shared by the authors and their contemporaries. But again there are problems. Bellamy's *Looking Backward* was immensely popular, but even if we add to the number of buyers a vague estimate of those who read or heard about the book, the resulting figure would be a small and probably unrepresentative segment of the entire population. Moreover, even though we have abundant evidence of readers' reactions to *Looking Backward,* it is impossible to determine precisely which attitudes were shared by Bellamy and his readers beyond the fact that they were both disturbed by the status quo of the late nineteenth century. For example, the members of the first Nationalist

Club in Boston claimed that Bellamy articulated their views. The Club included Boston reform editors, retired generals infatuated with the Industrial Army, Theosophists, Christian Socialists such as Howells, feminists, and self-proclaimed "cultural radicals," i.e., the members projected their diverse causes into the novel and then used it as a vehicle to publicize their views, which were not necessarily Bellamy's views. On the other hand, critics screamed about a book fraught with danger, a book reflecting the beliefs of a wild-eyed minority. And yet, the compilers of the Sweet Home Family Soap Album included *Looking Backward* in a select list of works— the "celebrants of traditional American values."[31] Who shared what with whom?

One other option is to follow the traditional humanistic method of assuming that the "best" works offer the most revealing insights into the attitudes of the authors' contemporaries. One advantage of this approach is that students of American literature and culture are familiar with utopian works by writers such as Twain, Howells, and Bellamy; therefore, it is easier to communicate arguments based primarily on these works than to attempt to synthesize and describe the spectrum of opinions expressed by the "lesser" writers. Furthermore, perceptive authors often use popular ideas and well-known literary conventions to reveal complex tensions beneath the surface of the familiar. Nevertheless, treating the authors of complex, respected works as "superior informants" has come under increasing attack. The almost religious awe of certain Great Works can seduce scholars into believing that the study of a few books can be a magic key, "a short cut around masses of historical data."[32] Needless to say, this can lead to an acute case of academic blindness that distorts objective interpretations of the past.

Giving equal weight to each book, emphasizing the popular novels, and revering the "best" works—three approaches riddled with methodological weaknesses. What's the solution? Probably there is no precise answer, but the most honest approach might be a combination of the three. Therefore, wherever it is possible throughout this study I will delineate the "average," the "popular," and the "most perceptive" viewpoints on the topic under discussion. (The "most perceptive" reactions will not always be represented by the well-known authors, since obscure writers often gave the most sophisticated views on specific aspects of America as utopia.) Besides honesty, another advantage to this multilevel approach is that it should invite speculation as to why all three viewpoints coincide on certain issues and split dramatically on others. In other words, it may help to determine which cultural values the utopian authors were most willing to change and which ones they strove to preserve. Of course, one disadvantage to a multilevel approach is that the conclusions may lack the compelling unity of studies of

American culture based on one interpretive viewpoint. But then again, American culture—past and present—may not be as compellingly unified as we once thought.

2

Time: Puritan History Revisited

*By measure hath He measured the times, and by number hath He
numbered the times, and He doth not move nor stir them, until the said
measure is fulfilled.*
—*Dr. Beverley O. Kinnear,* Impending Judgments *(1892)*

*Our "ship of state" is fast nearing the shoals upon which past civiliza-
tions have stranded, and, unless we put hard down the helm and steer
clear of danger, history will again repeat itself, and the dark, thick,
gloomy pall of ignorance and superstition will once more enshroud our
globe.*
—*Ardrey Rene, "A Glance at the Past and a Vision of the Future,"* The
Nationalist *(1890)*

*. . . we look back to the great Revolution as a . . . second creation of
man.*
—*Edward Bellamy,* Equality *(1897)*

One occupational hazard of being a narrator in a late nineteenth-century
American utopian novel is that soon after awakening or landing in utopia, one
usually meets a garrulous gentleman who is ever-so-willing to divulge his
version of the transformation from an evil, chaotic era to the present state of
bliss. The few narrators who escape this fate stumble upon an ancient volume
that covers the history of the transition period and includes seemingly endless
speeches and sermons. Some authors even blessed their narrators with both
guide and text.

As literary techniques, these surveys of the journey to utopia are less than stimulating, to say the least. But they do suggest important assumptions about how America could be changed into utopia, especially with regard to attitudes about when The Change will occur, where, and how individuals will react to the transformation. The narratives of the transitional period also signal a fundamental shift in the development of utopian speculation. No longer was utopia a nowhere, an imaginary place whose primary function was a critique of an actual society. The critique was still there but the terrors and the accomplishments of nineteenth-century America convinced the authors that utopia was a condition to be achieved; indeed it had to be achieved before it was too late.

J. O. Bailey, and more recently Frederick Earl Pratter, have revealed the variety of specific time settings used by nineteenth-century authors to describe the evolution of this utopian condition.[1] Despite this diversity, however, the American utopian authors did agree upon a frame of reference for the examination of the transition period. The frame was constructed of three implied questions, each one leading to the next: when will The Change occur?; what characteristics make this period ripe for change?; and do these characteristics suggest a theory of history that makes the confusion of the present meaningful in the overall context of the past, present, and future? With several important exceptions, the average, the popular, and the most perceptive authors agreed upon the answers to these questions. They especially agreed upon historical theories that involved dual perspectives of the present and the future—prophesies that implied both the utopian and catastrophic possibilities inherent in what was and what might be.

Thus a survey of the utopian authors' three-step approach to time should help to illuminate their ambivalent attitudes about America. Since there was a general consensus on this element of the journey to utopia, the historical question may also suggest assumptions that were shared by the authors and their contemporaries. Finally, the authors' attempts to make the signs of the future understandable to fellow Americans expose one of their most difficult problems. Like all prophets, they had to base their visions of the future upon contemporary ways of perceiving the past. Even "experts," such as the members of the American Academy of Arts and Sciences' Commission on the Year 2000 convened in 1965 and 1966, find this problem staggering. Hence it is not surprising that these amateur future-gazers assailed twentieth-century phenomena with conceptual tools similar to those used by the Puritans to explain their new world. The result was often a paradoxical view of history that simultaneously championed infinite Progress and longed for a static state, or promised utopia while predicting dystopia.

Several of the utopian authors were very specific about when The Change would occur. During the 1870s, for instance, William Fishbough, an expert on mesmerism, labored over a mammoth volume entitled *The End of Ages; with Forecasts of the approaching Political, Social and Religious Reconstruction of America and the World*. It finally appeared posthumously in the 1890s and contained some amazingly accurate (and lucky) predictions. For example, Fishbough believed that the forces of reform would face a crucial test in 1896, the year of the Bryan-McKinley campaign. As the title of Frank Rosewater's *'96; A Romance of Utopia* (1894) suggests, Fishbough was not the only one who singled out this year. In *Impending Judgments on the Earth* (1892) Dr. Beverley O. Kinnear even got down to months and days: the first phase of the Second Coming would begin in September 1896 and the second phase on March 29, 1899. Most of the utopian authors, however, balked at offering such a definite answer to when The Change would come, but almost all of them agreed that the answer to "when?" was "now." Over and over in their utopian works and in utopian articles in reform magazines the alarm resounded: you are living during a decisive, perhaps the final, transition period.

This warning was most often presented through fictional history or by looking backward from utopias or dystopias. Novels such as F. U. Adams's *President John Smith* (1897), James M. Galloway's *John Harvey* (1897), and J. W. Roberts's anti-utopian *Looking Within* (1893) were detailed historical narratives covering the period immediately preceding the 1890s, focusing on this tumultuous decade and the opening of the twentieth century, and finally looking toward or describing the new civilizations of the twentieth and twenty-first centuries. Other authors narrated the histories of imaginary countries such as Howells's Altruria and Samuel Crocker's island utopia, or other planets such as William Simpson's Mars or Cyrus Cole's Saturn. These fictional histories were usually obvious analogies to American history during the late nineteenth century and suggested the possible glories and trials of the near future. Narratives set mostly in the future pinpointed the transition period by hindsight. During the 1988 battle between the capitalists and the Brotherhood of Destruction, for example, Ignatius Donnelly's hero, Gabriel, is told, "You have arrived on the scene too late. A hundred years ago you might have formed your Brotherhood of Justice and saved society." Similarly, the narrator of *Looking Further Forward* (1890) bemoans the lost opportunity to create "co-partnerships or associations" during the late nineteenth century. Again, in both Bellamy's utopian novels Julian West looks back to the period starting in 1873 and culminating in 1896 as beginning a crucial transition in the peaceful evolution to the marvelous world of 2000 A.D.[2]

Of course, all 154 authors did not agree with Bellamy, who hoped that possibly his generation, and definitely the next, would live in an ideal America.[3] Amos K. Fiske and Charles Curtis Dail described slow evolutions, while Chauncey Thomas, the carriage builder, and Milton Ramsey, the carpenter, set their utopias respectively in the forty-ninth and eightieth centuries. Still, the overwhelming majority of utopian authors, including the popular Bellamy and Sheldon, proclaimed that they were living during a critical period and hoped that their great-grandchildren or possibly even their grandchildren could live in utopia.

By answering the question "when?" with "now," the utopian authors were, in part, attempting to convey a sense of urgency to their readers, a tactic employed by early Puritan divines as well as nineteenth-century Adventists and biblical chronologists such as Yale's professor of military science Charles A. L. Totten. The advantages of this view of the present are obvious: most people like to believe that they are living in an important era, but they often have to be reminded that they must act quickly before the opportunities of the present are lost. True, the emphasis on the 1880s and 1890s made the utopian authors' predictions more vulnerable than the less precise ideal worlds of a Plato or a Sir Thomas More. Hence Michael Harrington's general observation about idealistic visions can be applied to these utopian works: "paradoxically, the utopia must be kept distant in order to be practical."[4] But the late nineteenth century was an important period, a "watershed" era, to borrow Commager's term. Thus it is not surprising that the utopian authors felt that they were living during crucial times. Indeed, in their attempts to pinpoint the characteristics that made the late nineteenth century a transitional era in American history, they frequently singled out two problems that have attracted the attention of modern historians of this period—suffering and confusion.

Except for the few celebrants of the self-made man and the benefits of poverty,[5] these middle- and upper-middle-class authors felt that too many people were suffering from oppression or poverty or both. One result was mounting tensions and frustrations. As Howells's Mr. Homos reveals in his lecture on Altrurian history, the final tension point was reached "when the Accumulation's [the capitalist's] abuse of a certain [money] power became too gross." Bellamy elaborated on this general complaint with statistics. Julian West learns that by 1893 one-half of the nation's wealth was owned by 9% of the population. Publicizing these figures created the "necessary revolutionary temper"; they "were enough to turn the very stones into revolutionaries."[6] Similarly, narrators in other utopian works discover that during the late nineteenth century the rich got richer, the poor got poorer, and the middle-classes disappeared. This gap combined with horrid factory and slum conditions, a barrage of specific economic and social injustices, and the

38,303 strikes from 1880 to 1900, all seemed to indicate that the caldron was seething and about to erupt.[7]

Besides suffering caused by oppression and poverty, the utopian authors singled out confusion as the other major symptom of their critical transition period. In effect they said that the "answers" they were taught as children before the Civil War did not explain the experience of the late nineteenth century and that the groping for new answers was agonizing. Thus, both supporters and opponents of Bellamy agreed that the problems of their era inspired a host of contradictory panaceas. The result, according to Bellamy, was "a time of terror and tumult, of confused and purposeless agitation, and a Babel of contradictory clamor." In *The Great Awakening* (1899) Albert A. Merrill's Professor labels the period the "Chaotic Era," and even George Sanders, one of Bellamy's most vociferous critics, admitted that it was a time of "feverish unrest."[8]

The authors perceived confusion from two viewpoints, however. True, it was painful. True, during such a bewildering period, Americans might cling to obsolete beliefs, thus thwarting change. But many, including the Rev. Mr. Josiah Strong and the author of an article appearing in the first issue of *The Nationalist,* saw the brighter side of a dark situation: "Such periods are always characterized by uncertainty and anxiety, by difficult problems and by *great opportunities*"; "there seems to come a crisis, *a moment of opportunity,* which, if taken advantage of, would lead to a new order of social life."[9] (Italics mine.) Possibly the most interesting definition of the opportunities inherent in a confusing era was articulated by a Philadelphia obstetrician, Thomas Stewart Blair, who foreshadowed some of the modern theories of Thomas S. Kuhn:

> the evidence of the senses seems conclusive in favor of the old belief until the continued occurrence of difficulties which it fails to clear up, make it possible for the rival hypothesis to get a hearing.[10]

In other words confusion and rapid change were painful, but it was hoped that these unpleasant aspects of the present would jar Americans enough to make them foresake outdated ideas and listen to the utopian authors. Then confusion would lead to utopia rather than to more confusion and suffering.

This certainly was an optimistic way of perceiving confusion. But for most of the utopian authors it was not enough. They felt they had to go beyond exposés of the suffering and confusion that made their era unusual to develop a general theory of history that would define the late nineteenth century not simply as an important period but as THE FINAL TRANSITION. This reveals a basic weakness in the utopian authors' concept of time. Some of their specific observations about the 1880s and 1890s were certainly perceptive. But when the authors reached out for the new fundamental answers that would make their era truly understandable and meaningful to their contemporaries, they could only revert to a concept of history that had been satirized decades earlier by Herman Melville and expounded as early as 1630 by John Winthrop: "the tendency of each generation to consider its own hour as the beginning of the last scene in the last act of the world drama."[11] They even revived Winthrop's image of all the eyes of the world fixing on America: to quote Sanders, "The whole world seems to have left the destinies of the race with us, and is watching [for] the solution of the great question."[12] The "question" was whether America would survive the suffering and confusion of the present and rise triumphant as the model for all peoples, or fail and herald the downfall of mankind.

Dramatic interpretations of history offer readers the opportunity to view themselves as participants in cosmic crusades, and there aren't many crusades that are as sensational as a choice between the triumph or collapse of humanity. Since the utopian concept of history had roots as old as or older than the early Puritan settlements, the authors were also speaking a language that white, native Americans could comprehend, a language that would offer a sense of continuity, patriotism, and understanding. Therefore, like the conventions of the sentimental reform novel, sermons, lectures, and speeches, the utopian concept of history made the unfamiliar seem familiar and reassuring. Nevertheless, an examination of the authors' general theory of history—including the portrait of the eighties and nineties as Armageddon, the delineation of the differences between Old-World and New-World time, and the descriptions of the ultimate goal of the utopian timetable—should also suggest how the utopian concept of history limited its creators' vision and helped to perpetuate confusion about the nature of American history.

It may seem odd that two of the writers (Donnelly and Lease) examined in this book are also analyzed by Frederic Jaher in *Doubters and Dissenters,* a study of cataclysmic, not utopian thought. Another apparent oddity— Joaquin Miller's *The Building of the City Beautiful* (1893) was preceded by the dystopian *Destruction of Gotham* (1886). Finally, in a letter to Charles Eliot Norton referring to the Altrurian romances, Howells confessed that "all other dreamers of such dreams have had nothing but pleasure in them; I have had touches of nightmares."[13]

To most students of American utopianism these apparent contradictions would indicate nothing more than isolated deviations from the mainstream of American idealism.[14] They would argue that compared to European strands of utopianism and radicalism that predict inevitable class warfare and advocate violent revolutions as remedies, American utopian prophesies seem rather pallid and optimistic. And it is true that the late nineteenth-century

American utopian authors who seemed the most prone towards violence and catastrophism—men such as Ignatius Donnelly or Professor Von Swartwout—were careful to decry lawlessness and violence. Even Twain's Hank Morgan at one time hoped for a "peaceful revolution."[15]

But a close examination of the nature of the transition period reveals that a mixture of utopianism and dystopianism was typical—typical and central to the depiction of the late nineteenth century as Armageddon. *All* the utopian authors examined foresaw the possibility of serious strife during the transition period; over twenty pictured American society teetering in a delicate all-or-nothing crisis; and approximately one-third of the authors actually described outbreaks of violence ranging from local skirmishes to the destruction of America and Europe.

Even the peaceable Bellamy could imagine nightmarish futures. David Ketterer's analyses of coach, pyramid, and iceberg images in *Looking Backward* reveal hints of disaster.[16] Dr. Leete reminds West that many of his contemporaries thought that they were facing "an impending social cataclysm." Bellamy apparently changed his terminology to reflect his fear. In *Looking Backward* the transition was an "evolution"; in *Equality* it became "the great Revolution." And one of the most explicit warnings about the disastrous possibilities of the 1890s was written by Bellamy, our most famous utopian author:

> We are today confronted by portentous indications in the conditions of American industry, society and politics that this great experiment [America], on which the last hopes of the race depends, is to prove, like all former experiments, a disastrous failure. Let us bear in mind that, if it be a failure, it will be a final failure. There can be no more new worlds to be discovered, no fresh continents to offer virgin fields for new ventures.[17]

Of course depicting the present as Armageddon was nothing new to utopian thought.[18] What is significant is that the utopian authors apparently believed that they could best communicate their ideas to the American public by placing the transition period within the context of history as the final, all-or-nothing "act" that would determine the rest of American and world history. This period would either initiate a time when the rich (or socialists) would gain dictatorial powers followed by a bloody revolution and endless eons of chaos and darkness, or a period leading to a drastic and permanent improvement of man and his environment. A particularly fascinating characteristic of the way the authors presented this Armageddon of the late nineteenth century was their conscious or unconscious ability to utilize familiar Christian images as well as current fads to make their prophesies about the final battle of good and evil seem both traditional and modern.

To emphasize the cataclysmic possibilities of the present a few authors envisioned bloody revolutions such as Donnelly's battle of 1988, scenes of mass destruction such as Twain's Battle of the Sand-Belt, or global wars such as Dr. Kinnear's "Armageddon" (he even included a map of the battle-grounds). Most of the authors, however, used a variety of less explicit warnings. They described limited outbreaks of violence, hinted about the possibility of "a terrible era of violence," or gave their works titles and subtitles such as *Armageddon, Law and Order vs. Anarchy and Socialism, The Labor Revolution of 1920, Impending Judgments on the Earth: or, "Who May Abide the Day of His Coming,"* and *The Earthquake*. As the last two titles indicate, they also employed Biblical images of natural catastrophes, especially cyclones, earthquakes, floods, fires, violent storms and plagues. (Several of these acts of divine retribution were pictured in full page illustrations. See Plate 1.) In Walter D. Reynolds's *Mr. Jonnemacher's Machine* (1898) there was even a modernized version of the avenging flood. Embankments collapse around a lake of "aerial liquid," a substance similar to Kurt Vonnegut, Jr.'s ice IX. Thousands of corrupt politicians, dangerous revolutionaries, and innocent citizens are killed in the evil city of Philadelphia.

But by far the most common image of the turbulent and potentially destructive forces culminating during the transition period was the volcano. At least 31 utopian works, including Sheldon's popular *In His Steps* and Donnelly's ambivalent *Caesar's Column,* contain overt volcanic imagery and many others include passages alluding to the tensions of the period as the rumblings beneath or the pent-up subterranean forces. These images usually appeared several times in crucial sections of the narrative to suggest the explosive frustrations of the poor and oppressed or the frightening punishments awaiting the oppressors. (See Plate 1.)

Examples of the former are found in both co-operative and competitive utopian works. In *Caesar's Column,* Gabriel senses the anguish of the laborers (who literally work beneath the ground) and articulates his fears: "I could hear the volcanic explosions." These explosions soon burst like a "terrible volcano" destroying America. In a less violent novel, *John Harvey* (1897), John Galloway describes the tense lull before a threatened revolution as "Vesuvian fires burned beneath this awful quiet, and must result in earthquakes and convulsions." George Sanders mocks radicals and dreamers who "say we are living upon a volcano." Yet three authors who considered themselves critics of collectivist dreamers were all haunted by volcanic imagery:

> Like a volcano in the interior of Mars, the long pent up wrath worked violently in the breast of the enslaved people.
> —Richard C. Michaelis

Imagine a community that has lived for centuries on the fertile slopes of a volcano.
                                                —Arthur Vinton

I [the narrator] felt as if . . . only a slip of solid ground were left between me and
chaos, and that were shaking, as if a volcano were beneath ready to burst forth and
rend it.
                                —J. W. Roberts

Several passages in *Caesar's Column* contain volcanic images suggesting
the other type of warning about the fate of the oppressors and their underlings,
but the most extended use of this kind of volcanic imagery appears in
Alvarado M. Fuller's *A.D. 2000* (1890). A guide informs the narrator that in
1916 an accident at a Pittsburgh explosives plant touched off a chain reaction
of earthquakes and volcanic eruptions. (See Plate 1.) These in turn caused a
flood that completely inundated the Ohio Basin. Fuller more than implies the
identity and intentions of the supervisor of the catastrophe. It was carefully
observed by a "higher Power" and represented a "mighty effort of nature to
overcome the grasping endeavors of man to accumulate wealth. . . ."[19]

Both types of volcanic imagery, like the other predictions of natural
disasters, could have been read as a fulfillment of Biblical prophesy. As Jay
Martin has pointed out, such forecasts about calamities are similar to the
"purposeful and fruitful catastrophe[s]" which, according to *Revelation,*
were to usher in the millennium.[20] There were also well-known nineteenth-
century literary precedents for using volcanic imagery to suggest declines,
ideal worlds, and pent-up tensions: for instance, Edward Bulwer-Lytton's
best seller *The Last Days of Pompeii* (1834), James Fenimore Cooper's
utopian allegory *The Crater* (1848), and Harriet Beecher Stowe's description
of George Harris's temperament as volcanic in *Uncle Tom's Cabin* (1852).
But the utopian authors were also consciously or unconsciously capitalizing
on a late nineteenth-century volcano vogue. The eruption of Vesuvius in
1872 drew worldwide attention. (In the same year Twain incorporated his
long description of Kileuea into *Roughing It.*) Then in 1883 "the extinct
volcano Krakatoa was blown into the sky . . . while fifteen other volcanoes
simultaneously belched forth to keep her company." American interest in
these terrifying events was reflected in serious scientific studies and in
popular science articles. In 1885 the cover of the March 16th *Harper's
Weekly* depicted Vesuvius in action; in 1899 The International Scientific
Series published a full-length study of volcanoes; and in their search for
popular and representative prophetic articles on "Science and Invention"
appearing in American magazines from 1895 to 1905, Ray Brosseau and
Ralph K. Andrist selected "How the World Will End" by Hudson Maxim, an
inventor. The title of the article was printed over an illustration of a volcano,
and Maxim picked volcanoes as his first topic of discussion.[21] Yet another

reflection of the interest in volcanoes was the fact that one author of a partially utopian work, Frona Eunice Colburn, was an expert on America's largest volcano, Mt. Lassen; and one chapter of John Uri Lloyd's bizarre *Etidorhpa* (1895) is entitled "A Lesson on Volcanoes."

Thus, the utopian authors often achieved a compelling blend of Biblical, literary, and popular imagery in their visions of the dark side of the late nineteenth-century Armageddon. They also selected a familiar image to suggest the bright side, the possibility of triumphing over the forces of suffering and confusion in the present. To oppose the hellish images of man-made and natural destruction the utopian authors most often used a powerful Christian symbol, one that would be as easy to understand as floods and volcanoes—the Resurrection.

Christ's suffering, confusion ("My God, my God, why hast thou forsaken me?") and victory became an analogy for the suffering, confusion, and possible triumph of America. For example, when Howells's Mr. Homos describes the darkest hour of the Age of Accumulation, he declares that "the Son of Man must suffer"; and when Mr. Homos and many other narrators reveal the painful and miraculous victory of good during the transition, they use images or phrases recalling the dying Christ and Christ resurrected.[22] On a more personal level the popular Bellamy and Sheldon and the majority of utopian authors argued that the change of heart that would lead to the final defeat of the evils of the present would occur when each individual was willing to "die" and "be born again" to a new life.[23]

The Resurrection images combined with the glimpses of man-made and natural destruction—like Dante's paradise, purgatory, and hell, or Winthrop's city on a hill and Puritan trials—served several functions. Most importantly they helped to make the "ungraspable phantom" of the present graspable.[24] When perceived as a battle of frightful and hopeful images, the suffering and confusion of the present were not senseless; on the contrary, they were divine hints revealing the possible punishments and rewards awaiting God's chosen during the final act of a grand drama.

But the utopian authors wanted to do more than make the present graspable. They wanted further to emphasize the importance of the choices confronting their contemporaries by making the past and future understandable. To do this they placed the Armageddon of the late nineteenth century within the context of two different kinds of time. The centuries before the late nineteenth century were associated with a meaningless cyclical process. If the American public did not heed the warnings of the utopian authors, mankind would continue forever on this treadmill of Old-World time. If Americans listened, however, they could break the cycle and usher in a birth of meaningful, progressive time. Again, this way of perceiving history was nothing new. Early European settlers often perceived their voyages to the New World as an escape from the cruel and senseless repetitions of the past to a glorious new Garden of Eden.[25] The utopian authors evidently believed that a rekindling of these old prejudices about the Old World—an easy task considering the hostility towards the "new immigration" of the 1880s and 1890s—combined with a plea for the fulfillment of the original promise of the New World would help their contemporaries to see the way out of the quagmire of the present.

Three illustrations found in two obscure works offer good introductions to the utopian authors' concept of Old-World time. The frontispiece of D. Herbert Heywood's satiric "prospectus," *The Twentieth Century* (1889), is reminiscent of Thomas Cole's "Destruction" (1836) in his famous "Course of Empire" series. Supposedly the frontispiece depicts "The Ruins of Paris" in the twentieth century. The decayed and partially overgrown architecture is Classical Roman and the Parisians appear in robes. A few primitive ships have come to rest in a small harbor. It is not certain that they are war ships, but the mood of the painting evokes memories of a great empire which, because of internal strife or barbarian incursions, is in the process of rapid decay. Two similar illustrations appear in John Ames Mitchell's satiric anti-utopian novel, *The Last American* (1889). The scene is New York harbor in 2951 A.D. Centuries earlier America had been destroyed by greedy capitalists, imitators of European lifestyles, and a political dynasty led by the "Murfey" clan. The first illustration depicts an ancient Persian vessel sailing past the ruins of the Statue of Liberty, her base overgrown with a dense forest. (See Plate 2.) The skyline, darkly silhouetted in the background, is an irregular line of crumbling skyscrapers. The second illustration is more stark and menacing. (See Plate 3.) The small vessel passes beneath lonely piers that once supported the proud Brooklyn Bridge. Now they are spindly stumps of cracked masonry ridiculously stranded in the East River, entwined with rusted and broken suspension cables. The implications are similar to the implications of Heywood's frontispiece. The crumbling piers even evoke the Gothic image of decaying Roman pillars during the dark ages following the collapse of the Roman empire.

William Fishbough quoted combinations of mystical numbers to demonstrate the meaningless ups and downs of the past; Dr. Kinnear used biblical prophesies combined with maps, mathematics, and references to biblical chronologists and prophesy conventions in London; most of the authors simply offered general observations about history. But whether they used numbers, illustrations or generalities, the message was the same: since the expulsion from Eden, nothing new had really happened in the Old World. Instead mankind had acted out war after war and rises and falls in an insane cyclical drama. A few nations had been fortunate enough to rise to glorious peaks, but such achievements only seemed to be the cues for the ever-present hoards of barbarians waiting in the wings or, as in the case of Twain's *A Connecticut Yankee,* the villainous Church always "in the background, delaying the arrival of Utopia."[26] As Bellamy's Dr. Leete observes, many nineteenth-century students of history believed that

> Human history, like all great movements, was cyclical and returned to the point of beginning. . . . Tending upward and sunward from the aphelion of barbarism, the race attained the perihelion of civilization only to plunge downward once more to its nether goal in the regions of chaos.[27]

With all due respect to Dr. Leete, the typical utopian concept of Old-World history was not precisely a return "to the point of beginning." The authors had apparently received too great a dose of the Enlightenment in college to perceive history as a circle. Instead it might better be described as a wave-like line on a two-dimensional plane, the vertical axis representing progress and the horizontal representing time. As the line extended along the horizontal, the crests and possibly even the troughs rose slightly, implying that people at least learned a little from their periodic plunges into barbarism. Nevertheless, the authors agreed that since the beginning of history very little "progress" had been made in the Old World.

But what really frightened the utopian authors was the haunting spectre of crumbling ruins on the American landscape of the future. If Americans failed to heed their warnings, the suffering and confusion of the present would, according to Bellamy, herald the "recurrence in the New World of all the Old World evils."[28] As a *Nationalist* article entitled "A Glance at the Past and a Vision of the Future" warned:

> Our "ship of state" is fast nearing the shoals upon which past civilizations have stranded, and, unless we put hard down the helm and steer clear of danger, history will again repeat itself, and the dark, thick, gloomy pall of ignorance and superstition will once more enshroud our globe.[29]

This warning about the contamination of the New World with Old-World time was re-enforced in a variety of ways. Some utopian authors painted brief word pictures similar to Mitchell's illustrations. (Bellamy's Julian West expected Boston to be "a heap of charred and moss grown ruins" in 2000 A.D.)[30] Others used a time-lag vocabulary similar to Thorstein Veblen's. Thus, certain characteristics of America's economy, religion, or family structure were branded as "barbaric survivals" from the Old World. Finally, a few authors, especially the Christian mystic Thomas Lake Harris, launched into hyperbolic jeremiads:

American civilizee; parasite, producer, plutocrat,—prick the skin and we touch the savage still . . . savage of the age of steel, of dynamite, of electricity.
. . . the savagisms, the barbarisms of all the past lie latent in its [America's] animalized cupidities. Coiled like gigantic serpents, they wait. . . .[31]

Again history would repeat itself. Again a snake was loose in a new world's Garden of Eden.

No wonder the utopian works were haunted by the crumbling piers of the Brooklyn Bridge. No wonder one of Ignatius Donnelly's characters wails, "Oh, for some divine power to sunder the present from the past."[32] But in the midst of their despair the utopian authors found hope in the great opportunities of the late nineteenth-century Armageddon. They did not picture themselves as Cassandras because they expected everybody to listen to their warnings. (After all, *Uncle Tom's Cabin* "caused" the Civil War, and *Looking Backward* was awakening America.) Moreover, the restless forces of the period were so powerful that, after they had been harnessed and directed by utopian visions of the future, they could be used to achieve a unique event in history, a complete liberation from the undulating coils of the past. Looking backward to this period, Bellamy's the Rev. Mr. Barton describes the miraculous transformation (again using the time-lag vocabulary): "In the time of one generation men laid aside the social traditions and practices of barbarians and assumed a social order worthy of rational human beings."[33] Many of the titles of the utopian works and the utopian magazines celebrated the advent of this glorious epoch: *The New Time, New Era, The New Era, The New Republic, The End of Ages, Daybreak, The New Time* (edited by B. O. Flower and F. U. Adams) and *The New Nation* (edited by Bellamy). It must be emphasized that this time break did not simply mark the end of one Old-World cycle and the beginning of another. It constituted a new *kind* of time—a fulfillment of the motto on the American seal, *"Novus Ordo Seclorum."* To return to the analogy of the two-dimensional graph, it was as if the time-line stopped as it seemed headed for an Old-World nadir and then suddenly skyrocketed parallel to the progress axis freeing itself from the bonds of time. The "idea of progress in a right line" became a reality; and the event was heralded as the "second creation of man." Harris's strained feminine metaphor is unusual, but his enthusiasm is typical of reactions to this hoped-for event:

COLUMBIA herself, the myriad-bosomed, myriad-bearing WOMAN PEOPLE, is pregnant and heavy for a new and thrice auspicious birth of TIME.[34]

This celebration of Progress makes late nineteenth-century American utopian works representative of the earliest stages of modern evolutionary utopian novels as defined by Richard Gerber. Gerber links the new view of time to the acceptance of Darwin's theory of evolution:

> The idea of progress and human perfectability does exist in . . . early utopias, but since it is not supported by an adequate world-picture, it is not more than a seed. The progressive attitude only becomes really powerful and realistic with the emergence of a new view which sees progress not only as a moral postulate, but as a historical reality derived from observable facts. Then time expands into a timeless vista. . . .
>
> Such an adequate background for utopian humanism was provided by the theory of evolution. Here . . . men are no longer static, nor time empty. Everything is seen as an infinite evolutionary growth and flow, [with] the anticipation of a glorious future.[35]

And yet, this birth of infinite progress had a rather low ceiling in late nineteenth-century American utopias. Despite Darwinian claims that "a state of evolution beyond which no progress can be made . . . [is] absurd,"[36] when the utopian authors tried to describe the dynamic results of the liberation from Old-World time, some rather static qualities crept into their visions of the future. In *Looking Backward* Dr. Leete boasts that the "fundamental principles on which our society is founded settle *for all time* the strifes and misunderstandings which in your day called for legislation." (Italics mine.) To cite only a few other examples of this attitude, William Simpson simply labels the ideal Martian economy as "the stationary state"; Mr. Homos modestly believes that the present Altrurian "civic ideas are perfect"; and Chauncey Thomas's narrator describes the government of the forty-ninth century as the "Government of Settled Forms," the forms being "fixed inflexibly in the minds and consciences of the people."[37] Even if an author refrained from such explicit comments, the reader soon senses the static quality of the author's ideal world as he vicariously wanders past crowds of smiling, perfect physical specimens in noiseless cities, in perfectly efficient factories and on spotless boulevards. Returning to the two-dimensional graph for a final analogy, it is as if the time-line did indeed break away from the senseless crests and troughs of the past. But it only skyrocketed to a specific point on the vertical axis. Then it stopped and proceeded to parallel the *horizontal,* not the vertical axis.[38]

The overt celebration of infinite progress and the not-so-covert longing for a static state is the most glaring contradiction in the utopian concept of history. It is a reflection of at least three interrelated kinds of problems: literary, philosophical, and cultural. It is relatively easy to posit the possibility of unlimited progress in expository writing. One simply formulates an evolutionary hypothesis assuming gradual but absolute amelioration. This is exactly what Thomas Stewart Blair did in his 573-page treatise, *Human*

Progress (1896). His "Theory Of Human Progress" is based on the "Want Principle": "satisfaction of any want gives rise to the development of another want, and the new want is, under normal circumstances, *of a higher order than the want whose place it takes*."[39] Such a principle may seem logical, but it is difficult to dramatize in a novel. The characters and the settings have to be well defined and fairly consistent if the reader is to identify with them. This becomes a problem if the author is trying to depict continual change. Another problem is concreteness. An essayist can often achieve his goals by staying on a fairly abstract plane as long as his arguments seem reasonable. A novelist, however, is expected to communicate primarily through recognizable, concrete situations. If he is attempting to express unlimited progress, he may run out of recognizable details as he approaches the limits of what his readers consider possible.

This literary problem is related to at least two philosophical problems. One traditional function of a literary utopia has been to offer readers a vision that somehow unifies the mass of details called the present and then to project this unity onto the future. According to the nineteenth-century world view, unity still implied a rather static state; thus it was difficult to incorporate the concept of continual change into descriptions of utopia, even if change meant improvement. Even the "scientific" Social Darwinists and the spiritualistic Theosophists, whose beliefs influenced many Nationalist Clubs, implied a unified, idealistic end to progress. Another related problem is that once one has imagined a unified, better world—one that might even be perfect—and provided details to prove how wonderful this world is, why change it? Change might imply that the new existence originally imagined was deficient, maybe not that much better than the "real" world.

Of course, utopian authors have struggled with such problems for centuries. But these dilemmas became particularly acute for middle- and upper-middle-class authors writing for a late nineteenth-century American audience. The bewildering changes of the 1880s and 1890s might symbolically point towards the millennium; and, if harnessed correctly, they might free America from the coils of Old-World time. But still, they were frightening, especially to authors who suspected that childhood answers no longer worked and that their financial and social security of earlier years might vanish in the future. Moreover, if the authors incorporated too much rapid change into their utopias, they and their readers might feel that they were actually making the future more terrifying than the present, only fighting change with more change, future shock with more future shock.

One solution to this desire for—and fear of—change might have been simply to admit that unlimited progress was not so ideal after all. But this really wasn't a promising alternative for authors who hoped to reach a mass

American audience. William Morris could do it in *News From Nowhere* (1890), but he was an Englishman writing for Englishmen. Henry Adams might long for the Virgin and Chartres, but he was an "aristocrat" writing for a small group of friends. Admittedly there was a medieval cult among some intellectuals and a popular medieval vogue during the late nineteenth century;[40] and these challenges to the celebration of unlimited progress were reflected in the utopian literature. Donnelly's "Garden in the Mountains" was an attempt to turn back the clock to a simpler, pastoral existence; Howells's Altruria was in part inspired by Morris's utopia as well as memories of his small-town boyhood; in Harold Frederic's *Gloria Mundi* (1898) a wealthy aristocrat even recreates a model medieval village. Furthermore, the shapes and zoning divisions of the utopian cities bear striking resemblances to the shapes and sections of medieval or baroque cities. Still, the utopian authors were not medievalists. Their cities are loaded with technological marvels; Donnelly's hero keeps some sophisticated machines in his Garden; Howells's Altrurians travel on streamlined mass-transit systems; and the feudal system fails in *Gloria Mundi*. Progress was still a god in America, and the authors evidently felt that any attempt to dethrone him completely would have made their utopias dystopias for most readers. The utopian authors were trapped, so they lived with a contradiction. They mourned over the poor Old World and her endless cycles, warned about the spread of this disease in the New World, celebrated a unique liberation that promised unlimited progress, and then prescribed a ceiling for utopia which, if anything, was more stagnant than the undulating crests and troughs of the past. Time seemed restricted to a choice between "an antlike stability and eternal recurrence."[41]

One author, however, sought another choice, and his experiment serves as a tragic and important illustration of the tension and ambivalence underlying the utopian concept of history. For most of Mark Twain's *A Connecticut Yankee in King Arthur's Court* (1889) it appears as if Hank Morgan will be the hero of a tale about a miraculous liberation from Old-World time, a liberation similar to the triumph of Walter McDougall's hero among a lost Indian tribe in *The Hidden City* (1892), or the more astounding victory of Austyn Granville's hero, who transforms the lives of a lost species descended from Australian bushmen and kangaroos in *The Fallen Race* (1892).[42]

By chance, a factory worker's blow sends Twain's hero, Hank Morgan, back into one of the deepest troughs in the history of the Old World, sixth-century feudal England. But this resourceful Yankee quickly masters the situation and soon becomes "The Boss" of the entire nation. Using his technical knowledge and his flair for dramatics, he bedazzles both royalty and peasants and within a few years has nineteenth-century American civilization "blooming" in feudal England. It seems as if nothing can stop his era of limitless progress.

Twain even used one of the most typical utopian images in Hank's story. As Allen Guttmann and others have noted, *A Connecticut Yankee* abounds in volcanic imagery.[43] Hank's newspaper is the "Camelot Weekly Hosannah and Literary Volcano," the fireworks at the restoration of the fountain are described as "furious volcanoes," Morgan le Fay hides a "Vesuvius" behind a blooming exterior, her husband is "an extinct volcano," and several descriptions of Hank's machinery involve volcanic imagery, especially the following passage found in Chapter 10, which was added in 1888 after Chapters 1-20 had been written:

> [Hank's factories and workshops were] as substantial a fact as any serene volcano, standing innocent with its smokeless summit in the blue sky and giving no sign of the rising hell in its bowels.[44]

Only Donnelly came close to equaling this barrage of explosive images.

But something is very different about Twain's use of volcanic imagery, and this difference suggests Twain's inability to accept the utopian concept of history. Volcanic imagery was usually used to warn about the pent-up workers and the possible fate of their employers during the late nineteenth-century Armageddon. In *A Connecticut Yankee* all the significant volcanic imagery is instead associated with the hero; even Morgan le Fay's Vesuvian nature can be linked with Hank, since his last name is her first. In most instances the utopian heroic figure harnesses the turbulent forces of his age and directs them into constructive and peaceful channels. But here Hank ultimately becomes the explosive, blind Samson who destroys his enemies and in the process wrecks his own civilization and falls prey to the champion of Old-World superstition, Merlin. Instead of achieving a rejection of the past, this hero of Progress only succeeds in engineering a massacre that rivals any "senseless" Old-World war for its barbaric carnage, a battle that has been called "one of the most distressing passages in American literature."[45]

Disciples of R. W. B. Lewis and Leo Marx might venture to explain Twain's use of volcanic imagery and his denial of Hank's mission as an ironic manipulation of well-known images and beliefs. But the artistic use of irony requires a degree of distance and control that, as Henry Nash Smith and Roger B. Salomon have persuasively argued, Twain lacked while writing *A Connecticut Yankee*. He was the victim of a "divided artistic consciousness." In several unpublished essays completed during the composition of *A Connecticut Yankee* Twain expressed a faith in Progress similar to Hank's. Twain was seeking a vehicle to express his faith in American progress as compared to Old-World oppression and stagnation. But, like the other utopian novelists, "in developing fictionally his theme of progress, Twain was forced to deal with specific characters in concrete situations."[46] Unlike other authors, however, he saw only disaster in concrete situations where he was ultimately supposed to see hope. Popular authors, Bellamy and Sheldon for instance, could make the smoke belching from their volcanoes blend into the utopian landscape as easily as a George Inness could blend the fiery soot of a locomotive into a pastoral landscape. They feared it but hoped that the frightening energy would awaken Americans and help them to discard the past. Twain, on the other hand, seemed to be fully aware of the terrifying possibilities of pinning mankind's dreams of infinite progress on the all-too-finite limitations of the burgeoning technological civilization of the nineteenth century. He sensed that the champions of this type of progress— champions he admired, at times almost worshipped—might be as dangerous as the robber barons and eruptive masses of the New World or the kings and barbarians of the Old. Yet he couldn't come right out and say this. It would have been too painful for Twain the artist and Twain the American. Instead he floundered between contradictory extremes by dramatizing the night-marish possibilities of Progress and then rewarding his lord of misrule by hinting at a happy reunion with an Old-World beauty after death. (See Dan Beard's last illustration.) Reading *A Connecticut Yankee in King Arthur's Court* is like placing a magnifying glass over all the weak spots and sore spots in the utopian concept of history.

But it should be emphasized that Twain's tortured awareness was a minority report. The utopian concept of history was one of the few basic elements of the journey to utopia upon which the average, the popular, and most of the perceptive authors agreed. This does not necessarily mean that their view of time dominated American culture during the late nineteenth century. It does suggest, however, that the authors believed they had to present the past, present, and future in an understandable and inspiring way if they were to reach their contemporaries. By answering the question "when?" with "now"; by pointing to suffering and confusion to justify this periodiza-tion; and by presenting their era as an Armageddon that would culminate by either plunging American society back into an Old-World cycle or by launching it forward through a period of dramatic progress climaxing in a heaven-like, static state—by offering this interpretation of American history, the utopian authors suggested that this was the way Americans wanted to view history. The emphasis on the United States' role flattered Americans; the combinations of contemporary fads, patriotism, Adventism, Christian im-ages, and Puritan rhetoric transformed abstract theories into concrete, under-standable observations and predictions; and the emphasis on prompt action and utopian-dystopian possibilities made living during confusing times seem exciting and challenging.

The utopian concept of history also served at least two important psychological functions. First, during a period when impersonal forces, especially the depression of 1893, seemed to render the individual helpless, the utopian concept of history reasserted the responsibility and power of the individual. Again and again the authors proclaimed that if enough individuals acted now, the entire course of history could be changed. Despite this optimism, however, the other psychological function betrayed insecurity about the power of individuals. In a recent review of "radical" movies a critic has remarked that "the value of constantly predicting revolutions, civil war, [and] violent accountings is to give a sense of power to the powerless."[47] Alexander Saxton and Frederic Jaher have defined the psychological advantages of mixing catastrophism and utopianism in a similar manner: "[it represents a] double wish fulfillment through justification of the elect and confusion and torture of all enemies"; "relief was sought in future debacles or utopias where corruption would be crushed and the just . . . would rule."[48] The utopian authors were not helpless, poverty-stricken individuals. But, as the biographical data reveals, they were susceptible to the violent fluctuations of the economy, and they were frightened by the few who had immense power and the many whose poverty made them potentially dangerous. Hence, the visions of destruction and utopia that permeated their view of history and forecast the elimination of the rich and the poor allowed them to release their hatred of those "above" them and their fears of those "below" them and to rejoice in the hope that the right type of individual—people like the authors who were neither rich nor poor—would thrive in America as utopia.

Of course this dream of a middle-class utopia is still with us—as are many other elements of the utopian authors' concept of history. American politicians, religious leaders, teachers, and writers still describe the present as a crucial era, point to suffering and confusion as symptoms of fundamental change, and predict that we are on the brink of "utopia or oblivion."[49] Two implications of the persistence of this historical perspective are that American history, including the 1960s and 1970s, has been punctuated by a series of "future shocks" and that one response has been to popularize historical outlooks that confront the terrors of the situation but, like good evangelical sermons, offer possibilities of hope and understanding by making change seem familiar and controllable. Therefore, the utopian view of history is still useful to us today as a psychological buffer against the uncertainties of the future.

But as a basis for concrete action or as a tool for interpreting reality, utopian historiography seems even more obsolete than it was in the 1890s. The rejection of the past in favor of a New Era raises false hopes and obscures sources of contemporary problems and models for understanding the present. All-or-nothing expectations instill a sense of urgency, especially with regard to the problems of ecological survival and strategic arms limitation. Nevertheless, this attitude, augmented by the immediacy of television coverage, encourages a desire for fast and, ironically, superficial results. When instant utopias or dystopias are not forthcoming, or even when short-range goals—such as the end of military involvement in Vietnam or the end of the draft—are achieved, interest in reform often ebbs before long-range changes can be planned or implemented. Finally, the celebration of America's messianic role can blind as well as inspire. We are surprised when the Russians consider themselves the chosen people and predict that our grand-children will model their lives after communist saviors; hurt when Canadian students rebel against Americanization; angered when we can't "clean up" the "messes" in "little" places like Southeast Asia or the Middle East; infuriated when we hear applause for Red China in the U.N. or are forced to depend upon Arabian oil to make our cars go. Of course, late nineteenth-century utopian authors can't be blamed for our nationalistic view of world history. But the popularity of their works breathed new life into old Puritan expectations. World War I and, to some extent, World War II, kept the faith in America's messianic role alive and set us up for the frustrations of Korea and Vietnam. Hence the usefulness of the utopian view of time as a reassuring explanation of history is counterbalanced by its inability to cope with the changing roles of America in the twentieth century. Psychological buffers become blinders when ideology and reality are confused.

Plate 1: Volcanic Eruptions. Alvarado M. Fuller, *A.D. 2000*.

Plate 2: "The City of Ruins." John A. Mitchell, *The Last American*.

Plate 3: "The Two Monuments in the River." John A. Mitchell, *The Last American*.

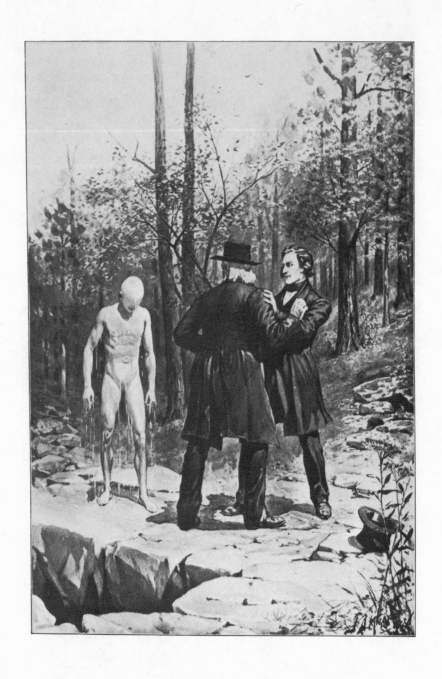

Plate 5: "Confronted by a Singular Looking Being." John Uri Lloyd, *Etidorhpa*.

Plate 6: Aeronauts Discover the North Pole. Alvarado M. Fuller, *A.D. 2000*.

Plate 7: Twenty-Second-Century Airplane. Albert Adams Merrill, *The Great Awakening*.

3

Space: Virgin Land Again?

He mourns his lost land . . . it was so fresh and new, so virgin before.
—*Mark Twain,* Notebook

There can be no more new worlds to be discovered, no fresh continents to offer virgin fields for new ventures.
—*Edward Bellamy, "Letter to the People's Party"* The New Nation *(1892)*

Despite Oscar Wilde's oft-quoted maxim, "A map of the world that does not include Utopia is not even worth glancing at,"[1] utopian authors seldom reveal the exact latitudes and longitudes of their nowheres. Instead, traditionally, they have followed B. F. Skinner's "first rule of Utopian romance: 'Get away from life as you know it, either in space or time, or no one will believe you.'"[2] Of course utopian authors give us glimpses of places: valleys, islands, lost continents, the earth's interior, or other planets. Sometimes they even provide detailed navigational information, though "some convenient storm and shipwreck [usually] interferes with navigation and provides the plausible evasion."[3] But the settings of conventional utopian works are rarely meant as descriptions of real locations. They are philosophical and literary devices that encourage readers to escape, to see a different life style in isolation, or to view their own time and place in a new way.

But again, late nineteenth-century American utopian authors strayed from the conventional utopian course. To borrow Arthur E. Morgan's phrase, their nowheres were somewhere; their geographical sites were as literal as their timetables. One of the characters in Warren S. Rehm's *Practical City* (1895) proudly displays the location of an ideal city "on our latest state map,"[4] and Charles Caryl's, John Galloway's and William Gilpin's celebrations of Colorado more than hint that utopia is hiding somewhere in the immediate vicinity of Denver. Most of the authors did not risk such precise pinpointing. Nevertheless, all but eight modified the original meaning of utopia by locating their ideal societies in the United States.[5] This was even true for authors who described utopias on distant planets, within the earth's center, or on imaginary islands, since these noplaces were analogies for a potential someplace, an ideal America. To quote Howells's Mr. Homos, "America prophesies another Altruria."[6]

This manner of presenting the ideal place to begin the journey to utopia was, of course, directly related to the utopian concept of history. Both capitalized on a wondrous coincidence. For centuries religious and secular leaders had visions of an undiscovered world where man could break away from the past. Sometimes this Earthly Paradise "was an island beyond the seas, sometimes a land situated underground, sometimes a country in the mountains; but wherever it was supposed to be, it was believed to be actually there and was traceable on mediaeval maps." Then, by chance, Columbus bypassed the edge of the world and stumbled upon a lost continent. Given such a coincidence it was inevitable that old visions of ideality and new reports about America would be linked. Thus, it seems logical that Sir Thomas More used Vespucci's travel accounts to inform his vision of Utopia or that Coronado straggled through Pueblo villages looking for El Dorado.[7]

The late nineteenth-century American utopian authors integrated this geographical accident and way of perceiving America with their view of history. First of all, they used a geographical rhetoric of escape and rebirth that complemented their notions of the undulating coils of Old-World time and the unique liberation of New-World time. For instance, the territorial governor of Colorado, William Gilpin, proclaimed that North America represented a "new and original condition" that would "stir up the sleep of a hundred centuries," end "the sanguinary gestations of the chaotic [old] world," and

> teach old nations a new civilization . . . carry the career of mankind to the culminating point . . . cause a stagnant people to be reborn . . . unite the world in one social family . . . and . . . shed blessings around the world.[8]

Such enthusiasm would be familiar to readers—it was part of a heritage stretching back to early Puritan settlements. Still, this wasn't enough. Anyone could see that America was no longer "new and original" in 1890. But ironically, the apparent failure of the original promise of American soil did not disprove the utopian concept of history. Indeed, it helped to prove it by enhancing the sense of urgency with concrete evidence of the approaching Armageddon. If Americans did not reform, all the New World would become as corrupted as the Old; and this would be a "final failure." As Bellamy proclaimed in his "Letter to the People's Party," "there can be no more new worlds to be discovered."[9]

If this were all there were to say about the utopian concept of space, the authors' descriptions of the American landscape could simply be classified as one type of evidence used to support their view of history. But once we go beyond the broad generalizations about the past and present meanings of the American continent, it becomes clear that the utopian landscape should not be tossed off as a footnote to utopian time. There was too much disagreement about exactly where to start The Change; and this disagreement not only reflects confusion about how to define the ideal place, it also suggests that most of the authors, including the popular and the perceptive, could no longer believe in simplistic expectations about the restorative powers of new worlds.

The Nationalist provides a good introduction to the controversy over the geography of utopia. It contained two different types of reform essays. Most, including contributions from Bellamy, warned that evils already existing in certain parts of America could contaminate the whole country. These reformers argued that Americans should cleanse these areas, not by looking for new "virgin fields," but by focusing a variety of reforms on the worst areas of corruption thus demonstrating that Americans could always live up to the promise of the New World because of their willingness to purge Old-World evils from their soil.[10] The other type of article was typified by Campbell Ver-Plank's "A Co-operative Commonwealth" describing the Kaweah utopian community in California. After the July 1889 issue, almost every number of *The Nationalist* contained a full- or half-page advertisement for Kaweah—"Bellamy's Dream Realized!"[11] Ver-Plank assumed that there would always be some niche of uncorrupted American land available to which Americans could flee. Once there, they could act out a small scale denial of the past, which, by the power of its example, would cleanse America and the world.

These two views of the links between history's grasp and American soil were found in the utopian works as well as in reform magazines. In the magazines neither viewpoint was clearly dominant. In the utopian books, however, the answer to the question, "Virgin land again?," was a rather decisive "no." Over two-thirds of the authors examined, including the popular Bellamy and Sheldon and the most perceptive authors on this topic, chose reform from within over the quest for new worlds.

Admittedly this statistic is somewhat arbitrary since in some cases it was difficult to determine whether an author was using a setting purely as a literary device or as a true expression of his faith in America's virgin land. But explicit statements in prefaces and afterwords usually clarified this ambiguity. Thus, it is safe to say that in general the reform-from-within outlook was dominant; if anything the two-thirds figure is a conservative estimate. Again those works with imaginary or distant settings were seldom exceptions to the majority viewpoint. Howells's Altruria may be located on some once virgin island in the Aegean sea (or in Australia), but the force behind the change from Accumulation to Altruism came from within by evolution, not from without by emulation. Similarly, on William Simpson's Mars, escape to the "unoccupied agricultural surface" was seen only as a temporary "truce" between available space and the corrupting influence of time.[12]

This apparent rejection of a faith in the revitalizing powers of America's open spaces may be surprising to some students of nineteenth-century American culture. It would seem that a celebration of our virgin land would be easier to communicate to readers and more consistent with the utopian concept of history than the appeal for reform from within. Biblical Edenic images, a familiar characteristic of utopian literature, could be used in setting descriptions.[13] The rhetoric of the frontier so brilliantly analyzed by Henry Nash Smith in *Virgin Land* would make utopian warnings and promises sound particularly American and exciting. The unity of the narratives would be greater since the authors could make the birth of new time coincide with the move to a new territory. The works would also be consistent in their inconsistencies: the longing for virgin land embodies the desire for Progress and a static state, the yearning for and fear of change, so characteristic of the utopian concept of history. And the authors who pictured model communities springing up in idyllic virgin territories did develop these possibilities. But most of the utopian authors could not because their emphasis was on reforming the corrupted parts of America.[14]

Although it is probably impossible to explain exactly why so many utopian authors de-emphasized the popular nineteenth-century habit of associating virgin land with renewal, enough evidence exists about them and their times to allow some speculation. One possible explanation involves the relative "testability" of general theories about human existence. The predictions the authors made about history eventually made their utopias vulnerable, but the nice thing about dividing the past into eras is that historical markers are often difficult to "disprove." So many different kinds of events occur in any given year that it is easy to "prove" hypotheses by selecting specific events that support one view of history. Thus, in *The End of Ages* (1899) William Fishbough could mathematically prove that American history was neatly parcelled out in twelve-year cycles by pinpointing "important" events that occurred every dozen years from 1776 to 1860. Such manipulations of reality become more difficult when the primary evidence is land and the artifacts upon it. Events, especially private ones, have a way of merging with the obscurities of the past, making them susceptible to manipulations. Land and artifacts can also be viewed from many angles; but it was hard for the utopian authors to deny that parts of what early settlers had called virgin were by 1890 slums that resembled the areas of the Old World from which many Americans fled. If this undeniable fact proved anything, it indicated that America's open spaces were just as hospitable to evil as were the cluttered landscapes of the Old World. Other more specific facts that could be used to test the powers of unoccupied land were the numerous utopian communities established during the nineteenth century. A few authors, notably Ralph Albertson, Alcander Longley and Thomas Lake Harris, followed this path to utopia. But most of the authors were aware that in spite of the dedication of men like Cabet, Owen, and Fourier very few of these experiments proved that a move to virgin territory meant a rebirth of humanity; and the gradual disappearance of easily accessible, cheap, fertile land revealed by the 1890 census reports seemed to hold little hope for the success of future large-scale utopian communities.

The relative testability of theories about time and space may in part explain why most of the utopian authors expressed little faith in lighting out for the territory. It is likely that their ambivalent feelings about rural and urban America also contributed to their decision. As Donald C. Burt has argued convincingly, the utopian authors longed for a return to rural America. They realized, however, that industrialized, urbanized America was here to stay. Moreover, the new order might make life more exciting and comfortable for most Americans. Faced with this situation, the utopian authors settled for a series of compromises between their nostalgia for an agrarian landscape and their hopes and fears about an urban landscape.[15] One reflection of this ambivalence is the utopian authors' continued faith in the promise of the New World (95% of them directly or indirectly predicted that America would be the future utopia) combined with their assumption that the corrupt city was the place to start The Change (at least for two-thirds of the authors).

But the two-thirds majority weren't the only ones forced to compromise. One of the most fascinating characteristics of the concepts of space found in the late nineteenth-century utopian works is that even the authors who advocated a return to the wilderness could not agree upon the exact role of virgin land. Furthermore, most of them advocated modernized, or at least modified, versions of traditional American attitudes about America's virgin soil. This diversity and the tendency to modify old attitudes combined with the rejection of a literal faith in the redemptive qualities of virgin land by two-thirds of the authors strongly suggests that the changes of the late nineteenth century were undermining popular, traditional beliefs about America's wide open spaces. Like many of their contemporaries, many of the utopian authors were born in rural areas or in small towns, so they probably were exposed to the rhetoric of America's virgin land as children. But as middle-aged city dwellers, they found that these answers no longer applied or that they needed an overhaul before they could offer solutions to contemporary problems. An examination of the four versions of the faith in virgin land combined with a running critique, based on the views of the most perceptive authors, should help to illuminate this reaction against one of the most persistent American beliefs.

Of the four versions of faith in virgin land, two were traditional and two were modifications. The two traditional versions expressed two interrelated assumptions. The first presented unoccupied land as a powerful stimulus to begin anew—to discard evils associated with settled land. The second showed less concern for virgin land per se than with its function as a necessary condition for the founding of model communities free from the corruption of the world. The two modified versions of these expectations explored ways of reclaiming once virgin land or of transforming introspective model communities into activist clusters that would eventually participate in national reform movements. That most of these authors chose the latter modification again indicates the decline of traditional beliefs about virgin land, at least among middle- and upper-middle-class urbanites.

Very few authors (6) championed the first traditional concept of virgin land by pointing to the existence of unoccupied territory as the greatest opportunity Americans had for escaping the past. To borrow Harold V. Rhodes's terminology, these authors believed in an "outward utopia": "utopia exists now—somewhere—but not here." Thus, the journey to utopia meant simply moving from "here to there," and "there" was, of course, America's virgin land.[16] The most enthusiastic proponent of this "outward" American utopia was the previously quoted William Gilpin. Born in 1813, he was older than most utopian authors and had personally participated in America's conquest of the West and parts of the Southeast as an Indian fighter and as the first territorial governor of Colorado (1861-62).[17] In *The Cosmopolitan Railway* (1890) Gilpin admitted that by the late 1880s America had used a great deal of "fertile and unoccupied land" and that the increasing number of strikes was a blight on the landscape. Still, there was plenty of land left, and the nature of that land promised the eventual salvation of America and the world. Utilizing the theories of Alexander von Humboldt, a German geographer, Gilpin argued that "physical nature" shaped "human communities." The American continent, for example, dictated a reversal of "the policy of the old world" because the basic geological formation of the Old World was a "bowl reversed which scatters everything from a central apex," whereas "North America opens toward heaven in one expanded basin to receive and fuse harmoniously whatever enters within its rim." (See Plate 4.) Gilpin even extended his descriptions of America's gigantic melting basin into the familiar metaphor of the grand American stage where the rejection of the past would be acted out: "Let us recall again the sublime amphitheater occupied by the American people, impregnably set in the midst of all the populations of the world."[18]

Besides the uncorrupted nature and the unifying shape of America's virgin land, Gilpin and the few who agreed with him argued that America was so fertile and rich in resources that its inhabitants were certain to lead lives of pious productivity. Even the possibility of the eventual depletion of the soil did not frighten them. After the American "race" had grown to perfection on American soil, their sacred duty was to expand the boundaries of America and acquire millions of acres of new land in other parts of the world. Gilpin predicted that the Siberian desert would bloom; the Kansas Populist Mary Elizabeth Lease longed for the "cool sea breezes" and "dew drenched fronds of palm and myrtle" that would make South America a coffee-producing Garden of Eden; and John Jacob Astor envisioned a mineralogist's Big Rock Candy Mountain awaiting future American interplanetary pioneers:

> . . . iron mountains, silver, copper, and lead formations, primeval forests, rich prairies, and regions evidently underlaid with coal and petroleum, not to mention huge beds of aluminum clay and other natural resources that made his materialistic mouth water.[19]

While lost in these expansionist rhapsodies, these authors seemed unaware that such acquisitions might constitute a repetition of the Old-World custom of coveting and then stealing one's neighbor's property. But the promise of America transformed these grasping endeavors into holy crusades, since an American was defined as a person who settled virgin territory only for noble reasons. He was to establish a godly, model community that would prove American superiority and encourage other nations to allow Americans to develop their virgin territories.

Americans were also model pioneers because they were productive. According to Gilpin, they deserved to possess virgin territories because the fertility of America's soil inspired them "to transmute the cinders and waste material of this world into fine gold which ministers to human culture."[20] This was a well-established excuse for taking Indian lands. It also reveals that even the most traditional view of virgin land expressed by utopian authors differed from perceiving virgin land as Eden. Virgin land was inspiring, but it could not be left alone. It had to be transformed into what Leo Marx has called a "middle landscape" in between the overcivilized cities of Europe and the howling wilderness of America. This new Garden of Eden is described well by James Galloway's narrator in *John Harvey* (1897) as he beholds a utopian settlement in Colorado from Pike's Peak:

> One seemed to be looking from the abode of pristine wilderness and nature into a wonderful garden, . . . Every portion of the land showed intelligent attention and loving care. . . . All noxious growth and things inimical to thorough cultivation, or offensive to the senses or repellent to ascetic tastes had been removed. . . . They had redeemed that land from primitive wilderness and made it to bloom as the rose. [21]

Of course, almost all utopian authors agreed that America was destined to be an exemplary garden. But only a few became so intoxicated with the fact of virgin land that it dominated their utopian visions. Moreover, their enthusiasm for exploiting the soil was criticized from within the utopian ranks by precursors of modern ecologists. Milan C. Edson, a retired soldier, believed that with proper irrigation and cultivation even the Great American Desert would bloom; but he also knew that unless settlers were willing to replenish soil with fertilizer, initiate "persistent tree-planting projects," and keep large tracts of land out of the hands of greedy industrialists, the country would be turned into a wasteland by shortsighted, exploitive Americans who would "rob us of all our fertile soil." Edson even went so far as to propose an alternate to the "middle landscape." He envisioned a magnificent series of wilderness preserves that would include the Sierra Nevadas, the Alleghenies, the Adirondacks and the "Pride-of-the-World-Park," the Rocky Mountains. [22]

Another type of criticism of Gilpin's celebration of virgin land came from at least 16 authors who sympathized with his basic assumptions and goals but felt that too much of America was (or soon would be) corrupted to be saved by the revitalizing powers of the remaining virgin land. These authors therefore imagined a second version of the faith in virgin land, a modification that might best be labeled a do-it-yourself virgin-land plan. Stated simply, they hoped to reclaim America's virgin land by cleaning away all the rubble that had collected in America since its discovery by Europeans. The cleansing agents came in a variety of shapes and sizes. According to Thomas and Anna Fitch a few spectacular urban renewal projects would do the job. The novelist Frank Stockton, the astronomer Simon Newcomb, and the journalist Stanley Waterloo predicted that the threat of powerful weapons that could literally scour the landscape would inspire a global reformation. Alvarado Fuller,

Samuel Walker, and Benjamin Rush Davenport called upon God for a divine purge that would make "ready the land for the springtime of a new freedom . . . and permanent happiness."[23] But the majority of these authors (8) including Ignatius Donnelly, had little faith in urban renewal, threats, or well-timed purges.[24] Instead they feared that someday America might be so soiled that only a war or a violent revolution would restore purity and free America from the contamination of Old-World cycles.

They justified these drastic means with two assumptions. First, they believed the violence could be discriminating, purging only the worst "stain[s]" on the otherwise "fair escutcheon of a great nation." For example, in Henry Salisbury's *Birth of Freedom* (1890) the narrator admits that "Glancing over the ruined city where many fires still burned, one consoling thought came to mind—most of its vilest plague-spots had been wiped out." In William Pomeroy's *Lords of Misrule* (1894) the worst devastation is visited upon east-coast centers of socialism which, after the revolution, can be distinguished as "black splotches" on the landscape. Even in Donnelly's *Caesar's Column* the destruction seems to be limited to evil American and European cities—proof that "God wipes out injustice with suffering, wrong with blood, sin with death." The second assumption was one shared by the professors of the traditional faith in virgin land: *only good* could spring from uncorrupted land. To quote Donnelly, "after destruction *must* come construction." (Italics mine.) The elect may have to leave their native land temporarily while it is purified, but they will return and America will again become the stage for a fresh start—only this time the promise of a new world will be fulfilled. The few "savages" who still inhabit this new wilderness will have learned their lesson and will become docile followers of the elect.[25]

The most poignant criticism of the do-it-yourself virgin-land approach did not come from the budding ecologist, Edson; it came from Mark Twain. In *A Connecticut Yankee* Hank Morgan, like his ancestors, initially perceives his new world as virgin: "I was just another Robinson Crusoe cast away on an uninhabited island, with no society but some more or less tame animals [the Arthurians]."[26] In a notebook entry Twain recalled this attitude in a passage describing the Yankee's return to England as an old man: "He mourns his lost land . . . it is all so changed and become so old, so old—and it was so fresh and new, so virgin before."[27] Eventually, however, the revolt against Hank forces him to admit that sixth-century England is inhabited. He reacts by trying to scour the Old-World political and religious stains from the landscape, and his crusade exposes the tragedy of assuming that purges can be controlled and that good always rises from reclaimed virgin land.

Hank wants to topple the king and the Pope. But as he carries out his schemes to rid the world of these plague spots, he discovers that undermining the king means war with Merlin, the nobles, the knights and possibly *"the massed chivalry of the whole earth."* Similarly, undermining the Church calls for an attack on kindly priests as well as fat, evil bishops and, in the end, the peasants, who remain loyal to their religion. Hank's righteous assault on evil even indirectly causes the deaths of his loyal followers and erases his own accomplishments from the English landscape. This hideous progression demonstrates that once one person or group is singled out as the enemy and the decision is made to solve the world's problems by eradicating that person or group, a really clean slate necessitates the elimination of the enemy, the enemy's close associates, then distant associates, until the widening circles of destruction engulf everyone including those who began the crusade. So much for limiting a purge.

But if the advocates of do-it-yourself virgin land were right, even after such an uncontrollable purge, good would arise. Not so in *A Connecticut Yankee*. After the Battle of the Sand-Belt, Hank—unlike Donnelly's hero Gabriel—does not rise above the carnage in an airship and go off to Africa to train a select group who will return to build a new and beautiful world. Instead of sensing the joy of a glorious resurrection, the reader sees Hank suffering and confused, surrounded by "three walls of dead men." Thus, the novel reverses Gilpin's prediction that man's destiny was to "transmute the cinders and waste" of nature into "fine gold." Hank proves that man can also reduce a civilization to piles of charred bodies, "cinders and waste." This alone would be a devastating blow to both Gilpin's and Donnelly's theories, but Twain concludes with a brilliant stroke that shows how cleaning the slate might lead to something worse than the nothingness of a wasteland. After the battle, Merlin sneaks into Hank's cave, and it is he who finally conquers Hank. Merlin, even more than Morgan le Fay, embodies both the evil superstitions and the satanic cruelty of the Old-World cycles. Hence, Merlin's final incantations and "curious passes" over Hank constitute a black mass that reverses the historical liberation symbolized by the Resurrection. Out of a reclaimed virgin land rises a powerful figure of evil instead of the risen Christ.[28]

The other two versions of the opportunities represented by America's virgin territory celebrated its revitalizing powers but were especially aimed at depicting virgin land as a necessary condition for the founding of model communities. Of course the idea of a model city was as old as the quest for undiscovered continents, as attested to by Greek city-states, Augustine's "City of God," Campanella's "City of the Sun," and the "Heavenly City" of the eighteenth-century philosophers. But as Loren Baritz has argued in *City on a Hill,* this idea had especially strong roots in America. Therefore, utopian authors who expressed their hopes and fears in this form could assume that their messages would at least be familiar, possibly even reassuring during confusing times. Nevertheless, most of these authors felt the need to update old answers suggesting that no matter how reassuring Winthrop's "Citty upon a Hill" was, it could no longer define America's problems and aspirations.

Only 7 utopian authors championed the traditional introspective model city, and of these, 4 (Albert Merrill, Corwin Phelps, Albert Chavannes, and King Camp Gillette) believed that in order to achieve Winthrop's goal of attracting "the eies of all people" something larger than a community was needed. Although Merrill's, Phelps's, and Chavannes's beacons to humanity began as small settlements of earnest Americans in Africa, they soon grew into prosperous nations pointing the way for America's future *national* development. Gillette's ideal city began as a huge metroplex and eventually absorbed all North America's population becoming the only "city on a continent, and possibly the only one in the world."[29] (See Plates 19-23.) Even the three who stuck closest to the traditional model envisioned very different communities. Ralph Albertson described an actual Georgia community guided by Christian love; William Bishop imagined a North Carolina city whose life style was determined by large communal-living complexes; and Charles W. Caryl offered detailed plans for an industrial and cultural center in Denver. (See Plates 25 and 26.)

But the diversity and the switch to a national model represented a search, not a denial. The authors were looking for new ways to present traditional beliefs. Each community still began on "virgin and unoccupied country" and was dedicated to breaking away from the past. Even the language used to describe the communities would have been familiar to Winthrop's followers: "a beacon to guide [humanity's] steps," "a guiding star," "a pattern for all the world to follow," and "all eyes were centered on it."[30] To ward off the possibility of corruption these models of purity and productivity, with the exception of Gillette's city, were also just as intolerant of outsiders and "heathen" as were many Puritan communities. The utopians erected tall walls, posted lookouts, and enforced rigorous immigration laws so that only "choice spirits" could enter. This exclusivism, moreover, points toward another fundamental similarity to Winthrop's model city—they were both introspective, passive. When William Bishop attempted to express the tremendous force his imaginary community would unleash upon the world, he did not consider missionary programs or other means of actively reaching out beyond his "Garden of Eden" valley. Instead he held aloft the old belief that the existence of such an example would be enough to change the world:

Just wait until the Twentieth Century dawns. We are going to tear down our fences then. There shall be at least one model community in the world. [31]

Like the other versions of a faith in virgin land, the city on the hill was subjected to some perceptive criticism. A reviewer in *The Nationalist* chided those who sought to change the world by "shutting themselves up in a community," and in *The New Nation* Bellamy observed that "the world has thus far shown itself decidedly more inclined to admire than to imitate [such] examples."[32] But the most sustained and thorough critiques of the introspective model community were expressed in three novels, all written by women: Adelia E. Orpen's *Perfection City* (1897), Eva McGlasson's *Diana's Livery* (1891), and Caroline A. Mason's *A Woman of Yesterday* (1900). Orpen's novel is especially interesting because she isolated two related problems facing late nineteenth-century communalists. A young college girl, Olive, marries one of a band of Perfectionists settled on the Kansas prairie. Though sympathetic to the communal ideals, she soon realizes that at this stage in American history communalists were sometimes forced to live on rather barren plots of virgin land—so barren that even the rhetoric of America's fertility wouldn't make things grow. Perhaps an even more serious weakness to the location is shown by the reactions of outsiders. The nearest village is a tiny hamlet. The townspeople perceive a "'fectionist" only as something to be ridiculed or ignored, certainly never imitated. As for the rest of the world: a wandering Englishman observes that Perfection City is a rather small and inaccessible "theatre in which to present before mankind the new principles of social life."[33] In other words, during the late nineteenth century the search for virgin land might drive utopians to such isolated areas that they not only failed as exemplary producers, they also failed to be any kind of example because they were too far removed from "the eies of all people." Their quest for the necessary condition, virgin land, doomed their ultimate goals.

Still, even if no one was looking, the communalists might at least gain a sense of satisfaction from the piety of their community as compared to the evils of the rest of the world. All three authors admitted this. McGlasson's Pleasant Hill, Kentucky's Shakers, Mason's band of Christians, and Orpen's 'fectionists, like Hawthorne's reformers in *The Blithedale Romance* (1852), initially compare favorably with outsiders. Yet it seems impossible to maintain this level of purity. Exclusiveness bars unwanted troublemakers, but it also helps to create a narrow view of life while encouraging a fanaticism that divides the idealists and frightens outsiders. But the most fundamental threat to purity is simply the inability of the communalists to live with one another on a day-to-day basis over an extended period of time. At first the flush of enthusiasm and the hostile environment unite these backwoods saints; but eventually in all three communities petty jealousies, lovers' quarrels, and the constant frustrations of living on a barren land outweigh the spirit of brotherly love. Thus, by focusing on three idealistic communities, these authors could suggest that the very things communalists seek—virgin land, isolation, and exclusivism—can undermine even small-scale attempts to reject the past.

The fourth concept of virgin land was an attempt to respond to doubts similar to those expressed by Orpen, McGlasson, and Mason. Most of the familiar assumptions and expectations were still voiced: the ideal condition of a "great virgin continent" would facilitate the growth of a community that would be a "beacon light" to "the waiting and watching world." F. H. Clarke even capitalized on the meaning of the name of the state in which he located his colony—Idaho, "Light on the Mountains." And, as usual, the ultimate goal of the move to open spaces was a liberation from "the conditions which exist in the old world."[34] But a "Letter to the Editor" of *The Nationalist* written by Alcander Longley, a well-known communalist, underscored the basic difference between the "new" model community and the traditional city on a hill. He defended his book, *What is Communism?*(1890), by declaring that he never intended that his followers should remain shut up in an isolated community. After one had achieved some degree of success, he envisioned the founding of satellite communities that would eventually "consolidate" into a national political party dedicated to the elimination of corruption on nonvirgin land.[35]

Again there was diversity. At one end of the spectrum Bellamy's brother Charles focused mainly on an isolated Western community and spent little time describing missionary activities in *An Experiment in Marriage* (1889). In *Altruria* (1895) and *San Salvador* (1892) Titus K. Smith and Mary Tinckner placed more emphasis on outside contacts, and in Henry L. Everett's *The People's Program* (1892) the hero organizes a "Geometrical League," the equivalent of a word-of-mouth, chain-letter reform movement. Several imaginary communities, including Donnelly's "Garden in the Mountains," were designed to train leaders to eventually transform the outside world. Finally, in F. H. Clarke's *The Co-opolitan* (1898) an Idaho community becomes the hub of a grass-roots political movement which, by 1917, controls several Western and Southwestern states, has elected forty senators, supports municipal ownership throughout the country, and has created five national railroad systems.

These various outward-looking communities did not solve the fundamental problems of actually finding cheap, accessible, fertile land or making people live together harmoniously; but they did bring the city on a hill down to earth where the idealists were forced to mix with the heathen. They also represented the most popular version of a faith in virgin land. In at least 22 utopian works the authors depicted outward-looking, activist communities.

This shift to outward-looking communities reflected a more complex mode of perception than did the other three versions, which, to use Leo Marx's observations about pastoral escapism, tended "to confuse a transitory state . . . with the universal condition of things."[36] Land in a state of original or reclaimed virginity or a geographically isolated event (a community) on such land became confused with perpetual renewal. Conversely, Alcander Longley's brand of communalism was closer to Leo Marx's concept of complex pastoralism: an awareness that the retreat to the wilderness is temporary. It is a means of gaining new perspectives that can be used when the idealist returns to the ever-changing, corrupt world. In their enthusiasm for the founding and growth of the initial community even these utopian authors sometimes lost sight of what was temporary and what was not. But occasionally—after they had allowed the reader to escape momentarily to Idaho or Colorado or wherever and then reminded him that the removal was only preparation for a return—these authors fulfilled one of the functions of the best utopian literature: forcing the reader to look at something different so that he can see his own world differently.

An overview of the late nineteenth-century American utopian concept of space does suggest, however, that these authors' views of the ideal landscape were limited as compared to the imaginary places envisioned by the best British, European, and Classical utopian authors. Whether they rejected, clung to, or modified the faith in virgin land, their concept of the ideal place was limited to America. Thus, like the utopian concept of history, the utopian concept of space was more vulnerable than the geography of Sir Thomas More's crescent-shaped Utopia. Since the utopian view of space re-enforced the utopian view of time, it also encouraged Americans to indulge more fervently in cosmic navel staring—the belief in America's messianic role that has limited Americans' ability to understand twentieth-century international relations.

The utopian concept of space does, nevertheless, suggest that these authors were aware that Americans needed new ways to perceive the American landscape. The centuries-old quest for that "green land" that thrilled the Dutch sailors who haunt the concluding page of Fitzgerald's *The Great Gatsby,* had inspired generations of Europeans and Americans. But most of the utopian authors concluded that this earthy Holy Grail had too often receded "year by year" before the eyes of the devout. Their choice of the corrupt city as the place to start The Change argued that the urban landscape was the frontier of the twentieth century; and the rejection of the faith in virgin land by two-thirds of the authors made it clear that for them a "mere difference in latitude and longitude cannot achieve miracles."[37] And this position was maintained in the face of repeated challenges making the utopian stance even more praiseworthy. To quote one representative critic: "There are thousands of acres of good government lands left, where Mr. Bellamy and his friends may settle and show the world what they can do."[38] The decision by most of the authors not to do this, not even to write about doing it, underscored their belief that twentieth-century Americans who ran away from the problems of industrialization and urbanization would only be fooling themselves. The direct and indirect criticism voiced by authors such as Edson, Twain, and Orpen illustrates that some of the authors were also capable of tours de force that picked apart weaknesses in the several versions of virgin land as salvation. Finally, the fact that almost half of the authors who clung to the promise of virgin land chose to narrate the histories of activist, outward-looking communities suggests that even the "true believers" were searching for alternatives to a simplistic faith in the revitalizing powers of an unoccupied piece of turf.

Their search and the search of the other utopian authors may not have been much more than inspired groping laden with ambivalence about rural and urban America. But their solutions are still important warnings to Americans who react to contemporary problems with napalm do-it-yourself virgin-land tactics in small countries, self-righteous, introspective communes, mass exoduses from central cities, and dreams of the Good Life on Arizona "ranchettes."

4

The Individual: Converted, Led, Whitewashed and Conditioned

Turn, turn from the cave's dark hollow!
Look up to the light and see,
Though thine eyes be dazzled in the glory,
the man that is yet to be!
—*Rennell Rodd, "For the Future"* The Nationalist *(1889)*

The French reviewer was impressed. Bellamy's Boston of 2000 A.D. was an enchanting "dream," but. . . . The rub was that "unless man's heart be entirely transformed," the dream would remain only a dream.[1] For late nineteenth-century American utopian authors this criticism represented the most imposing obstacle on the journey to utopia. They hoped that utopia would be more than a dream. They wanted a glorious "accomplished fact."[2] But if they were going to convince their readers that dreams could be facts, they had to explain how average citizens could be transformed into utopians.

In essence the French critic, Emile de Laveleye, was saying that American idealists might indulge in inspired speculation about a reformed or virgin New World as the hallmark of a liberation from the past. But what was to keep the inhabitants of this sparkling landscape from making old mistakes, fouling the land, and sending America right back onto the roller coaster of Old-World time? The only insurance seemed to be what Joaquin Miller called the *"new man* of the *new world."*[3] That's fine; but this answer spawns a knotted string of questions: Does human nature need to be changed to create the new man? If so, should it and can it? If it should and can, must each individual change before society really changes; or is it possible for part of the population to change first, thus helping to build an environment that will convince stragglers to reform?

Literary problems and again the issue of testability made these questions even more perplexing. The authors had to create utopians who were noble enough to prove that people could change, and human enough to be believable. Otherwise the readers would not identify with them and might brand the utopian authors as naive optimists who imagined beautiful worlds while taking for granted a degree of human perfection beyond the limits of human nature. What made this artistic challenge particularly difficult was that readers could consider themselves experts on human nature even if they doubted their ability to judge the utopian concepts of time and space. General theories about history were difficult to prove or disprove because of the ease with which events could be selected and arranged and because the readers' own experiential knowledge covered but a tiny segment of time. Space was much more concrete and testable. Still, unless readers had attempted to purify a corrupted area or joined an isolated commune, how could they "know" which utopian concept of space was "right"? Of course, the readers' experiential knowledge of human nature was limited, but this represented a different kind of perception. Readers existed in time and space, but they existed as humans and spent much of their lives watching other humans. Therefore, no matter how limited their contacts were, they could still consider themselves experts on human nature, or at least they could believe that they were in a better position to evaluate the utopian concept of the individual than the utopian views of time and space.

Again these were dilemmas utopian visionaries had battled for centuries. They were especially bewildering, however, to late nineteenth-century American utopian authors because part of the confusion they perceived as symptomatic of America's Armageddon was uncertainty over the fate of the individual. On the one hand, there was a sustaining reservoir of hope springing from the Enlightenment's assumption of the perfectability of man. Closer to home was a democratic faith in the average individual, a celebration of the American Adam in much of our literature, and a continuing belief in the self-made man.[4] On the other hand, the Puritan heritage of man's innate depravity, the inadequacies of Adamic innocence in a corrupted land, and mounting evidence that individuals could not make themselves, all seemed to belittle the role of the individual. The last doubt was chronic. Less than 10% of the authors maintained that by industry, frugality, and skill alone could any American be a success.[5] The rest believed that impersonal forces, especially money power and economic cycles, played an important role in shaping individuals. And this struggle between the individual and circumstance was presented as the key to Armageddon. Either the outrageous effects of unjust forces would inspire individuals to create an environment that would encourage instead of discourage personal development for the majority, or individuals would yield under the yoke of impersonal pressures and change into barbarians or serfs. (In Benjamin Rush Davenport's *"Uncle Sam's" Cabins* (1895) Americans literally become serfs.) Thus, the fate of the individual would determine whether America broke with the past or plunged back into Old-World feudalism and barbarism.

As this all-or-nothing attitude implies, the utopian concept of the individual, like the utopian view of space, was closely linked to the authors' concept of history. Hence, as might be expected, when they wrote about changing individuals, they weren't thinking of just any individuals; they meant Americans. It would be Americans who would change first and pave the way to glory or destruction for the world's population. Consequently, the utopian authors' definition of human nature was as narrowly nationalistic and as vulnerable as their views of time and space.

Nevertheless, the utopian authors realized that transforming the individual was the most difficult step on the road to utopia. They knew that human beings were complex creatures who had to be approached from several different angles. Therefore, like some of the best classical and British utopian authors surveyed by Richard Gerber, these authors agreed that "moral, intellectual, and material improvement [had to] work . . . together" to change man's heart.[6] Thus they utilized all their talents for mixing the traditional and the modern, the religious and the secular, and the serious and the faddish, to come up with a formula that combined four different views of human nature.

The following examination of these four approaches is different from the analysis of the two major and four minor utopian concepts of space. It is fairly easy to divide the authors into several groups advocating different geographical perspectives. Similarly, it is not difficult to select specific authors who emphasized one view of human nature over others—as a matter of fact, this is one of the most interesting things about the utopian concept of the individual since we can see several striking differences between the average, the popular, and the most perceptive portrayals of the ideal individual. For example, the most experienced authors were more aware of the difficulties involved in changing people. Bellamy and Howells dramatized the trials suffered by converts to new-world views (West and Eve); Twain and Donnelly foresaw terrible possibilities in reform leaders turned tyrants; and Twain questioned the possibility of ever conditioning goodness into adults. Nevertheless, all the authors used at least three of the four approaches in varying degrees. Therefore, it would be misleading to associate specific works with only one view of human nature.

Although the four approaches can not be directly linked with certain groups of works, they can be placed on a spectrum that ranges from a close examination of each individual's psyche to an aggregate overview of the relation between man and his environment. At one extreme the individual is altered by a sudden, inward conversion similar to the excruciating but ecstatic experience analyzed by Jonathan Edwards, an associate of Bellamy's great-great-grandfather. At the other extreme is a much more gradual process dependent upon man's ability to consciously manipulate the environment and thus predetermine which characteristics of human nature are most likely to develop fully. In between these extremes are the glorification of a culture hero who inspires mass conversions and the implication that dominance by one preferred "race" and the conscious elimination or neutralization of others will improve the human environment by screening out undesirable traits.

Given such a conglomerate view of human nature, it is not surprising that the utopian concept of the individual contained some of the most perceptive and humane ideas found in the utopian works as well as the most simplistic and narcissistic. This suggests a truism—one that is more truth than platitude: it is sometimes the most difficult problems that inspire the best and the worst thought by reformers. It also reveals how difficult it was for authors whose backgrounds did not fully reflect the changing makeup and diversity of their population to envision a utopia large enough to include individuals whose backgrounds were radically different from their own—even if they were sincere in their desire to help all mankind and even if they offered multisided answers to the complex question of transforming people.

The first side of the conglomerate approach to changing the individual was the conversion experience: a sudden and dramatic transformation that enabled a person to discard "preconceived notions" and see the world in a new way.[7] It was a painful process because seeing things differently meant losing part of one's old identity and facing ridicule from the unconverted. Thus, each conversion was a miniature Armageddon, a personal drama that reflected the general suffering and rebirth that heralded the Resurrection of the transition period. Another link to the utopian concept of history was that the conversion experience was not described as a purely mystical event unrelated to the outside world. Like the Puritan conversions analyzed by Jonathan Edwards, these perception revolutions were most likely to occur during times of great suffering and confusion when the old ways of seeing simply did not work. According to the utopian authors, the late nineteenth century was such a time, so it was not unreasonable to expect conversions.

Most of the authors gave only vague glimpses of conversions, which allowed the converted to perceive both the horrors and the opportunities of Armageddon. They often compared these transformations to religious revivals by pointing to sudden mass awakenings. In *Equality,* for instance, economic changes are accompanied by a "Great Revival," and religious and evolutionary rhetoric combine to celebrate a new vision of mankind:

> . . . the moment [when] men allowed themselves to believe that humanity after all had not been meant for a dwarf . . . but that it stood upon the verge of an avatar of limitless development. . . . It is evident that nothing was able to stand against the enthusiasm which the new faith inspired.[8]

In *In His Steps* and *Looking Backward,* however, we find more than general references to mass conversions. Here we have in-depth portrayals of individual conversions. It may be a coincidence that these two novels were the most popular utopian works—a coincidence that the only nineteenth-century reform novel to rival *Looking Backward* and *In His Steps* in popularity was *Uncle Tom's Cabin*, which also includes a dramatic (re)conversion experience. (Tom reaches a low point at Legree's plantation, but a holy vision revives him.) Possibly it was a coincidence or the fact that conversions made exciting reading material. Still, Sheldon's and Bellamy's popularity might also be related to the willingness of nineteenth-century readers to accept a conversion as a familiar, understandable, and believable way of revealing how people change.

In Sheldon's *In His Steps* the conversion experience is presented in a traditional religious context; but, as in other utopian works, the experience is precipitated when the suffering of the late nineteenth century is dramatically revealed. Startled by the collapse of a tramp in his small-town church in Kansas, the Rev. Mr. Henry Maxwell realizes that "to revolutionize the world" humanity must be "regenerated." To Sheldon's hero this specifically means that each individual must suffer through a "crisis of character" that not only calls for a new way of perceiving others and Jesus, but also necessitates the re-evaluation of every single act performed by the individual. This is a painful task for the converts. At first a few influential parishioners convert and preface every act with the question, "What would Jesus do?" But the majority of the townspeople treat the minister and his followers as madmen. One poor fellow even loses his job and the love of his family for seeing the world as a Christian should. Yet the town is eventually transformed because the conversions give Maxwell's followers the insight and dedication to withstand ridicule and to make their surroundings conform to their vision of Christ's utopia.

Bellamy presented his portrayal of a conversion experience from a different angle. His narrator, like the first readers of *Looking Backward,* is suddenly transported to a new world where he finds his old perceptions practically useless. He must learn to see anew. Thus, through Julian West's experience—which is so vivid and personal that it seems as if Bellamy were recalling his own conversion as a Baptist teenager[9]—Bellamy could suggest the nature of the suffering and joy that motivated the reformers who built the America of 2000 A.D.

In the numerous imitations of *Looking Backward* the narrator's confused reactions to the new America became literary clichés not unlike the standard anguished responses of the narrator to strange events in popular Gothic novels. He is confused upon awakening and several times throughout the story he utters stock statements about being a frightened creature caught between two worlds. By contrast, West's transformation from being a "rich and also educated" Bostonian of the 1880s to becoming a Nationalist at the opening of the twenty-first century is not a literary cliché. Repeatedly he complains that he is suffering "mental torture" and an "emotional crisis." He must fight "for sanity." He even begins to believe that he is "two persons," that he has a "double" identity. These crises lead to violent psychosomatic reactions seldom included in proper Bostonian novels: crying jags, burning eyeballs, insomnia, running and shouting wildly through the streets, and fits of nausea. At one point his description of a crisis sounds as if it came from a case study by a psychoanalytical anthropologist:

> In my mind, all had broken loose, habits of feeling, associations of thought, ideas of persons and things, all had dissolved and lost coherence and were seething together in an apparently irretrievable chaos. There were no rallying points, nothing was left stable.[10]

As Howells observed in the *Atlantic* obituary for Bellamy, the ultimate crisis occurs in "that moment of anguish at the close, when Julian West trembles with the nightmare fear that he has only been dreaming." In a dream he returns to the Boston of 1887; but now he sees the same reality, especially the suffering of the poor, in a totally different manner. He, like Maxwell, also feels guilt ("I found upon my garments the blood of this great multitude") and must suffer ridicule. He is called a "madman" and a "fanatic" by his old friends, his fiancée, and her father. This he can stand, and he continues to appeal to them until he is thrown out. Then, suddenly, he comes to a crushing conclusion. It is not just that his new perception gives him a different perspective from his old friends; his world view has been so radically changed that his words are "meaningless" to them. The old "habits of feeling, associations of thought," "the rallying points" he had formerly used to communicate with others had all "dissolved" from his mind. The horrifying corollary to this awakening is that his old identity is no longer a meaningful reality to him. He is confused, he experiences physical pain, and finally he gives way and breaks down: "Tears poured from my eyes. In my vehemence

I became inarticulate. I panted, I sobbed, I groaned. . . ." But miraculously and suddenly, as in a religious conversion, his pain and confusion are alleviated and turn to euphoria: ". . . I sobbed, I groaned, and immediately afterward found myself sitting upright in bed . . . and the morning sun shining through the open window into my eyes." He is still quivering and the tears are still flowing, but now these physical reactions express his relief and joy instead of his anguish.[11]

Most of the utopian authors made less of the pain and confusion of a conversion, which may have made their portrayals less believable. Almost all the authors did, however, point to a crucial personal awakening that signaled the beginning of The Change. The only two obvious exceptions, Solomon Schindler and William Dean Howells, demonstrate the influence of an author's background and the ability of an experienced author to question the possibility of conversion. *Young West* (1894) narrates the life cycle of Julian West's son. Near the conclusion of the novel Young West discovers his father's "Confessions," which reveal that West never really enjoyed utopia because no one can completely change his way of perceiving the world. Such a change, argues West, only comes with a gradual process of internalizing new ideas over several generations. In part this criticism of the conversion experience may have been due to the background of Young West's creator. Rabbi Solomon Schindler was one of the few non-Protestant utopian authors. To him the Protestant concept of conversion was simply not a probable way of explaining how people change.

William Dean Howells was Protestant, but in his relatively unknown *Letters from an Altrurian Traveller* (*Cosmopolitan*, 1893-94) his desire to convey realistically the reactions of an upper-class woman led him dangerously close to denying that a sudden awareness of the horrors of the present and a vision of a better world could transform the heart. Mr. Homos, an Altrurian visiting America, manages to fall in love with a wealthy young girl, Eve, who agrees with his views. After they have declared their love for each other, however, she is shocked when he asks her to give up her lifestyle, friends, and money and go to Altruria with him. For a brief moment love triumphs and she agrees; then she reconsiders and reacts as did Maxwell's and West's old friends. She is too much of a lady to call Homos a madman, but she does call him a silly "goose" and refuses to go. Homos reacts by first depicting her as a victim of "false conditions" that have "warped" her. Then he realizes that the real reason for her decision is that if she did accept Altruria, she would be "in a manner ceasing to be." She had invested so much of her intellectual and emotional self in an upper-class way of seeing America that to deny this would be an act of self-destruction.[12] Unfortunately, when Howells returned to this situation and extended the story in Part 2 of

Through the Eye of the Needle (1907), the complexities of her dilemma are obscured by her enthusiasm for life in Altruria.

In a sermon near the conclusion of *Looking Backward* the Rev. Mr. Barton alludes to a "stormy epoch of transition when heroes burst the barred gate of the future."[13] Yet Bellamy did not create a champion of Nationalism who inspired mass conversions. Nevertheless, about half the utopian authors, including Sheldon, gave leading roles to heroic figures in the drama of American history. (Here I am specifically referring to individuals who lead mass movements during the transition period. Narrators and other major characters are not included unless they meet this qualification.)[14] These authors implied that the conditions of the nineteenth century might not be enough to inspire conversions. But the leadership of a hero who had converted would make Americans see the realities of the present and the possibilities of the future. In *Aristopia* (1895) Castello N. Holford defines the role of this type of hero by placing him within the context of the utopian concept of history:

> . . . a man of great wisdom, foresight, and genius, with an unselfish devotion to the welfare of humanity, placed with immense power at the parting of the ways in the course of human events, seizing the opportunity to turn the march of bewildered and struggling humanity into the path leading up and away from the dangerous marshes . . . of ancient errors, and . . . antique evils.[15]

Having a hero lead the march to utopia made sense from a literary viewpoint. Most of the utopian authors were inexperienced at novel writing and, as one *Literary World* reviewer put it, having a hero around was very handy when an author "needed some gigantic puppet to hold the threads of a well-nigh unmanageable plot."[16] Nineteenth-century readers, moreover, expected heroes in their novels, especially "solitary" figures battling an "alien tribe."[17] Since the authors were narrating a grand historical drama, it would also be natural to find some Founding Fathers in the early scenes. Then too, heroes could be rendered familiar and believable with comparisons to real heroes who appeared in times of need: Washington, Lincoln and Grant were used, and hadn't Jesus inspired millions to change their ways of seeing things?

These authors had to be careful, however; Americans love heroes, but they hate kings and dictators. Therefore they had to find some way to make their heroes powerful leaders and true-blue democrats simultaneously. In an English single-tax utopian work, *The Story of My Dictatorship* (1894), Lewis Henry Berens and Ignatius Singer skirted the issue with the familiar dream motif. Just as the hero is beginning to enjoy his tremendous powers, the narrative is interrupted with "'Get up, my dear, get up; you must be quite stiff, sleeping all night on that hard chair.'"[18] For the American creators of utopian heroes there was no need to vanquish their heroes with literary evasions. Their solution suggests an attitude that has characterized numerous American reform movements and emergency policies, such as Greenbacks during the Civil War, guidelines and price freezes during periods of depression and inflation, and the wartime powers of a president, the utopian hero was perceived as a *temporary* means of solving a *specific* crisis. To illustrate, the one author who came closest to advocating a personal dictatorship, Dr. William Von Swartwout, envisioned an ideal state headed by a president (himself) with tremendous powers. Still, "a Leader, a Joshua" was only an "absolute necessity" during "the Transition." Thereafter a democracy would be restored.[19] The hero was transient because his mission eliminated his function. Once he had converted the masses, all Americans would participate in a society of heroic equals. As the narrator of Alcanoan O. Grigsby's *Nequa* (1900) boasts,

> a time came when the effects of their teachings [several Christ-like heroes] was to produce a multitude of such characters, and then the entire people made one great bound upwards, and now we are all saviors.[20]

According to the utopian authors, many different types of heroes could inspire this "great bound upwards." The following list surveys the occupations of most of the heroes. Admittedly this is a very crude introduction to the utopian heroes. Any such listing tends to lump dissimilar heroes together. But the list does at least indicate the occupational diversity of the heroes. The names under the categories are the authors of utopian works in which heroic figures lead the journey to utopia. (For descriptions of these works, see the annotated bibliography.) Several novels include more than one type of hero; therefore several names appear under more than one category.

ENGINEERS, INVENTORS, MINERALOGISTS, AND SCIENTISTS
  Astor, Caryl, Fitch, Fuller, Galloway, Granville, Griggs, Grimshaw, Holford, Houston, McDougall, Moore, Newcomb, North, Phelps, Reynolds, Schindler, Twain, Waterloo, Welcome, Windsor.
MINISTERS AND RELIGIOUS LEADERS
  Cole, Daniel, Davenport (*"Uncle Sam's" Cabins*), Everett, Grigsby, Lubin, Sheldon, Thomas, Tinckner, Windsor, Woods.
POLITICAL LEADERS AND ECONOMIC REFORMERS
  Adams, Child, Griggs, McCoy, Pomeroy, Satterlee, Swift, Von Swartwout.

LABORERS
Donnelly (*Caesar's Column*), Hale, McCowan (2), Porter, Salisbury, Woods.

MILITARY MEN AND SEA CAPTAINS
Bradshaw, Craig, Davenport (*Anglo-Saxons, Onward!*), Fitzpatrick, North, Satterlee.

AUTHORS
Clarke, Crocker, Franklin, Leggett.

BUSINESSMEN
Peck, Reynolds, Stockwell, Walker (J.B.)

JOURNALISTS AND EDITORS
Everett, Griggs, Morris.

FARMERS AND LIVESTOCK OWNERS
Edson, Donnelly (*Caesar's Column, Golden Bottle*).

VERY WEALTHY HEROES AND HEROINES
Athey & Bowers, Bartlett, Bishop, Craig, Crocker, Donnelly (*Golden Bottle*), Edson, Fitch, Frederic, Galloway, Griggs, Holford, Howard, McDougall, Phelps, Stockwell, Tinckner, Walker (J.B.).

The variety of occupations suggests that the utopian authors did not look to any one profession as the source of heroes. Even some of the obvious trends might be considered literary conveniences. For example, if an author imagined a national reform movement or a large, isolated community, a wealthy leader was a handy explanation for the necessary funds. He might also make the narrative more believable since several of the successful nineteenth-century communes did have wealthy founders.[21] The popularity of moralistic inventors, engineers, and scientists reflects nineteenth-century America's respect for such professions. An earnest hero who could plan both the spiritual and physical sides of utopia was also an economical means of unifying the plot.

But the all-encompassing nature of the leader was more than a literary shortcut. It was central to the concept of the utopian hero: a desire for what Michael Kammen has called the American Everyman-Superman. Except for the few aristocrats, most of the utopian heroes had humble or average backgrounds. Their names even reflect their commonness. By far the most popular name was John; F. U. Adams went one step further with his *President John Smith* (1897), and Archibald McCowan named his heroic coal miner's son Abraham Lincoln Homeborn! But as this last name suggests, these were certainly uncommon commoners. They were earnest, brilliant, and skilled, especially at making speeches.[22] And what's more they had haloes. Again the names are indicative: names like Joshua, Emanuel, Gabriel, and Moses; even the Johns could find biblical authority in John the Baptist. Furthermore, many of the heroes justified their programs by claiming that they were merely applying Christ's teachings. Several authors went beyond this: Chauncey Thomas's John Costor has the same initials as Jesus Christ; Cyrus Cole's hero's name, Creeto, sounds like Christ and the birth of this "Son of God" was called a "Second Coming"; and in William Windsor's *Loma* (1897) thirty representatives of the "Associated Philosophers" journey to the birthplace of the hero bearing gifts!

The names and biblical comparisons sufficiently deified these commoners; but many authors added one final touch, again demonstrating their ability to blend traditional images and popular fads, in this case religion and the aura of ritualistic fraternal orders. The hero's organization was often a mysterious "brotherhood" unified by secret rituals, oaths, and symbols. Reform groups met in secluded places and enforced strict secrecy; the leaders sometimes even dressed in monk-like robes as do Caesar and his two assistants in *Caesar's Column.* John Costor's followers wear crystal buttons symbolizing the crystal clear truth of Costor's religion; and John Harvey's supporters sing such songs as "Hymn to the Nationality." Several heroes wrote books that were revered as modern bibles, and all the brotherhoods had inspirational slogans such as "Equality or Death," one used by black students in Dr. Griggs's *Imperium in Imperio* (1899). Henry O. Morris's readers even found a cross-like "mystic symbol" as the frontispiece and cover design for *Waiting for the Signal* (1897).

To twentieth-century readers the biblical analogies and the rituals might be so much fraternal mumbo jumbo thrown in to add a touch of sacred melodrama to otherwise dull books. But in essence the utopian authors created heroes who resemble the culture heroes described by Anthony F. C. Wallace in *Culture and Personality* and *The Death and Rebirth of the Seneca.* Using the example of the Seneca leader, Handsome Lake, Wallace argues that during times of cultural collapse, a purely rational and practical leader may fail to "revitalize" his people. What is needed is a person who combines common sense with the ability to present his message as if it were an integrated, divine revelation, a whole new world view to fill the vacuum left by the decay of old values.

Surveying the occupations, names, and rituals associated with utopian heroes gives some idea of the nature of these practical saviors. But to really understand their makeup it is necessary to take a closer look at a couple of typical heroes.

In Chauncey Thomas's *The Crystal Button* (1891) the hero, John Costor, has Scandinavian parents, grows up in the Midwest, marries and starts a farm in the Northwest. His rather uneventful life is shattered when his wife and children are killed by a band of Indians enraged by broken treaties. Instead of seeking revenge, Costor goes into the wilderness, lives with the tribe and tries to help them. While living with the Indians, "stripped of all the robes with which civilization . . . covered its moral deformities," Costor has a conversion experience, and, like the missionaries from the outward-looking utopian communities, he leaves his friendly tribe and goes out to confront the alien tribe of nineteenth-century Americans. He becomes the sole "prophet" and "moral teacher" of a new religion requiring each individual to re-evaluate every act performed in relation to its "truthfulness." His truth societies crop up all over America and around the world, attesting to the power of his person and his gospel. This rapid moral revolution saves America from outbreaks of violence between workers and employers and lays the foundations for the utopia that the narrator discovers in the forty-ninth century.[23]

At first glance James M. Galloway's hero in *John Harvey* (1897) seems to be a completely different type of individual. At about the same time in his life as John Costor is losing his wife, John Harvey, a bright young "wizard" of an engineer-mineralogist-inventor, is busy discovering a Colorado mine that produces hundreds of millions of dollars in gold and two new miracle metals. He keeps the mine a secret and quietly proceeds to buy "a vast body of land now lying waste" in the West which, under his direction, is transformed into a just and productive Nationalistic confederation. Harvey's vision of a new kind of society, his technological skills, and his devotion to his vision inspire several thousand settlers to change their lives. Although his message is not specifically religious, his devotion to a vision of a just society soon makes him a deity among his followers. The manuscript that tells his life story is treated as if it were a Holy Gospel, and after his death he is encased in an elaborate tomb worthy of a lesser Pharaoh. Symbolically, he even rises from the grave to advise his flock. Near the end of the novel his confederation is threatened by the capitalists of the east coast. A select group of his most devoted followers and the narrator enter his tomb and perform elaborate rituals and oaths accompanied by mysterious organ music and chants in the presence of an ominous black statue of Harvey. The rituals enable the followers to open a hidden compartment containing the formula for a secret weapon to be used only during times of dire necessity. The compartment is empty. The apostles realize that Harvey's final act must have been the destruction of the formula; his posthumous message was that no crisis was worth the possible destruction of mankind. He is right, of course. The workers on the outside of the confederation support the Nationality, and a civil war is averted. The novel concludes with the narrator and Harvey's daughter looking upwards toward the dome of an administration building where "in a halo of light on its summit, [we] saw the statue of John Harvey."[24]

Despite the obvious appeals of their money, skills, devotion, and haloes, it must be remembered that only half the utopian authors included heroes in their histories of the transition period. Handsome Lake could revitalize the Seneca, but half the authors felt that in a country as large and diverse as America it was foolish to expect that one individual could capture the imagination of the people and make them see things a new way.

Furthermore, the perceptive authors who narrated the exploits of heroes during The Change tended to portray them as pathetic or frightening figures. In Book III of Caroline Mason's *A Woman of Yesterday* (1900) the hero's fanatic devotion to Christianity destroys a utopian community; and in Elizabeth Orpen's *Perfection City* (1897) a heroine who possesses both wealth and religious fervor succumbs to personal jealousy and abandons her community, which collapses without her funds and guidance.

But the most poignant criticism of dependence on heroic figures came from three of the more experienced authors—Joaquin Miller, Donnelly, and Twain. In Miller's *The Building of the City Beautiful* (1893) one hero (there are two) dreams of founding a model community on a virgin mountainside. Unfortunately, John Morton's retreat to the wilderness—his isolation and introspection—lead to delusions of grandeur. Thus, as in many of the utopian works about experiments on virgin land, a private, temporary vision is imposed upon the rest of the world. John thinks he is building a glorious city upon a hill, when in fact he is only cultivating a few scraggly olive trees and no one really cares. Ignatius Donnelly's Caesar is not isolated and does achieve his goal of rallying the masses to overthrow the money kings of 1988. But once he unleashes the powerful forces he organized and inspired, he discovers that he cannot control them. He even fails to control one of his closest associates, a Russian Jew, who flees the country with one hundred million dollars. This powerful hero in whom thousands had placed their trust eventually loses control of himself, becomes drunk with power and then literally drunk upon the liquor once owned by one of the former financial kings. His own followers become enraged with his behavior, murder him, and place his head on a spike. Donnelly's feelings of fear and disgust associated with the potentially destructive results of dependence on a heroic figure are fully revealed in the final glimpse he offers of the once inspiring Caesar: "I [Gabriel] could see the glazed and dusty eyes; the protruding tongue; the great lower jaw hanging down in hideous fashion; and from the thick, bull-like neck were suspended huge gouts of dried and blackened blood."[25]

Then there is Hank Morgan, who combines the good intentions, the lack of control, and the isolation of John Morton and Caesar. If F. U. Adams's John Smith can claim that he is "an American of Americans," Hank can boast that he is "a Yankee of Yankees."[26] Also like other utopian heroes he is a commoner (a factory foreman with a common name); he has exceptional skills—especially a dramatic flair for bedazzling the Arthurians; he is careful to keep his organization a secret; he is revered as a "superior being"; and he is religiously devoted to Democracy and Progress. And, like Caesar, he leads a successful revolution, then loses control of his followers (except for Clarence and the fifty-two boys). Unlike Morton or Caesar, however, Hank's knowledge of advanced technology allows him to perpetuate his delusions of grandeur. This represents an important criticism of the utopian hero. Twain perceived that when modern leaders controlled sophisticated weapons, the completion of their mission did not necessarily mean their disappearance. So much for a *temporary* solution to a *specific* crisis. Beyond this Hank embodies the pathetic loneliness of the modern solitary hero and suggests the dangers of hoping for an Everyman-Superman. Despite Hank's rambles through the countryside, he is never really in touch with the people because he views them as "tame animals." After the Interdict, technology enables Hank to isolate himself completely behind dynamite barriers and rings of electric wires. In his deadly womb-like enclave this democrat loses contact with the people—they become things to be eliminated. Only once does he go to the people, and ironically he only visits corpses and dying knights. Hank gazes through the bars of an electrocuted knight's helmet and is horrified by the thought of the charred contents obscured by shadows. Later in an act of kindness, he attempts to help a wounded knight who stabs him for his compassion—Hank's horror and sympathy come too late. Like the revelation of Ahab's humanities in "The Symphony" chapter of *Moby-Dick,* the descriptions of Hank's human and humane reactions only serve to heighten the tragedy of a misguided hero by exposing his confusion and loneliness. Near the end of the Battle of the Sand-Belt Hank becomes painfully aware of this isolation. As the electrocuted knights silently drop around him, he admits that "this sort of thing . . . was very creepy, there in the dark and lonesomeness."[27] Instead of the decisive tones of a mature individual who dispels suffering and confusion and inspires mass conversions, Hank's confession is the pathetic whine of a bewildered child. Through this man-child Twain expressed his deepest fears about allowing the Everyman-Superman to lead the way to utopia.

Thus, even though half the utopian authors, including Sheldon, hoped for the appearance of an Everyman-Superman who was a "Scholar, Sage, Humanitarian, Reformer, Patriot, Author, Orator and Statesman" rolled into one,[28] the other half, including Bellamy, preferred to emphasize different means of transforming the individual. And Miller, Donnelly, and Twain had glimpses of Hitlers, Stalins, and even a Nixon-like modern leader who buries himself behind the power and complexity of mass government and in isolation gnaws upon private delusions.

In *Equality,* Bellamy proclaimed that the ultimate aim of reform was the elimination of the "accident of birth." Yet, in the same book he made it very clear that there were certain unchangeable accidents of birth. In a section on "the colored race and the new order" he argued that blacks should have economic equality, but

> Even for industrial purposes the new system involved no more commingling of races than the old one had done. It was perfectly consistent with any degree of race separation in industry which the most bigoted local prejudice might demand.[29]

This is just one indication of an assumption underlying the utopian concept of human nature: there were certain types of individuals who could never really be converted, and they certainly could never lead others to conversions. Therefore, reformers should shape the future of mankind by eliminating or at least neutralizing such individuals. This represents the utopian authors' third approach to transforming the individual.

Over the past two decades a controversy has grown over whether late nineteenth-century reformers were more racist than their contemporaries.[30] Such debates are difficult to evaluate since conclusions are almost certain to be predetermined by the samples used. It would be easy to select specific passages from the utopian literature to prove that the authors were racists, but it would only be a bit more difficult to pick out humane comments on ethnic and racial problems. Possibly the only reasonable conclusion is that certain groups were more adept at articulating the prejudices shared by most white, native Americans. Whatever the truth behind this unanswerable controversy is, the utopian works do reveal that it was very difficult for middle- and upper-middle-class reformers to conceive of ideal individuals whose ethnic and racial backgrounds deviated from their own white, Protestant heritage. Instead of trying to adapt to the increasing diversity of America's population by imagining a pluralistic utopia, they recoiled and hoped for homogeneity. Thus, the utopian concept of human nature was as ambivalent as the utopian concept of time. Reforms were sincerely proposed on behalf of all mankind. But if "all" became too inclusive, the authors might risk resolving the confusing diversity of the present with more diversity in the future. It was safer to restrict "all" to the size of a full-length mirror.

Very few utopian authors (5) chose to write books like Benjamin Rush Davenport's *Anglo-Saxons, Onward!* (1898)—books championing the

Anglo-Saxonizing of mankind either by creating superhuman "Aryan" heroes, by envisioning the successes of armed combat, missionary movements and colonization, or by simply assuming that once dark-skinned people got a glimpse of the white, American way, they would reject their cultural and racial heritages and clammer to be "whitewashed."[31] This celebration of the white man's burden is very similar to hero worship. Again people are seen as heroes or villains; they are all "white" or all "black." (As a matter of fact all the heroes save two were white.) A quasi-utopian adventure story, Frona Colburn's *Yermah the Dorado* (1897) appropriately dedicated to the "'WHITE KNIGHTS' of all times", even praises one character and elevates him to a heroic stature using phrases that would have delighted the leaders of the Nazi Lebensborn experiment. He is a young, blond, "pure-blooded" "Aryan"—"the Ideal man of all time, and of all people."[32] *Yermah* is also interesting because it makes explicit an assumption shared not only by Davenport and the other Anglo-Saxonists but by most of the utopian authors: at one time in the dark recesses of the past, there existed a pure light-skinned race that enjoyed a unified, noble civilization. Unfortunately, during the Old-World cycles, this race was corrupted and partially destroyed by hordes of barbarians and natural catastrophes (in *Yermah* the sinking of Atlantis and volcanic eruptions in California). But possibly in the future, after the liberation from Old-World time, there could be an end to the confusing nationality and racial diversity of the present and a return to the original, understandable homogeneity.

Many authors implied this longing by sprinkling praises to the "Caucasians," "Anglo-Saxons," and "Aryans" throughout their works. But there were only the five militant Anglo-Saxonists. The rest of the authors were much more concerned with justifying why certain strands of humanity had to be strained out or purified to insure more homogeneity and the birth of the ideal individual. The undesirables most frequently mentioned in this weeding out process were the new immigrants from Southeastern Europe and the Orient, Jews, American Indians, and blacks.

During the late nineteenth century, thousands of immigrants flocked to America from Southeastern Europe, and utopian authors feared the results. In some cases new immigrants were seen as proof that America was headed towards an Old-World nadir. In *Equality,* for example, West is told that the evils of the transition period were compounded by an invasion of "the lowest, most wretched, and barbarous races of Europe—the very scum of the continent";[33] and in *Armageddon* (1898) Stanley Waterloo predicts that once Catholic foreigners, especially the Spanish, gain power, they will reinstitute the Inquisition! Usually such compliments were saved for the new immigrants (violent labor agitators were swarthy-complexioned Italians;

Donnelly's Caesar was Italian), but John A. Mitchell's fictional history singled out the "Murfey Dynasty," a twentieth-century political machine, as one of the main causes for the ruins of the Brooklyn Bridge. (See Plate 3.) It was the Chinese, however, who received the worst treatment from the utopian authors. They had been excluded from America since 1882, but the "Yellow Peril" was still seen as a serious threat and as the closest thing to a barbarian horde in the modern world. In at least two works, Arthur Vinton's *Looking Further Backward* (1890) and John Bachelder's *A. D. 2050* (1890), the Chinese actually mass an attack on the United States; and in Vinton's story Americans have become so dissipated under Nationalism that the Chinese are victorious. Two brief comments found in *Caesar's Column* and Davenport's *Anglo-Saxons, Onward!* are more indicative of anti-Chinese feelings. In Caesar's world the farmers' profits were slashed by capitalists who bought bonanza farms and hired "vile hordes of Mongolian coolies" with their "effeminate limbs." Davenport's young hero has, in the past, had some contact with Chinese women. To him they were simply "incomprehensible." Of course, he made no effort to understand them; Chinese were supposed to change and become comprehensible.[34] In fairness to the utopian authors, at least one of them, Castello N. Holford envisioned an ideal America that was especially proud of its immigrants and its "heterogeneous" nature. But even in his *Aristopia* (1895) immigrants from Switzerland were preferred.

In popular nineteenth-century fiction Jewish immigrants and bankers were often portrayed as strange and evil beings who were leaders of mysterious money conspiracies. As Norman Pollack and John S. Patterson have pointed out, however, attempts to link reformers with anti-Semitism can be misleading. Donnelly attacked national, racial, and religious prejudices in newspaper articles and speeches; hence, it is unjust to pass judgment on him because of "a few passages" found in one novel.[35] Unfortunately, this one novel, *Caesar's Column* (1890), was his best-selling work and one of the four most popular utopian novels written during the late nineteenth century. (By January 1891, 1,000 copies were sold each week; and a year after publication, it topped the 60,000 sales mark.)[36] In it the Jews are pictured as part of the worst of two "Semitized" worlds. On the one hand, the "bloated," lustful and sinister money prince, Cabano, has a Hebraic face and almost all the moneyed aristocracy is of "Hebrew origin." On the other hand, the mastermind of the Brotherhood of Destruction is a deformed Russian Jew who, during the revolution, absconds with a hundred million dollars and flees to Judea where he plans to become king of Jerusalem. Overall, however, there was not much blatant anti-Semitism in the utopian works. Only one novel, *An Ideal Republic* (1898), contains the full-blown Jewish-banker-

Lombard-Street conspiracy defined by Richard Hofstadter in the *Age of Reform*; and the author, Corwin Phelps, was a retired Civil War soldier who was convinced that Jewish bankers had been involved in shady deals that deprived soldiers of necessary supplies. (It is interesting to note, though, that Phelps received an extremely favorable review in *Arena*.)[37] One other novel, Alexander Craig's *Ionia* (1898), describes a utopia which, in part, was achieved by forbidding Jews to marry each other and by sterilizing any Jew—man, woman, or child—convicted of a crime. Still, the prejudice expressed by Phelps and Craig should be balanced against Joaquin Miller's views in *City Beautiful*. Here the real hero is a dark-skinned, beautiful, all-knowing Jewess who succeeds in building a perfect city, while her American, "Anglo-Saxon" counterpart is an utter failure.[38]

There may not have been much rampant anti-Semitism in the utopian works, but if a Jew wanted to enter utopia, he had better convert. General Leggett criticized Judaism as a corrupting influence upon Christianity and pictured Jews as "Christ-killing," "murderous Jews."[39] No other utopian author was such an outspoken proponent of this cruel stereotype, but all the utopian works—with the exception of books written by three Jews and four other authors[40]—described *Christian* utopias; there were no synagogues on the utopian landscape.

It would be difficult to determine whether the American Indian or the American Negro was the most confusing to and most unwanted by the utopian authors. According to William Gilpin, the "black population" was "in every way inferior," a "blot on our institutions" and "a curse to the country."[41] If blacks were permitted to enter utopia at all, they came, at best, on an equal but definitely separate basis.

Still, they were allowed in, whereas the real invisible men of utopia were the first Americans. Most authors simply could not imagine any place for a race that was supposed to vanish before utopia was realized. Therefore, the Indian was usually ignored. When he was mentioned, it was either in derogatory comparisons, as an example of a disappearing inferior race, or as the topic for long racist tirades. Twain's Hank Morgan is fond of comparing the Arthurians to Indians when he wants to emphasize their childishness or savagery, and Bellamy's critics enjoyed calling Nationalism large-scale tribal communalism. In Walter McDougall's *The Hidden City* (1891) a model, joint-stock community financed by gold discovered on Indian land will transform the world. But the Indians have no place in this glorious future since they are "dying off the face of the earth because civilization is too powerful for them to resist, and they are too weak to accept its customs."[42] Finally, Thomas and Anna M. Fitch's "Lo! the poor Indian," Chapter 10 of *Better Days* (1892), is a sustained racist harangue. Admittedly, they focus on a particularly warlike band of Apaches, but the general attitude is that most Indians should be rubbed out and that the rest are, at best, "dirty," "gentle" creatures who will eventually crawl off into some hovel and die. Better days? Certainly not for Indians.

But again the few tirades were balanced by occasional admiration for the co-operative spirit of tribalism. Since Joaquin Miller lived with the "Digger" Indians and took an Indian bride, it is not startling to discover that instead of modeling her ideal city after the tribes of Israel, Miller's beautiful Jewish heroine is guided by the example of Indian tribalism.

No author advocated modeling utopia after African tribalism, though in one obscure South Sea romance, Mrs. M. A. Pittock's *The God of Civilization* (1890), white visitors were so impressed by the money-free culture of a group of Oceanian Negroes that they adopted their customs. In most of the utopian works, however, comments about blacks were limited to well-known stereotypes: they were docile, lazy people prone to lying, stealing, and letting their "animalistic" passions rise too near the surface. In Orpen's *Perfection City,* for instance, the heroine, Olive, has a small black helper who loves to sleep. One day the child shows particular relish for a story involving a hanging. Olive concludes that "he was just a black savage, still rejoicing in the vivid details of horrors and cruelty."[43] Maybe if Olive and her creator had known a few more children or read some of Twain's "boy stories," they would have realized that most kids, black and white, enjoy gore and a good snooze. Several authors, including Alcanoan Grigsby, even perpetuated old wives' tales about skin color and "improvement." In Grigsby's *Nequa* (1900) missionaries are sent off to a "dark country" where the native mothers worship their white ways. The result: babies get lighter and lighter, and after a few generations the blacks are white! (Of course, this is caused by spiritual and mental contacts, never sexual.)[44]

Despite the stereotypes, the Negro did at least have a place in utopia unlike the invisible Indian. Sometimes that place was nothing more than being "excellent and willing servants"; but a few authors, including Bellamy, did offer economic equality and three implied social equality by predicting widespread intermarriage—one author half-jokingly advocated a pro-miscegenation, "pepper and salt party."[45]

Still, the only sustained treatment of blacks, one that made them the primary leaders on the journey to utopia, is found in *Imperium in Imperio* (1899). It was written by Dr. Sutton E. Griggs, the only black utopian author, whose works were "probably more widely circulated among Negroes than the works of Charles W. Chesnutt and Paul Laurence Dunbar."[46] *Imperium in Imperio* is the story of two black heroes, one a politician (a mulatto) and the other an orator-journalist-educator, who struggle against prejudice and lay the foundation for a black utopia. Some of their specific achievements, such as a schoolboy speech on "The Contribution of the Anglo-Saxon to the Cause of Human Liberty," might not seem so heroic to blacks today. But their general goal certainly was: they wanted to dispel the image of the "cringing, fawning, sniffling, cowardly Negro" derived from minstrels, washerwomen, and comic strips and show the world "a new Negro, self-respecting, fearless, and determined in the assertion of his rights." The culmination of their efforts is a secret, ritualistic organization based in Waco, Texas. It is funded by the inheritance of a black colonial scientist and, like John Winthrop's city, "seven million eyes [black Americans'] are riveted upon [it]." The plan that Griggs seemed most sympathetic towards was a mass migration of blacks to Texas where they would work out their "destiny as a separate and distinct race" under a "perfect" form of government. But the majority of the members of *Imperium in Imperio* are for a revolution, and the novel ends with warnings about subterranean smolderings similar to the cataclysmic danger signals that pervade the utopian literature.[47]

Although *Imperium in Imperio* shared many characteristics with the model-community utopian works, Griggs's treatment of blacks as real human beings, who were not only capable of conversion but could contribute significantly to America's salvation, gave his utopian vision a broader view of human nature. This is the prime illustration of a trend in the utopian projections of the ideal individual. It seems as if the only authors who could achieve a concept of human nature that transcended the white, Protestant, native American experience were those few who by birth or circumstance (Joaquin Miller's contacts with Indians) deviated from this racial and cultural heritage. Thus, it is not surprising that it was not Bellamy or Sheldon or Howells or Twain but David Lubin, a Jewish businessman-agriculturist, who conceived of an ideal America as a rich blend of human diversity:

> As in an intricate and beautifully woven piece of tapestry, strands of diverse shades are scattered here and there, all with the end of producing harmony of design as a whole; thus, it seems to me, has the All-Artist, the Master Designer, woven this nation, with warp of ideas from all races, and with woof of peoples of all nations.[48]

The fourth approach to transforming the average American into an ideal individual implied that it was possible to plan, create, and control a new identity for mankind. Conversions were spontaneous reactions dependent upon each individual's perception of his environment. Hopes for a hero who could inspire mass conversions rested upon the faith that "in God's providence the right man always comes forward when needed."[49] Even encouraging the elimination or the whitewashing of certain strands of humanity did not represent a conscious attempt to produce a new kind of man; the authors were simply assuming that everyone should behave like one of the old strands. But almost all the authors agreed that after the initial awakening—brought about by some combination of conversions, heroic inspiration, and the neutralization of dark-skinned peoples—it was America's duty to continue the process by carefully manipulating the environment so as to encourage the "good" qualities in man. Then the improved individuals could create even better environments, and the beneficial effects of environmental conditioning would spiral upwards until they hit the stable ceiling that marked the uppermost limits of the utopian concept of history.

This awareness of the interaction between the individual and his environment suggests that the utopian authors were in touch with some of the most advanced social thought of their day, Reform Darwinism. They realized that a person's identity was not simply determined by whether he had good "character" or "pluck"—two favorite nineteenth-century words—but that his physical surroundings and his cultural environment were tremendously important shaping influences. This was certainly a believable theoretical framework for the discussion of the ideal individual since the effects of environmental conditioning were readily observable. Moreover, the utopian authors perceived that the influence of environment could be seen from the cradle to the grave. Most of their explicit statements about conditioning explored the relationships between adults and their surroundings. But they also believed that the "proper utilization of [man's] prolonged infancy," childhood, was crucial to the development of the ideal individual.[50] There was even a bit of Skinnerian and Huxleyan speculation about manipulating infancy and tampering with those noble Anglo-Saxon genes. (The specific means of conditioning adults, children, and infants will be examined in Chapter 6. But the basic assumptions underlying these methods can be traced briefly here.)

The utopian authors' general theory of adult conditioning was best summed up by Bellamy's version of John D. Rockefeller's parable of the American beauty rose. For years the rose endured as a sickly plant; all attempts to strengthen it failed. Then the rose was transplanted from its bog to the "sweet, warm, dry earth," and it flourished proving that "the stock was good enough . . . the trouble was in the bog."[51] In explicit terms this belief—which derives as much from Enlightenment philosophers as from Reform Darwinism—could be stated thusly: the present environment encourages the wrong type of behavior. If the environment were altered properly, good behavior would be encouraged; so, change the environment. Though logical, this formula begs a question: just what is the "good" in man?

During an era when the self-made man and the rugged individualist were popular models for the ideal individual, it could be predicted that quite a few authors would choose the "Parable of the Talents" as their text. To these authors the good in man was his own particular skills, and his strongest motive was self-interest. Therefore, the ideal environment would be a highly competitive one that encouraged each person to develop his own talents for his own benefit. Gradually the most brilliant and skilled would rise to the top and the less capable would be weeded out. These utopian works were replete with Social Darwinistic clichés about "fit" individuals and "storm beaten oaks." S. Byron Welcome even conceived of a utopia that would have delighted Ayn Rand and Robert Nozick: businesses, hospitals, the judicial system, and the number of students in a classroom are regulated purely by competition.[52] Needless to say, any form of large-scale co-operation or socialism was dystopian to these authors. Such environments would only make the lazy lazier, allow the weak to thrive, and encourage sin. In *Looking Further Forward* (1890), for example, Richard Michaelis predicted that under Nationalism thousands of innocent maidens would flock to Washington bureaucrats offering their bodies as payment for personal favors. What a corruption of America's virgin territory!

Despite the popularity of the attitudes expressed by these authors, they were overwhelmingly outnumbered by the rest of the utopian authors. About 85% of them, including the popular Bellamy and Sheldon, chose "Love Thy Neighbor" as their text. They argued that the good in man was his desire to help others, especially the weak. Hence, they denounced capitalism as a "wisely calculated and prudently guarded system for the outlet and satisfaction of egotistic lusts," particularly the desires of those who were on top not because of inherent talents but because they were lucky enough to inherit money.[53] The solution was an environment that made each individual aware of the needs of others: systems such as co-operative associations, Altruism, Christian Socialism, or Nationalism. In spite of the emphasis these environments placed on helping others, the authors argued that individuals would develop talents faster than in any other setting since the efficiency of the new systems would free them from worries about necessities and a pride in a social identity would spur them on to new heights. As the economist Laurence Gronlund put it, "I must make myself valuable, for if myself is paltry, so is every other self, so are all selves put together."[54]

Such claims for co-operative environments were enthusiastic and sincere but troubled. Authors tended to hedge on terms. Very rarely did they use "socialism"; instead they preferred more American-sounding names such as Nationalism or co-operative individualism. And Bellamy's young Bostonians—competing fiercely for colored ribbons awarded to those who helped society most—indicate the lengths to which authors would go to prove that a socialistic economy would not produce a race of sluggards. Further-more, some of the most popular and perceptive opponents of capitalism, Bellamy and Howells for instance, used confused and troubled narrators and characters (West and Eve) to dramatize how difficult it was to adapt to a co-operative environment; and Twain expressed doubts about conditioning adults to any new environment even before the Battle of the Sand-Belt.

At the very end of Chapter 31 in *A Connecticut Yankee* Hank becomes ecstatic when he discovers a common charcoal burner who, after careful prompting, responds by forsaking his training: he admits he is glad that his cruel feudal master is dead. Hank breaks into a eulogy dedicated to the potential of the individual: "A man *is* a man at bottom. Whole ages of abuse and oppression cannot crush the manhood clear out of him." This passage is found in the last paragraph of the chapter. In the very first paragraph of the next chapter, the same charcoal burner strolls along a public road with Hank, and they pass several travelers. The burner is obsequiously polite to a monk and a gentleman, "gossipy" to his peers, and sticks his nose in the air when a slave passes by. Hank's reaction to the behavior of his "man" goes beyond his usual comments about training: "Well, there are times when one would like to hang the whole human race and finish the farce." This incident could, of course, be linked with the burner's training. But the close juxtaposition of the incident and Hank's eulogy, Hank's reaction to the incident, the repeated acts of vicious cruelty scattered throughout the novel, and, finally, the fact that Hank—an individual with thirteen more centuries of training than the Arthurians—perpetrates the most colossal slaughter witnessed in the book, all support a comment entered into one of Twain's notebooks during the composition of *A Connecticut Yankee*: "The thing in man which makes him cruel to a slave is in him *permanently* and will not be rooted out in a million years."[55] By the end of the novel it appears that there were times when Twain would have liked to rephrase his statement about the type of beings who could be noble one moment and cruel the next. Possibly he would say, "A man *is* a man at bottom. Whole ages of ideal environments cannot crush the cruelty, jealousy, and superstition clear out of him."

But, as usual, Twain was voicing a minority report. The utopian authors argued that adults could be conditioned by an improved environment, and the overwhelming majority took a seemingly "un-American" stance by attacking capitalistic environments. This decision may in part be explained by their belief that capitalism was fostering the brutal and senseless greed and poverty they saw around them. Their concept of a complex, interdependent American culture also suggests that they thought that the nineteenth-century idea of a society of individuals going their own ways not caring for others was cruelly obsolete. Basing their conclusions on the membership of some of the urban Nationalist Clubs and the popularity of communism among upper-class intellectuals during the 1930s, some critics might also argue that advocating socialism was a fashionable way to express disgust for the nouveau riche in America. But such a theory would not explain the opinions of the businessmen-authors, or the attitudes of the majority of the authors since it was not too fashionable to have socialist leanings in the 1880s and 1890s.

Actually the two most basic reasons that the utopian authors chose to champion socialistic conditioning may be only indirectly related to their theories about economic systems and social class structure. A persistent belief in Christian brotherhood certainly influenced them. It seemed obvious that Jesus would have preferred Americans to help weak individuals. The other force inclining them towards co-operation had less to do with a specific belief system than with the fears implied by their concept of history. Competition was not only cruel, it was chaotic. There was no order; everyone seemed to be working against each other. The results were often senseless duplications and haphazard cutthroat savagery. On the other hand, Nationalism or Christian Socialism or whatever they wanted to call their co-operative systems at least appeared orderly and understandable. Again we see the ambivalence that characterized the utopian concept of history. The chaotic environment of the present was perceived as evidence of spreading Old-World barbarism, but the social self and the security and order of the co-operative environments were not too far removed from the medieval concept of the individual as a dependent component in an organic society.

When the utopian authors extended their arguments about conditioning beyond adults to children and infants, the tension and ambivalence became even more evident. On the one hand, they realized that children and babies were more susceptible to conditioning than adults because they had internalized less experience and thus had fewer assumptions and expectations to change. As Hank Morgan's assistant, Clarence, explains,

> [I chose youths as the most trusted followers] because all the others were born in an atmosphere of superstition and reared in it . . . with boys it was different. Such as have been under our training from seven to ten years have had no acquaintance with the Church's terrors, and it was among these that I found my fifty-two.[56]

General Mortimer D. Leggett even found an appropriate Christian justification for cultivating young minds: didn't Jesus say, "Suffer the little children to come unto me"?[57]

Nevertheless, once the utopian authors who supported co-operative conditioning entered the schoolroom and especially the nursery, they discovered that they were running head on into something as dear to the hearts of nineteenth-century Americans as Christian brotherhood, namely Mother. As they approached this shrine, they were besieged by violent attacks from reviewers and Bellamy's critics. The usual associations between socialism and the destruction of the family were made, and apostrophes to mothers "sainted in heaven" became blanket responses to suggestions that mothers should set examples for their children by working in co-operative societies.

Several satirists, including the well-known Oliver Wendell Holmes, went beyond these typical responses. Paul Haedicke envisioned an age of absolute equality achieved by an intensive "process of equalization." Children, called "Pi-Pars," are raised in communal nursery barns, eat from troughs, are taught nothing, and are free to indulge their sexual lusts (pregnant twelve-year-olds are quite common). At puberty ingenious combinations of body weights, surgery, selective bone breaking, and induced rickets insure absolute physical equality. If anyone persists in being above the average physical and mental standards, he is exiled and forced to live in a hole. In J. W. Roberts's future Massachusetts the process of physical conditioning is carried one step further with infant body molds. After a few generations this innovation is so successful that no one knows his children, his wife, or her husband from other children, wives, and husbands. The resulting kidnappings and wife swappings throw Massachusetts into a state of complete confusion. Finally, Holmes presents the ultimate in the effects of a socialistic environment. His Saturnians are so equal that the only agitation on the planet comes from the "Orthobrachians," who demand equal rights for the left hands of the planet, and the "Isopodics," who want equality for the lower limbs. (They secretly practice what they preach by going on all fours at their meetings.)[58]

These reductio ad absurdum satires were lighthearted attempts to reenforce popular assumptions about the effects of conditioning in a noncompetitive environment. Advocates of co-operative utopias responded by either ignoring such criticism, by claiming they never intended physical and mental equality, or by placing Family and Mother on the highest available rhetorical pillars. There was one author, however, who hinted at types of conditioning as imaginative as the satirists' visions of the reformed men and women of the future. It is this brand of speculation that makes John Uri Lloyd's *Etidorhpa or The End of Earth. The Strange History of a Mysterious Being . . .* (1895; the title is derived from Aphrodite spelled backwards) a fascinating precursor to the dystopian and utopian worlds of Aldous Huxley's test-tube babies and Charles Reich's Consciousness III.

Lloyd was a Cincinnati pharmacist-chemist who admitted to having experimented with combinations of morphine, cannabis, alcohol, and chloroform that would "pall the effects of hashish or opium." In *Etidorhpa* he narrates a Dante-esque voyage to a land of ideal love. The main guide is an example of "a possible future in consciousness" controlled and created by man. Lloyd predicts that developments in the physical and mental sciences will enable man to understand the complexities of sensory perception so well that a new species of human being will be created. Despite the many illustrations and descriptions of scientific experiments in *Etidorhpa*, Lloyd is vague about how the transformation will occur. At one point he suggests that: " . . . man should reflect whether or not his brain may, by proper cultivation or artificial stimulus, be yet developed so as to receive yet deeper nerve impressions." This statement combined with his willingness to experiment with alcohol and drugs hints that he might be proposing mind-expanding experiments that would alter the chemistry of the brain. During the course of the narrator's journey, however, he passes through a hellish "Drunkards' Den" where former alcoholics spend eternity as disembodied heads, hands and legs; and a footnote warns that the indiscriminate use of drugs by the average individual could lead to the extermination of mankind. Thus Lloyd's definition of cultivation and stimulation was probably some ideal combination of mental training, carefully controlled use of drugs, and, above all, the stimulation of love (but not lust—the narrator also passes through a cavern of evil sirens). Despite Lloyd's vagueness about the specific applications of future knowledge, he does give the reader a good look at the end result. (See Plate 5.) The narrator's main guide is

a wonderful being; an eyeless creature, and yet possessed of sight and perception beyond that of mortal man. . . . a cavernbred monstrosity, and yet possessed of the mind of a sage; he was a scientific expert, a naturalist, a metaphysical reasoner, a critic of religion, and a prophet. . . .[59]

It is more difficult to give an overview of the utopian concept of the individual than to give overviews of the utopian concepts of time and space because, as the contrasts between Sheldon's converted Christ figures, Bellamy's social selves, Colburn's blond "Aryan," Griggs's black heroes, Miller's beautiful Jewess, and Lloyd's eyeless wonder indicate, the utopian authors' views on the ideal individual were quite diversified. Perhaps the diversity itself is the key to an overview if we can determine how to look at it and what it means. On the one hand, it can be taken as evidence that the utopian authors realized that questions such as the one posed by the French reviewer of *Looking Backward* could not be answered with the usual accolades to America's historic mission or the promise of American soil. Instead the authors responded by creating utopian citizens who had been transformed by a variety of phenomena ranging from a sudden, personal awareness of a new way to see the world and enthusiastic emulation of heroic figures to more gradual processes of racial selection and environmental conditioning. Moreover, the most perceptive authors, who in this case included the popular Bellamy, were not afraid to admit that exchanging a nineteenth-century American identity for a utopian one could be a painful experience—again the awareness that the road to utopia was paved with nightmares as well as pleasant dreams.

A contrary but equally revealing way of interpreting the diversity is as another indication of how confused the utopian authors were about the late nineteenth century. In part, as with their concepts of time and space, this was a language problem. In their attempts to reach a wide audience and to reassure themselves, the authors repeatedly drew upon traditional images and ideas, especially Christian images and ideas. This seemed appropriate, particularly when describing the conversion experiences that were so important to the two most popular authors, Sheldon and Bellamy. But the traditional language was strained when the authors proposed controversial "new" ideas about conditioning in co-operative environments. Then came the battle of the words—brave assaults swathed in clichés. So Mother rode her pedestal to work and kept track of the kids in the co-operative commonwealth.

But there was more to the confusion than an inadequate vocabulary. The utopian concepts of time and space were limited by the authors' tendency to define the east and west coasts of America as the edges of the world. Their view of the ideal individual was even narrower, extending only to certain light-skinned inhabitants between these shores. This nearsightedness again raises questions about the ability of any one group to establish meaningful goals for a population as diverse as America's. The utopian authors were sincerely dedicated to helping all mankind, but they were also frightened by the "alien tribes" on Ellis Island, on the Western prairies, and migrating up from the South. Apparently the only way they could cope with their confusion was to blind themselves to diversity by holding security mirrors in front of their eyes.

Diversity is confusing. But diversity in a state of flux is more confusing. This is what these reformers with relatively limited backgrounds had to face. In *People of Paradox* Michael Kammen has labeled this condition "unstable pluralism." One of the many results of such flux has been a double view of individuality, a "collective individualism." This concept may offer a final way to grasp the fundamental meaning of the diversity and confusion that often characterized the utopian concept of the individual. On the one hand, the authors hoped for sudden, individual conversions leading to a spiraling cycle of changes enabling each person to develop his talents as quickly as possible. But if everyone was continually changing, it would be difficult to know anyone, even oneself. The future might be more frighteningly unstable and pluralistic than the present. Therefore, the desire for changing individuals was tempered by the reassurance that one could know which strands of humanity were the best and that the ultimate goal of transforming human hearts was a secure and ordered society where individuals would be part of a close community of understandable identities.

5

Filling the Belly and the Soul

[All that] makes life worth living . . . depends first, last, and always on the manner in which the production and distribution of wealth is regulated.
—Edward Bellamy, Equality *(1897)*

. . . had [the mechanical wonders] been ten times more marvelous, they would still have impressed me with infinitely less astonishment than the moral revolution illustrated by your new social order.
—Edward Bellamy, Equality *(1897)*

In *The Scientific Romances* H. G. Wells offered the following advice to utopian authors: "As soon as the magic trick has been done the whole business of the [utopian] writer is to keep everything else human and real. Touches of prosaic detail are imperative [as is] a rigorous adherence to the hypothesis."[1] The "magic trick" is the journey to utopia, and for late nineteenth-century American utopian authors, this journey and "the hypothesis" involved their general concepts of time, space, and the individual. In spite of the familiarity and appeal of these concepts for nineteenth-century readers, the utopian authors, like Wells, realized that to make their utopias believable they had to flesh out their abstract ideas by creating the aura of a day in utopia—an immediate, concrete feeling that would convince readers that their utopias were more than vague impossibilities.

As hostile reviewers were fond of noting, it was easier to "flesh out" after the "magic trick" had been accomplished: there were usually more detailed descriptions of utopia than precise explanations of how to reach utopia. The greater emphasis placed on the transition period in Bellamy's second utopian novel, *Equality,* indicates that even the most influential utopian reformer felt that the reviewers were right. Nevertheless, because the utopian authors conceived of utopia as a condition to be achieved, they did emphasize the means used to attain utopia more than classical, medieval, or renaissance utopian visionaries did; Lewis Mumford and most other students of utopian thought have mentioned this change. Furthermore, the contemporary criticism about the vagueness of the journey to utopia wasn't altogether fair since it expressed misunderstandings of an important characteristic and a central function of utopian literature. Detailed descriptions of utopia support general concepts, but they also suggest specific methods of achieving utopia. Thus, if a narrator is introduced to a female utopian who is a leading political figure, the implication is that woman's role must be changed before utopia becomes a fact. This doesn't necessarily explain exactly how to change women, but it does pinpoint a specific precondition for utopia. The central function that the critical reviewers ignored is even more important to an understanding of utopian literature. As Bellamy often argued, it is foolish to start changing things before we have a clear and *complete* idea of what we want. Otherwise we may waste energy on piecemeal reforms leading who knows where.

Friendly reviewers were as fond of praising this detailed "completeness" as unsympathetic reviewers were of questioning the vagueness of the journey to utopia.[2] In part the inclusive nature of late nineteenth-century American utopias was a result of the tendency to write utopian fiction instead of utopian treatises. Treatise writing permits authors to dwell upon pet proposals. Most of the utopian authors had such pet schemes, often economic programs. But even if an author was certain that the efficient production and just distribution of goods were the keys to an ideal future, the fictional formula forced him to drag his narrator away from economic dialogues and speeches to see utopian cities, schools, churches, factories, and homes; and he would, of course, meet a beautiful utopian lady since part of the popular format was a wedding-bells ending. Thus authors were encouraged to imagine how their favorite reforms would relate to a multitude of cultural areas.

A comparison between the listings in the fourth edition of George P. Murdock's *Outline of Cultural Materials* (1965) and the spectrum of topics examined in the utopian works reveals how successful the utopian authors were in imagining these interrelationships. Every one of Murdock's eighty-eight major cultural categories (excepting the initial scholarly items such as bibliography) is discussed in the utopian literature. Moreover, most of the authors were not satisfied with sporadic glimpses of utopian wonders, though in *Sub-Coelum* (1893) Addison Peale Russell's chaotic samplings ranging from utopian oysters to fishponds proves that a few authors chose this route. Most of the authors, however, including the most popular and the most perceptive writers, strove to demonstrate how changes in one sector of a culture would affect the rest of that culture. To quote Henry Olerich, a Midwestern reformer-educator who wrote one late nineteenth-century and several early twentieth-century utopian works:

> For examples, a change in a locomotive implies or produces a change in the roadbed, in commerce, in speed, in mercantile business. A change in land tenure and in the medium of exchange produces corresponding changes in all other human institutions and conduct; if not, one land tenure and medium of exchange would be as good as another. A change in sex-relations is accompanied with a corresponding change in dress, food, dwellings, education, modes of travel, amusements, individual freedom, in manner of rearing offspring, and in countless other ways. A system in order to be a natural and harmonious [one], must be a connected whole. Hence we can see at once that every act of endeavoring to learn or discuss a single topic unconnected with others is a sign of mental incompleteness.[3]

This desire to examine interrelationships certainly helped to flesh out the authors' abstract "hypotheses" about time, space, and the individual. The inclusiveness of the utopian visions also makes these works valuable to students of late nineteenth-century culture; possibly no other type of primary source—including newspapers, magazines, diaries, court records, voting statistics, speeches, photographs, or examples of material culture—offers such a broad range of information. The attempt to project complete utopian civilizations also helps to illuminate the forward-backward looking nature of the utopian literature. On the one hand, the holistic outlook of the authors suggests that they realized—or the fictional format forced them to acknowledge—that it is difficult to isolate change in complex industrialized societies and that localized piecemeal reforms are often inadequate answers to modern problems. On the other hand, predictions about totally integrated cultures—Olerich's "harmonious . . . connected whole[s]"—expose an understandable but backward-looking desire to escape America's unstable pluralisms. Instead these authors could have concentrated on projections of ideal societies that reflected the potential richness and dynamism of America's pluralisms—visions such as David Lubin's blend of American nationalities, religions, and races.

The utopian authors' attempts to embellish their utopias with "human and real" detail and to pull diverse cultural areas into connected wholes will be presented in a survey of the specific topics that appeared most frequently in their works. Eight major and several minor areas will be analyzed in order of importance to the authors. The ranking will therefore suggest specific trouble spots in their society and specific characteristics of an ideal American civilization. This ranking, however, is not exact. It is based in part upon a content analysis of the utopian works, a task that was greatly facilitated by Charles J. Rooney, Jr.'s efforts.[4] But the number of times an author mentions a specific subject doesn't necessarily reflect his most fundamental concerns. Therefore statistical surveys must be complemented by subjective impressions of the authors' world views. The first two topics examined—economic reforms and a moralistic outlook—should help to clarify this approach.

Near the beginning of Bellamy's *Equality* Edith Leete declares, "[All that] makes life worth living . . . depends first, last, and always on the manner in which the production and distribution of wealth is regulated." One of the first things Julian West tells Dr. Leete in *Looking Backward* is that the most pressing problem of the nineteenth-century was "the labor question."[5] These comments about the glories of the future and the trials of the past reflect the types of goals and problems most frequently discussed in the utopian works. Robert L. Shurter even argues that the major reason for the outpouring of utopian speculation during the late nineteenth century was a dissatisfaction with economic conditions and that the main reason for studying utopian works is that they are excellent indices to late nineteenth-century American economic attitudes.[6]

Yet, two of the most perceptive Bellamy scholars, Joseph Schiffman and John L. Thomas, have emphasized the religious, not the economic thought of the most popular utopian author. Schiffman claims that "Bellamy's strongest motives were religious," and Thomas calls *Looking Backward* "a religious fable."[7] Furthermore, the numerous Christian images, symbols, and analogies used to express the authors' concepts of time, space, and the individual suggest that Schiffman's and Thomas's view of Bellamy could be extended to include all the utopian authors: the millennial spirit of America's role in history, the association of The Change with the Resurrection, the religious fervor of the communalists in the city-upon-a-hill utopias, the conversion experiences, the Christ-like heroes, and the comparisons between socialistic aims and Christian ethics. Add to these the many religious titles and subtitles and the fact that the two most popular authors were the scion of a long line of ministers (Bellamy) and a minister (Sheldon) and the utopian works begin to look more like religious tracts than economic treatises.

Of course, it could be argued that the utopian authors were only paying lip service to religion, capitalizing on the long-standing popularity of religious publications (especially Christian reform novels like *Uncle Tom's Cabin*) using religion to familiarize and justify their economic proposals. After all, this was an era when both critics and defenders of the status quo strove to sanctify their pleas. William Jennings Bryan inspired Populists and Democrats with his "Cross of Gold" speech; in his famous sermon "Acres of Diamonds" Russell H. Conwell told thousands that it was their Christian duty to be rich; and Jacob S. Coxey's "army" marched behind a banner adorned by Christ's image and the slogan: "Peace on Earth Good Will to Men. He Hath Risen, but Death to Interest Bonds."

Admittedly, like Bryan, Conwell, and Coxey, the utopian authors were trying to sell their wares in a way they thought would appeal to the American public; they often attempted to make "foreign" or "radical" economic reforms sound as familiar as Christ's teachings. Thus Bellamy called Nationalism an "intensely Christian movement"; Thomas Lake Harris labeled his socialism "THEO-SOCIALISM"; and Laurence Gronlund saw economic co-operation as the *"carry[ing] out of God's thoughts."*[8]

But the use of religion wasn't just a con game; and if it were, the authors were trying to con themselves as much as their readers. A religious-moralistic outlook was at the heart of the authors' pessimism and optimism. Long discussions of production and distribution attest to the authors' sincere interest in the complex routes that lead to a full belly. Nevertheless, the most fundamental criticism of nineteenth-century economic systems was not that they were inefficient, but that they were morally wrong. These middle-aged reformers—most of whom were born from five to fifteen years before the Civil War—wanted to see secular ills from a moralistic viewpoint the way many of their parents had perceived slavery.

Furthermore, like the Social Gospel ministers of the 1880s and 1890s, the utopian authors not only painted the evils of the present in moralistic tones, they also envisioned the ultimate goals of the future as being religious. In *Equality* Edith Leete may have said that all depends on the new economic system, but her father qualifies her comment by delineating the fundamental relationship between economics and religion: "economic systems . . . furnished the necessary material basis for all other changes that have taken place." Once this foundation was established, however, the major concern of Americans became "the science of the soul," the study of how people can express their love of God through godly thoughts and acts in their daily lives.[9] Certainly this vision of God's kingdom on earth—which was shared by the majority of the authors—was not the type of heavenly vision St. Augustine celebrated in *The City of God*; nor was it a branch of the pearly-gates optimism popularized several decades earlier by Elizabeth Stuart Phelps Ward's *The Gates Ajar* (1868); nor the literal Adventism preached by a few authors such as Dr. Kinnear in *Impending Judgments on the Earth* (1892). But it was a vision that clearly depicted economic reforms as *means,* tremendously important means, but they were not presented as ends per se. Thus at the risk of overstatement, the utopian works can be viewed as books in which abundant lip service was paid to sometimes sophisticated, sometimes half-baked economic means, while the ultimate goal was the creation of a moral civilization where true Christianity could be practiced by every person every day. The following analyses of specific economic and religious problems and solutions should further illustrate the utopian authors' attitudes about what they believed to be the two most important cultural areas in an ideal society.

At least 85% of the utopian authors perceived the moral wrongs of the nineteenth-century economic environment as a dangerous threat to the development of the ideal individual. These injustices—like practically every weakness in specific cultural areas—were also presented as Old-World evils contaminating the New World. America was supposed to be the land of equality, but the gap the authors saw between the rich and the poor seemed to prove that the "European spectre of Inequality" was haunting their land.[10] To emphasize this threat, villainous millionaires and capitalists were often depicted as money emperors, kings, princes or barons. But this inequality was not simply a matter of dollars and cents; it also involved social injustices. Ideally, America was to be a land where all honest work was respected equally. In the 1830s when Alexis de Tocqueville visited the New World, he was so impressed with the reality of this aspect of the American dream that he wrote a chapter in *Democracy in America* entitled "Why Among the Americans all Honest Callings are Considered Honorable." Sixty years later when another visitor, the imaginary Mr. Homos, came to America in Howells's *Altruria,* he was shocked to find that there were "some kinds of honest work that are not honored." One candid banker even revealed both his social and racial prejudices by admitting that "You are no more likely to meet a working man in American [high] society than you are to meet a colored man."[11] The European spectre of inequality seemed to be taking the specific form of the class oppression that had divided the Old World into warring factions and helped to inspire a desire to escape to America.

Still, it wasn't only the inequalities of the economic systems that smacked of the Old-World. Bellamy's well-known parable of the coach in the first chapter of *Looking Backward* dramatizes the inequality of the wealthy riders and the human beasts who pulled them. But it also portrays economic and social conditions as being as chaotic and senseless as the ups and downs of Old-World history. The system was inefficiently unjust because the riders did nothing while the workers labored to a point of unproductive exhaustion. Moreover, no clear reasons, such as superior skills, were offered to explain why some were up and others down. Everyone simply assumed that this was the way it always was and would be. Ironically, even the riders could not enjoy themselves. Competition for the top spots was so fierce and the road so uncertain that at any instant a rider might fall from the highest position into the muck of the toilers. If anything, this whole situation seemed more chaotic than the economic and social conditions of the Old World. There, nobility and rank would at least prohibit such sudden tumbles.

Specific criticisms of the inequalities and the chaos of nineteenth-century economic systems filled many pages of the utopian works.[12] The utopian authors' major criticism of the American laissez-faire system, however, was that it allowed a few individuals to accumulate so much wealth that they could prohibit the majority of Americans from ever rising much above a subsistence level. What made this undemocratic condition worse was that unless they were suddenly toppled, the rich could perpetuate their economic superiority by using means not unlike those used by the Old-World nobility. They could buy standing armies of Pinkertons and strike-breakers. In *The Lords of Misrule* (1894) William C. Pomeroy even included an illustration of a castle fortress owned by a millionaire. Monopolies and the ability to control the means of production, politicians, lawyers, and judges further enhanced the powers of the wealthy. The authors perceived this situation not only as a threat to the poor, but as a danger to their own socio-economic group. If conditions were allowed to persist, the middle and upper-middle classes would soon disappear. No longer could every American aspire to climb the ladder of success: the middle rungs would be missing, leaving the majority trapped at the bottom.

But there was more to the utopian authors' criticism than stripped ladders, bad guys, and weak guys. Rich, evil individuals were villains in this economic tragedy, but The Villain was a bad environment that encouraged people to develop the wrong habits. According to the majority of the authors, the economic conditions of the late nineteenth century, which made money all powerful, nurtured the release of man's savagery in a wide variety of ingenious and brutal ways. Capitalistic environments especially encouraged "the outlet and satisfaction of egotistic lusts" that exposed "the savagisms, the barbarisms of all the past [that were] latent" in businessmen and workers.[13] Then too, the chaos and the insecurity of economic cycles fostered inefficiency and waste. The impersonal "hitch and joggle" (Howells's phrase) of booms and busts could not only topple the rich, it could suddenly throw thousands of industrious executives, white collar workers, and laborers out of work wasting millions of dollars in investments and millions of man-hours of productive energy. In *The World a Department Store* (1900) Bradford Peck, a Maine businessman, even "documented" this irrational waste with an encyclopedic listing entitled "Conservative Table Representing the Estimated Wasted Energy in Every Department of Life at the Close of the Nineteenth Century." He concluded that in an average year over nine billion dollars was senselessly thrown away.

To some, Peck's claims might seem a bit farfetched, but his and the other utopian authors' attempts at tackling the overall economic situation are praiseworthy. Instead of simply concluding that economic ills were caused by greedy individuals, they tried to discover the conditions that fostered immoral and irrational behavior. Like several late nineteenth-century economists and sociologists—notably Richard T. Ely, Thorstein Veblen, and Lester Frank Ward—and the literary "naturalists," they knew that economics involved a complex network of people and things extending far beyond the individual's empty belly—and his industry and pluck.

The utopian authors also realized that the solutions to the inequalities and chaos of the nineteenth century called for extensive, systematic changes in the means of production and distribution as well as changes in attitudes about economic goals. But as should be expected when surveying so many reformers, the authors proposed a wide variety of specific programs and philosophies. S. Byron Welcome envisioned a single-tax utopia in which everything including schools and hospitals was regulated by fierce competition. Albert Merrill, Frank Rosewater, Corwin Phelps, and George Farnell recommended extensive monetary reforms; and Dr. Von Swartwout believed that the immediate abolition of money was the answer. William Child and Isaac Swift advocated confiscating money from the wealthy; Frederick Worley emphasized the benefits of a guaranteed annual income; Henry F. Allen lauded the potential uses of statistical studies in a planned economy; Ignatius Donnelly proposed a variety of Populist reforms; William Dean Howells advocated Christian Socialism; Edward Bellamy described a socialized state organized around an Industrial Army; the economist Laurence Gronlund merged his co-operative commonwealth with a Nationalistic state; and James Cowan proposed an economic system that would enable individuals to use cars, tools, even houses whenever and wherever they found them, all gratis. This enumeration barely scratches the surface of the various economic systems advocated.

Despite the diversity, Rooney and others who have thoroughly examined the utopian economic attitudes agree that there was a definite trend—including the popular Bellamy and the most perceptive economic critics—towards a centralized economy that was planned and directed by experts subject to the wishes of the people. About 20% of the authors advocated socialistic systems, although they usually used Bellamy's term, Nationalism or some other American-sounding name. Over 50% envisioned combinations of national co-operative business associations regulated by government controls. Less than 10% described economies controlled by totalitarian governments, and only a little over 10% described capitalistic systems modified by government regulations such as inheritance taxes and limits placed on personal income. Thus, even the most "conservative" proposals embodied reforms, such as limiting a person's wealth, that might be considered "radical" today.

The trend towards a centralized, planned economy was especially clear in Bellamy's popular *Looking Backward*. Like most of the other proposed economic systems, it was designed to eliminate the chaos of a laissez-faire economy and to dispel the spectre of inequality. Therefore, problems of production and distribution were handled by ten large departments staffed by experts; the work was done by the Industrial Army (in which everyone served from young adulthood until forty-five years of age according to his or her particular talents and interests); every individual received the same annual income transferable through a credit card system. A particularly interesting characteristic of Nationalism was that it served as an example of how the new America could grow directly out of the potentially catastrophic present since Nationalism is described as a result of one of the worst symptoms of inequality, the trust. According to Dr. Leete, trusts continued to engulf small companies throughout the 1890s and the early twentieth century until finally all the means of production in the United States were controlled by one gigantic monopoly. But there were advantages to this tragedy. It forced workers and employers to adapt to the procedures of large-scale production, and, after the majority of the population had awakened to the new vision of the future, it was simple to transfer the ownership of the Great Trust from a few private individuals to all the people by nationalizing it in a democratic election. Thereafter, the economy could be efficiently and justly managed by the ten administrative departments.

Though Bellamy's Nationalism was certainly not the first celebration of nationwide socialism in America (Laurence Gronlund's *Coöperative Commonwealth* appeared in 1884), it was the one that captured the public's attention, becoming an economic paradigm for utopian authors to praise, modify, or attack. But despite the numerous alterations, four basic elements of the paradigm were defended by a clear majority of the authors, even by some of the proponents of modified capitalism. First was a more equal distribution of wealth on moral and economic grounds since it was assumed that once customers had more purchasing power, they would buy more and bolster the economy. Second was the co-operative-centralized nature of the economic environment—a direct response to the savagery and chaos of competition. Third was a tendency to delegate important decision-making powers to "disinterested" experts instead of private entrepreneurs and politicians, a trend foreshadowing the Brain Trusts, Advisory Committees, and computers of the twentieth century. Finally, the utopian economic systems represented a rejection of the American tradition of stopgap economic reforms. The programs proposed were to be *permanent*. This represents both a criticism of piecemeal, temporary measures and the general longing for a stable, orderly society that characterized the utopian concept of history.

In spite of all the moral, practical, and psychological appeals of the utopian economic systems, the authors were aware that any reforms embracing a permanent, centralized economy would encounter hostile responses. Thus, in order to convince the readers (and themselves) that they were right, they had to reach out beyond the limits of specific economic issues to seek authority on a more general plane. Usually their justifications were reactions to four interrelated criticisms voiced by reviewers, political leaders, and several utopian authors including Michaelis, Roberts, Bachelder, and Wheeler: a co-operative-centralized economy would threaten individuality, the work ethic, American values, and Christianity.

The utopian authors replied to the warnings about individuality by claiming that their critics begged the question: they assumed that the status quo allowed people to develop fully and freely whereas in reality the majority were simply too burdened with eking out a living to ever develop. On the other hand, in their utopias the fairness and the efficiency of a co-operative-centralized economy would give people the time and the facilities to cultivate individual talents and interests (though one problem in completely socialized economies was freedom of occupational choice—the authors contrived numerous come-ons such as job rotation, shorter hours, and honors to attract workers to unpleasant or dangerous occupations).

The authors' answers to the question of individuality only egged some critics on to another challenge: if the utopians had so much free time to develop themselves, they must be a race of drones who avoid productive labor; besides everyone knows that in a co-operative society the lazy would have all sorts of excuses not to work. The advocates of co-operative economies replied that after Americans had been freed from the worries of sustenance and believed that every person could develop fully, the utopians would find new motives for work: for example, the enthusiasm for jobs they really liked as experienced by Howells's Altrurians, or a pride in their country and themselves as experienced by Bellamy's Bostonians and Gronlund's commonwealth utopians. Furthermore, even though in many utopias technological advances allowed work hours to be reduced to four per day, the standard of living and the rate of production were much higher than in the nineteenth century. The authors also stressed that everyone who had not retired performed some useful task. There were no idle riders perched atop the coach, nor were there unproductive middle-men. Improvements in technology combined with national planning and statistical studies would eliminate the need for salesmen and other nonproducers; thus telephones and conveniently located display warehouses or co-operative department stores would eliminate unproductive sellers, buyers, advertisers, and salesmen. Finally, since everyone worked, honest labor would be respected by all. In other words there would be a return to the egalitarian society that impressed de Tocqueville. Such a society of workers was, moreover, presented as a truly Christian society, since according to the Protestant ethic, one of the most concrete and constructive ways of expressing love and devotion to God was by faithfully following a "calling."

Nevertheless, in one sense the critics were right. The utopian authors' economic systems did challenge the popular American work ethic. Although over 90% of the authors emphasized that productive labor was a good and a necessary part of life, with shorter working hours and earlier retirement, producing things or ideas for personal survival or for society became a much smaller segment of the human experience. Most of the authors were afraid to examine the consequences of this change. Two did, however, and their concepts of work posed basic challenges to the nineteenth-century work ethic that were not fully evident until the middle of the twentieth century. At forty-five Bellamy's utopians retired, but that didn't mean that they spent half their lives in indolence. If anything, they worked harder since it was during this period of their lives that they were free to "fully devote [themselves] to the higher exercise of [their] faculties, the intellectual and spiritual enjoyments which *alone* mean life." (Italics mine.) Besides stressing the anti-materialism of Bellamy's utopia and questioning the stereotyped view of Americans as doers, this statement suggested that it was work that was done purely for self-development that was the most important. Ironically, Bellamy's awareness of the changes that would come with increased leisure made his utopia much more private and personal than the typical capitalistic utopia, such as David H. Wheeler's described in *Our Industrial Utopia* (1895) where each person spent most of his life producing for society.[14] William Dean Howells also modified the popular work ethic with a concept of labor similar to the one William Morris depicted in the ideal English setting of *News from Nowhere* (1890). In Altruria everyone performed useful tasks, especially farming, but the real value of work was in "the pleasure of doing a thing beautifully." Howells realized that mass production was often accompanied by a decrease in quality and an increase in ugliness. Therefore, the Altrurians work at refining and beautifying their products; they even tear up some of the railroad tracks from the landscape.[15] Howells thus had a glimpse of the 1960s and early 1970s when Lordstown, Ohio auto workers struck because they were not allowed to do meaningful, quality work, and when many longed to rip up the miles of freeways and billboards that sprawled across the countryside.

Despite their questioning of the American work ethic, Bellamy and Howells—like all the authors, with the possible exception of Charles Willing Beale[16]—still abhorred laziness. And this stance combined with the claims for new opportunities for individuality helped them and the majority of the utopian authors to confront the third general criticism, that their utopias were un-American. But the authors knew that statements about individuality and industry were not enough when critics charged that co-operation and centralization were alien to American soil. To counter this attack and to establish the Americanness of their economic systems, the utopian authors scoured American history for precedents. The Declaration of Independence was the most quoted document used to justify economic equality. Hadn't the Founding Fathers proclaimed that "all men are created equal"? The most popular historical precedent was the Civil War. It was celebrated as a holy crusade fought against the forces of inequality and as an example of the advantages of massive government spending, extensive planning, and large-scale organization. (This precedent reflected the Northern and Western biases of the authors.) Other precedents mentioned were the "White City" at the Chicago Fair of 1893, the co-operative spirit of the American Indian, the New England whalers' lay system of profit sharing, government mints, Naval shipbuilding projects, and the Post Office—the last three were even government owned and regulated industries. The utopian authors hoped that the cumulative effect of citing precedents would be to make readers believe that planned and concentrated economic systems represented original American values and goals, whereas a laissez-faire economy was a corruption of the American dream.

Still, even if critics conceded that the utopian economics had American roots, they could come back with the final blow: anything that smacked of socialism was un-Christian. Wealthy characters in the utopian novels were fond of reminding reformers that Jesus had said, "For ye have the poor always with you." Any attempts at economic equality would thus be blasphemous. Utopian guides and narrators replied that Christ had also asked his followers to help the poor. More importantly, He had singled out "Love Thy Neighbor" as the second greatest Commandment. Capitalism encouraged seeing others as hated rivals, whereas a co-operative economy inspired people to perceive others as brothers or at least as co-workers. Thus, in *Equality* the Rev. Mr. Barton could speak of the "Republic of the Golden Rule," and one of the few trained economists among the utopian authors,

Laurence Gronlund, could stress the spiritual benefits of a co-operative economy in his little-known work *Our Destiny. The Influence of Nationalism on Morals and Religion.*

This final line of justification leads directly into the authors' religious views since these reformers claimed that the final goal of replacing the economic inequality and chaos of the present with the equality and order of the future was to establish an environment conducive to practicing Christianity every minute of every day.

The utopian authors' ultimate goal was a Christian society. Only a handful of them were antireligious;[17] even Twain's vicious attacks were against the Church, not Christianity itself. But the average, the popular, and the most perceptive analysts of religion wanted a Daily Gospel and a New Trinity instead of a continuation of Christianity as practiced in America during the late nineteenth century.

Actually, that was the whole point. Christianity wasn't practiced, according to the utopian authors. Their major criticism was that religion was completely out of touch with the daily lives of most Americans. This meant that the establishment of a Christian utopia called for more than new economic systems; a religious revolution akin to Luther's reformation or Puritanism was needed.

The utopian authors were especially concerned with three symptoms of the irrelevancy of American religion. First of all, religion either naively refused to admit to the existence of evil in everyday life, or if it did, the evil was justified and sanctified as part of God's plan. For example, in an early notebook Bellamy recalled a typical incident at a camp meeting he and his father, a Baptist minister, attended. A large sign nailed to a tree proclaimed, "The Earth is the Lord's." Right beneath it was a real estate poster announcing, "Lots forty by sixty feet, for sale at $250."[18] In a more serious vein, the Rev. Mr. Sheldon in *In His Steps* admitted that the saloons and beer gardens, which his hero attacks with vigor throughout the novel, gave more comfort to the poor than many churches. One explanation many of the authors gave for this situation was that the poor found little solace in hearing sermons that defined suffering as a necessary precondition for the afterlife or justified the domination of the rich over the poor by quoting scripture. This criticism was especially evident in *In His Steps,* in Katharine Woods's *Metzerott* (1889), and in the satiric treatment of upper-class Protestantism typified by Ignatius Donnelly's Professor Odyard who delivers a sermon based on two familiar texts: "Many are called but few are chosen" and "For ye have the poor always with you." Both are used to sanctify the widening gap between the few rich and the many poor.[19]

Another diversion away from reality was a tendency Ben Franklin had noted in his *Autobiography* one hundred years earlier: religion seemed to be preoccupied with internal matters such as complex dogmas and creeds, petty sectarian quarrels, the ecclesiastical power structure of the institution, and religious trimmings such as church buildings, statuaries and music. In *A Dream of a Modest Prophet* (1890), for instance, General Leggett argued that Christianity was burdened with confusing and cruel sacrificial notions inherited from Judaism and that power-hungry Catholic priests and bishops and backbiting sectarian Protestants had contributed much to the decline of American Christianity. William Simpson felt that conniving "ecclesiastical bodies" had manipulated complex creeds so that the faithful would strive selfishly for otherworldly salvation rather than striving to help others on earth. Finally, in a seldom noticed section of *Caesar's Column,* Ignatius Donnelly imagined the ultimate outcome of the preoccupation with the trappings of religion. Gabriel, the virtuous visitor from an idyllic country, attends a church service in a gigantic, ornate cathedral. The interior is decorated with "sensuous" paintings and "naked" statues, the most notable being a voluptuous "nude Venus." The congregation is mainly composed of well-endowed women ("splendid animals, and nothing more") dressed extravagantly (only the wealthy were allowed to attend). The sermon justifies the gap between the rich and the poor and concludes that physical "Love is God." The women respond to the message and to swells of emotional music with wild applause and "palpitating bosoms." Gabriel is shocked and attempts to tell the congregation that they have strayed from Christ's teachings. He is pelted with ornate Bibles and thrown out of the cathedral, while the orgiastic frenzy of the faithful crescendos accompanied by the preacher's defiant shouts: "On with the dance! . . . Though we dance above the graves." Gabriel can only conclude that he has witnessed the death of Christianity and the "rebirth of Paganism."[20]

Though not emphasized as much as the other two weaknesses, a third reason religion had lost touch with the present was one closely related to the nineteenth-century controversy over Darwinism. In an America besieged by relics of the past a major function of religion seemed to be the conservation of Old-World superstitions and the rejection of modern scientific discoveries. In *The Man from Mars* (1891) William Simpson conceived of early religions as infant sciences whose main function was to explain phenomena beyond the grasp of human perception. Sudden and violent storms were perceived as evidence of an angry deity. The proper rituals and prayers would appease the god and sooner or later the storm would stop, proving that the rituals had worked. Such pseudoscience may have been useful to primitive tribes and Old-World peasants since it helped them to "understand" their universe; but as man's knowledge of the material world increased, the "ecclesiastical bodies" that supervised the development of religion tended to cling tenaciously to the old superstititions until religious knowledge and scientific knowledge were completely "divorced" from one another. The result: churches refused to acknowledge scientific interpretations of the material world and instead nurtured their flocks on "supernatural pablum."[21]

The religious revolution that would make Christianity Christian was similar to the economic reforms since most of the utopian authors believed that fundamental, permanent changes were needed to completely reorient the priorities of established religions and in effect create a New Trinity of religious principles: first, and by far the most important, utopian religion was to be especially concerned with day-to-day existence and expressed primarily in deeds; second, religious beliefs should be unified and simple, being limited to such teachings as Love Thy Neighbor and the Golden Rule; and third, religion should encourage—even glorify—scientific studies of God's works, thus reuniting divorced bodies of spiritual and physical knowledge.

Bellamy's Julian West is surprised to find that "you still have Sundays and sermons" in utopia.[22] Actually, if he had browsed through a collection of late nineteenth-century utopian literature, he would have known that the first principle of the utopian religion was that Christianity "know[s] no holidays":[23] instead of Sundays and sermons it was everyday and actions. "Open the book of God; read, mark, learn, and believe. *Then act,*" insisted Dr. Kinnear in *Impending Judgments.*[24] The whole point of Sheldon's popular *In His Steps* was that every individual should preface each act by asking "What would Jesus *do?*" (Italics mine.) If Jesus were a singer, would He sing comic opera or would He use his voice to bring comfort to the poor? Or would He, as a railroad employee, conceal a fraud; would He, as a college president, remain in His ivory tower; would He, as an editor, report prizefights and cower before money power? Sheldon continued this questioning until he had examined almost every occupation in the Rev. Mr. Maxwell's Kansas town. The answer to each question was basically the same: if Jesus were alive today, He would act to help those who were treated unjustly. Other authors expressed their everyday faith in a wide variety of ways: they gave their economic and political systems Christian names; required utopians to swear "to be true and honest in every act, word and thought";[25] and created heroic, action-oriented clergymen who set up co-operative associations in ghettos, lived with the poor, and fought for them though they risked ridicule and reprisals from conservative superiors, wealthy parishioners, and powerful politicians.

The second characteristic of the new religion, its unity and simplicity, re-enforced its everyday nature. In Bellamy's *Equality,* during the Great

Revival of religion, the obsolete creeds that cluttered up Christianity and the sectarian divisions were "swept away and forgotten" as the Religion of Solidarity captivated Americans—a religion that stressed a belief in God as . manifest in humanity and the daily practice of "Love thy neighbor." Likewise Cyrus Cole's Saturnians all believe in one religion, "Unitarianism," the "onehood of the universe"; William Simpson's Martians follow "one religion," based on the example of Christ's life; and General Leggett's Martians have replaced the diversity of Judaism, Catholicism, and sectarian Protestantism with one "simple religion," purified Christianity.[26]

The desire for unity was again expressed in the third aim of the new religion: the reunion of spiritual and material knowledge. This longing usually took the form of an abhorrence of superstitions and an acceptance of Darwin's theory of evolution, described as "the eternal Spirit working in material substance"[27]—an outlook not unlike late nineteenth-century American Theosophist views. The authors also felt that a truly religious person should be so interested in the nature of God's creation that he would keep abreast of new scientific developments. As one citizen of Simpson's Martian utopia boasted, "learning has become the chief part of our religion."[28] A few authors went beyond descriptions of general attempts to bridge the gap between religion and science by imagining such scientific religions that it was almost impossible to tell where religion stopped and science began. M. Louise Moore presented Biblical stories as allegories representing scientific facts. General Leggett maintained that since both religion and science sought to explain God's works, it was the responsibility of religious leaders to "test the accuracy of alleged facts in theology as in chemistry or geology." Cyrus Cole even demonstrated how this could be done. On Saturn Creeto's "great religion" was based on "certology," a mathematical, cosmic theory that defined "immortality" as the universal and eternal process of combination, separation, and recombination of atoms. David Lubin's Ezra might not have been the mathematical genius that Creeto was, but his ideal religion was as science-oriented as certology. To emphasize symbolically that God was "manifest in plants" his ideal temple of worship was a virtual hothouse. Busts of famous doctors and scientists were also prominent. But nowhere was Ezra's reverence for science more obvious than in the various religious holidays he planned for future Americans, including Chemistry Day, Invention Day, Metal Day, and Insect Day![29]

The three major goals of the utopian religion reflect some of the most controversial religious activities and issues of the late nineteenth century: the Social Gospel movement, Theosophy, dissatisfaction with hairsplitting creeds and sectarian squabbles, and the challenge of Darwinism and popular lecturers such as John Fiske and Robert Ingersoll. But they also reveal something characteristic of the utopian authors' views of specific cultural areas. They felt that contemporary belief systems did not give meaning to everyday experience. Economic expectations about the land of opportunity failed to explain inequality and chaos; and religious justifications for suffering, petty arguments about creeds and sects, or bullheaded resistance to science also seemed to be out of touch with reality. The authors' efforts to give meaning to experience thus represented a valiant attempt to revive a culture that they feared was not fulfilling the function of making common conditions and activities understandable and significant to the majority. Still, these praiseworthy efforts also exposed a limited outlook. The authors assumed that because the contradictions they saw between economic or religious theory and reality were irrational that the theories must be dysfunctional for most people. All they had to do was to point out the rational and moral correctness of their arguments and the readers would realize how much more useful and ethical the utopian positions were. Except in perceptive flashes of psychoanalysis, such as Bellamy's portrayal of West's conversion, most of the authors were not fully aware that unproved expectations such as the land of opportunity and suffering as preparation for heaven sometimes give the impoverished the only hope available in a bleak world; similarly diversions such as sectarian squabbles and crusades against Darwinism often provide scapegoats that relieve pent-up emotions. Of course, this does not mean that such assumptions and actions are right or just. But they can be functional and thus survive rational and moral attacks.

Another yearning evident in the utopian attitudes about economics and religion was a desire for order and unity. The authors wanted more than meanings for specific experiences, they wanted these meanings to connect into a coherent whole. In economics this meant a planned, centralized economy; in religion it meant perceiving each act and thought as part of a unified moral vision. Again the utopian authors displayed an awareness of crucial twentieth-century problems, especially the need for the controls and foresight to cushion sudden shifts in the economy and the longing for something that would counteract the fragmented, dislocated feelings so often reflected in modern music, art, and literature. But the desire for order and unity also exposes ambivalence and a limited perspective. On the one hand, the authors' assault on inequality was an expression of their sincere desire to help all mankind. Yet their idea of the fundamental beliefs that would give real significance to life, after material necessities were no longer a concern, was quite restricted. Instead of that "great and everlasting First Congregation of this whole worshipping world" envisioned by Melville's Ishmael, the utopian religion was basically an Americanized, simplified, action-oriented

Protestantism; in only a few cases were Catholicism, Judaism, Islam, Buddhism, and other major religions included in the formula. Even Bellamy's noble Religion of Solidarity with its sense of the dignity and unity of mankind and a oneness with God and the universe might not have welcomed a devout archbishop or a Queequeg.

This does not mean that the utopian authors were stupid bigots. It does suggest, however, that in a diversified population during a time of rapid change, the understandable desire for a meaningful, unified American culture made it difficult for these sincere reformers to imagine ideals that would make America meaningful and unified for Americans who did not share their backgrounds.

Plate 8: "Aerial Navigation." Arthur Bird, *Looking Forward*. Reproduced from Arno Press Inc. reprint (1971) with permission.

Plate 10: "Farming in 1999." Arthur Bird, *Looking Forward*. Reproduced from Arno Press Inc. reprint (1971) with permission.

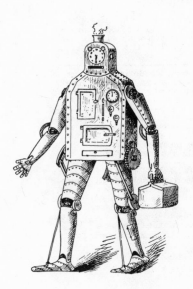

Plate 9: "The Automatic Valet." Arthur Bird, *Looking Forward*. Reproduced from Arno Press Inc. reprint (1971) with permission.

CLASSIFIED ADVERTISEMENTS.

INDESTRUCTIBLE FOOD—Our odorless rubber oysters are all the rage; cheap and durable; especially adapted to use in restaurants and at church fairs; will always wear; we refer by permission to the Ladies' Aid Society of the Church of the United Brotherhood, which purchased sixteen gallons of our oysters five years ago, and is using them still; will remain in a stew five hours without corroding. Perennial Bivalve Company, 149th street.

LOST—From the upper deck of a suburban airship, a lady's picture hat; the hat was caught in a whirlwind and is believed to have landed somewhere near Fort Collins; its return in good condition will insure a generous financial acknowledgment to the finder.

MISCELLANEOUS.

DON'T GO TO CHURCH—Have one of our kinetophones placed in your house; connects with all leading churches; you can shut off sermon whenever you wish. LONG DISTANCE RELIGIOUS COMPANY; factories in Denver and Brooklyn.

GENTLEMEN—Buy our Breath Deodorizer; fumes of Bourbon, old rye and lager removed instantaneously: splendid thing for those contemplating attending evening parties or the theater.

LADIES, READ THIS—Cinderella Shoes will make a No. 6 foot that requires an E last look like a narrow No. 1; comfortable and durable; each pair has a patent hypnotizing attachment that deceives even the most envious and spiteful women who catch a glimpse of the shoes when worn.

NO HOUSEHOLD COMPLETE WITHOUT ONE—We absolutely guarantee that our Electric Equalizer will dissipate any domestic storm and insure harmony in families; so simple that a child can operate one; so delicate in adjustment that the first angry word sets free a soothing magnetic current; for sale by every drug store and dry goods shop. Manufactured by the Anti-Divorce Mercantile Company.

Plate 11: "Classified Advertisements." Arthur Bird, *Looking Forward*. Reproduced from Arno Press Inc. reprint (1971) with permission.

Plate 12: "Hello-Central!" Mark Twain, *A Connecticut Yankee in King Arthur's Court.*

Plate 13: "Etidorhpa." John Uri Lloyd, *Etidorhpa*.

Plate 14: A Monorail. William R. Bradshaw, *The Goddess of Atvatabar*.

Plate 15: "Map of the United States of the Americas. 1999." Arthur Bird, *Looking Forward*. Reproduced from Arno Press Inc. reprint (1971) with permission.

6

Shaping Time, Space and Individuals
with Machines, Schools and Mothers

*. . . olive-trees, orange-trees, birds, bees, blossoms—a railroad depot in
the middle of all this, and yet all things so like one perpetual Sunday.*
—Joaquin Miller, The Building of the City Beautiful *(1893)*

*To educate some to the highest degree, and leave the mass wholly
uncultivated, . . . made the gap between them almost like that between
different species, . . .*
—Edward Bellamy, Looking Backward *(1888)*

. . . the housekeeper's millennium . . . a woman's heaven.
—William Henry Bishop, The Garden of Eden, U.S.A. A Very Possible
Story *(1895)*

In *A Strange Voyage* (1891) Henry F. Allen's narrator and a Venusian
maiden sit in "sweet content . . . for long hours, discussing many phases of
the economic question."[1] But what was "sweet content" on Venus could lull
earthly readers to sleep. Those long economic dialogues and the equally long
sermons about the ultimate moral and spiritual nature of utopia convinced
Forum and *Literary World* reviewers that utopian fiction was "all political
economy" peopled by characters who did "nothing but preach."[2] Fortunately, authors tore their narrators away from their weighty discussions and gave
them tours of utopia that most often included seeing wonderful machines,
visiting schools, and learning about sex roles—especially if the narrator fell
in love. Besides adding variety to sometimes dull narratives, these jaunts

made it clear that economics and religion weren't the only forces that shaped time, space, and the individual in utopia. Technology, education, and sex roles were also important influences.

The descriptions of these cultural areas are, moreover, some of the most interesting passages found in the utopian works. They reflect numerous hotly-debated issues ranging from factory conditions and the "new woman" to Latin courses and knickerbockers. They include some very perceptive criticisms and solutions: often authors whose economic schemes were naive showed an awareness of complex educational problems or of alternatives to "normal" family structures that may surprise modern readers. Furthermore, the authors' attempts to demonstrate how technology, education, and sex related to economics and religion again indicates an understanding of the far-reaching effects of specific changes in a complex, modern culture. By contrast, many Populists and Progressives shunned this broad outlook in favor of isolated political or economic reforms. Finally, comments about machines, schools, and especially sex roles expose some of the most sensitive spots in the utopian visions. Technological advances posed a difficult problem since Americans were supposed to celebrate the very machines that often put them out of work and strengthened the powers of the rich. Education involved the fundamental problems of how to define and pass on the knowledge that was considered necessary if an individual and his culture were to survive. But the touchiest issue was sex. Most anthropologists agree that it is easier to adapt to economic and technological innovations or even to changes in religious creeds and learning processes than it is to accommodate new kinship ties and sex roles. Thus when a narrator met his guide's family or fell in love, he was leading his author into a direct confrontation with a network of values more basic than any economic ideology.

The American officers shout enthusiastically. Behind them is an American flag whose ripples seem frozen in the eerie light. Their complex flying vehicle rests safely at its landing site, and in the distance jagged formations are just visible. The officers' celebration is momentarily interrupted by a telephone call from the President of the United States who congratulates them on their momentous feat. (See Plate 6.)

No, this is not a description of the first landing on the moon and the call from President Nixon. It is the climax (before the inevitable weddings) of Alvarado M. Fuller's *A. D. 2000* (1890), a typical example of the accuracies and inaccuracies of the utopian technological predictions. The situation is amazingly similar to the first moon landing; but the achievement is the discovery of the North Pole which, along with contacting distant planets, was often considered the ultimate technological accomplishment. Thousands of other technological wonders astonished narrators, and many of these, like Fuller's discovery of the North Pole, seem either surprisingly accurate or ridiculously outdated: for example, plastic, contact lenses, computers, Polaroid cameras, spaceships, solar power, cars with a top speed of twenty-one miles per hour, and twenty-second-century planes resembling Orville and Wilbur Wright originals. (See Plates 7, 8, 9, 10, 11, 14.) In spite of this diversity, three technological marvels were mentioned more than any others: electricity, aluminum, and high-speed railroads.[3] In our Automobile Age this technological trinity may seem as obsolete as the utopian biplanes. But gasoline shortages and pollution problems may soon make us all long for the streamlined, aluminum, electric trains of these utopias.

The many glimpses of inventions in the utopian works reflected the intense, late nineteenth-century interest in technology popularized in publications such as the Frank Reade Library, personified in eulogies to Thomas Edison, and enshrined in machinery displays at the 1893 World's Fair. Thus the descriptions of mechanical advances should be of interest to historians of science and technology.[4] Ironically, however, discussions of machines usually re-enforced the moral and religious nature of the utopian visions. Only a few authors—notably Robert Grimshaw, an engineer, Simon Newcomb, an astronomer, and Chauncey Thomas, a master mechanic—predicted utopias dominated by technology. In part this was because most of the authors knew little about machines. They limited their sketches of technological advances to vague descriptions; engines were invariably hidden beyond the narrator's sight. More importantly, technological achievements, like the new economic systems, were perceived primarily as means that would help to establish an environment suitable for the daily practice of Christianity. Even Chauncey Thomas called his ideal future the "Crystal Age of Truth" symbolizing the significance of John Costor's religion of truthfulness.[5]

Nevertheless, technological advancement was a very necessary means to utopia; its effects were similar to the benefits ushered in with new economic systems. First and foremost, the machine would enable Americans to work so efficiently and the cost of mass produced goods would be so low that everyone would be able to afford comforts which, throughout the history of the Old World, had been available only to the aristocracy. As Henry Matthews Williams argued in an *Arena* article, "The Mission of Machinery," such developments would help eliminate the widening gap between the poor and the moneyed aristocracy in the New World by making "wealth abundant to all."[6] Bellamy implied the same argument in *Looking Backward* when he described the marvelous system of mechanical umbrellas that covered all the sidewalks of Boston when it rained. Formerly, only the rich could afford umbrellas. Closely related to the expected upward leveling of material comforts was the assumption that machines would help to make all types of work equally respectable by eliminating the stigma of manual labor. In *Equality* Edith Leete explains to Julian West that it is perfectly respectable for a woman to be a factory hand, a mechanic, or a farmer (her present occupation) because technology has made these occupations exact sciences requiring brain work but practically no back work.[7]

Thus, technological advances, like the new economics, would encourage average Americans to change into utopians by narrowing the gap between the rich and the majority and by making all work honorable. Labor-saving devices would also provide more time for self-improvement and rearing children. But the individual wasn't the only element of utopia to be reformed by technology. Time and space would also be remodeled.

Barriers between different places, eras, and seasons would disappear allowing people to experience numerous spaces and times during one life. The most spectacular examples of the conquest of space appeared in interplanetary travel adventures such as John Jacob Astor's *A Journey in Other Worlds* (1894), C. C. Dail's *Willmoth the Wanderer* (1890), and Milton Ramsey's *Six Thousand Years Hence* (1891). A more typical prediction about how space would change was suggested by the title of Henry Olerich's *A Cityless and Countryless World* (1893). Advances in construction, production, communication, and mass transit would minimize the differences between urban and rural America. New types of high-rise buildings would allow the preservation of nature within the city; machines would reduce the drudgery for farmers and factory workers; television would bring urban "culture" to the country; and high-speed trains would allow people to live in the country and work in the city or vice versa. Time barriers would also vanish. We find nothing as compact and dramatic as H. G. Wells's time machine or Disneyland amusement parks that allow visitors to walk through different eras. But in Dail's *Willmoth the Wanderer* technology (spaceflight) allows the narrator to trace man's evolution; and in Harold Frederic's *Gloria Mundi* (1898) dedication, money, and technology enable an aristocrat to build and populate a medieval village. The most common assaults on time, however, resembled the seasonal transformations examined in Daniel J. Boorstin's *The Americans: The Democratic Experience*. For example, in Will N. Harben's *The Land of the Changing Sun* (1894) two adventurers stumble upon a suboceanic world with a perfectly controlled climate complete with a psychedelic sun that changes color every hour. The ruler, a scientist, knows that perpetual temperate weather would be boring, so he constructs enclosed pleasure parks with specialized climatic conditions and perfects simulated thunderstorms with multicolored lightning. Even if it were 100° in the outside world, a utopian could wake up to a springlike 68°, go skiing in the morning, and watch a summer cloudburst in the afternoon. Each day could be all seasons; astrodomes and plastic snow would not have surprised Harben.

The utopian authors' predictions about how machines would change time, space, and the individual indicate their awareness of the tremendous impact of technological progress. People would be more equal, drudgery would disappear, and the amount of experience that could be packed into one day would increase dramatically. This exciting vision of the future had little room for the trauma of continual experiential bombardment described by Alvin Toffler in *Future Shock*. Nevertheless, the average, the popular, and the most perceptive authors did not perceive technological advances as being *intrinsically* good, and a few of the penetrating authors hinted that machines could be intrinsically bad.

Most authors believed that if the wrong people controlled machines under the wrong conditions, advances in technology only increased the gap between the rich and the poor and turned free laborers into slaves. This was especially true if machines helped to increase the power of private monopolies. Before Frank Norris made the image of the octopus famous, Bellamy likened the combination of advanced technology and monopoly to "the body of the spider [that] swells as he sucks the juices of his victims."[8] One direct effect of this immense power was that honest workers engaged in honest trades were reduced to being "the slaves and hirelings of the owners of [machines]."[9] Advances in technology controlled by the wealthy also became associated with technological unemployment and senseless periods of overproduction. In Walter D. Reynolds's *Mr. Jonnemacher's Machine* (1898) by 1997 there are plenty of goods for sale, but few buyers. Two-thirds of the workers have been replaced by machines and can't find new jobs. But the most heart-rending result of increased mechanization was that machines made most tasks so easy that even women and children could perform them, and they did for twelve to fourteen hours a day under horrid working conditions. Thus, it is not surprising that many of the utopian heroes attacked machines as soulless monsters. As F. U. Adams's John Smith put it: "Great was the machine. It supplanted man, dethroned labor and ruled the world. Everywhere there was heard the whizzing of belts and pulleys and the ceaseless clatter of tireless metal."

But Smith went on to say that the suffering was not the machines' fault. The real problem was the cruel and chaotic environment of the late nineteenth century: "Run the old hulk into dry dock, take out the magnificent engine and place it where it belongs, in an environment fitted to stand the strain of a mechanical age."[10] This response represents the popular and the typical utopian attitude. Bellamy and most of the authors assumed that once the proper economic and moral climate was created, machines would change from tyrannical masters into benign genies offering the gifts and wonders of a technological utopia. In the socialistic utopias technology is controlled by industrial, agricultural, and trade departments; and in most of the other utopias local or national co-operative associations supervise technological advances. Again, as with the new economic procedures, decision-making powers are transferred from a few private individuals to experts subject to the will of the majority and morally dedicated to helping mankind. Thus in utopia, as in the Frank Reade stories, "inventions [are] always used for good purposes":[11] washable metal floors, robots, and plower-planter-harvesters make life easy for housewives, factory workers, and farmhands; blimp-shaped bombers and antigravity weapons insure peace; television brings true religion and the arts to the masses; and in William Bradshaw's Atvatabar mechanical ostriches solve rapid transit problems.

Not all the utopian authors shared this optimistic view, however, and some of the dissenters offered the most perceptive glimpses of modern technological successes and failures. Usually these insights were not as explicit as the attacks suggested by George Orwell's *1984* or Aldous Huxley's *Brave New World*. Instead they were implied by ambivalent attitudes that simultaneously celebrated and abhorred technology. Twain's Hank Morgan (who has been compared by one critic to Jacques Ellul's slave of technology and technique)[12] is trapped between his love of gadgets and a latent but growing awareness of the terrors of sophisticated weapons; Howells's Altrurians vacillate between tearing up railroad tracks and enjoying the country-city life made possible by them; and Simon Newcomb, Stanley Waterloo, and Cyrus Cole among others praised machines while envisioning devastating technological warfare or robot revolts. But possibly the most interesting foreshadowings of novels such as Arthur C. Clarke's *The City and the Stars* (1953) are found in the visions of modern technological achievements and problems in an obscure work written by an equally obscure Georgian novelist.[13]

As mentioned previously, Will N. Harben's *The Land of the Changing Sun* (1894) narrates the adventures of two travelers in a suboceanic utopia, Alpha, controlled by a scientist-king. The striking quality of this work is that Harben not only suggested the just and unjust uses of machines, he also implied *intrinsic* benefits and dangers associated with technological progress.

The visitors, Johnson and Thorndyke, are impressed by the high standard of living fostered by the wise and just uses of technology and by the inherent beauties of machinery. They listen to symphonies piped into their rooms, see the equivalent of modern slides, movies, and color television, and wonder at the dome of the king's palace: "a marvel of kaleidoscopic colors formed by a myriad of electric-lighted prisms." The chef d'oeuvre, however, is the gigantic electric sun that illuminates the suboceanic cave world. It is solid crystal, five hundred feet in diameter and is suspended from cables connected to trucks that run on rails spanning the roof of the cavern. With each hour of "daylight" this locomotive-chandelier changes color, making the Alphian landscape a wonderland of varying hues.

Throughout most of *The Land of the Changing Sun* the visitors remain dazzled by mechanical wonders, but they also become very aware of the possible misuses of technology. Weak and undesirable Alphians are victims of an inhuman policy of eugenics. They are flown off to starve in a secluded wasteland. The scientist-king's dictates are enforced by a police force equipped with a television scanner that would have delighted Big Brother. Technology is also used to brainwash suspect individuals. The scientist-king is reasonably sure that Thorndyke will make a good Alphian. Nevertheless, to insure his obedience, Thorndyke, like Orwell's Winston Smith, is sent to a special room for a bit of mental conditioning. First he is deprived of his senses and mobility: the walls are padded, there is no light or sound, and he is clamped to a chair. After he has spent several minutes in this senseless state, a tiny bright light appears. The light projects a luminous, revolving circle on the floor, which—like Poe's pendulum—slowly approaches its victim. Just before it reaches Thorndyke's heart, the light is extinguished, and he is left in absolute darkness again. Thorndyke's next trial is an encounter with a frightening combination of Frankenstein's monster and Coleridge's Ancient Mariner. A "faint hum of hidden machinery" is heard, and a mechanical man rises from a nearby couch: "pale lights shone in the orbits of [his] eyes and the sound of harsh automatic breathing came from the mouth and nostrils." After "a sharp, whirring noise," the monster speaks: "My voice shall sound on earth for a million years after my spirit has left my body; and I shall wander about my dark dungeon as a warning to men not to do as I have done." His sins were a tendency to question the scientist-king's motives and an attempt to escape Alpha. His punishment is a living death. His internal organs have been replaced by complex machinery that enables him to repeat his warning forever. Hence in Alpha the king can hand out eternal punishments as well as create a sun. Another period of darkness is followed by Thorndyke's removal from the dungeon. He is immediately ushered into the king's throne room: "the beautiful women and handsome men moving about the throne were to him like glimpses of Paradise." Juxtaposed with his recent terrifying experience, this "glimpse" is obviously designed to teach Thorndyke the differences between the fates that await the loyal and the disloyal Alphians.

Intensive mental conditioning may be an effective way of handling suspect individuals, but the scientist-king realizes that it would be impossible to apply this tactic to every Alphian. Therefore, he has devised more subtle methods of conditioning and pacifying the masses. The educational system is carefully planned to teach young Alphians just enough about the outside world (disease, harsh weather, war) to discourage escape and just enough about the artifical sun, moon, and stars to make their cave world a wonderful mystery. The latter characteristic of the educational training is indirectly related to another method of social control, which again involves the use of technology. Like Twain's Hank Morgan, the scientist-king is a good show-man with an excellent sense of timing. Near the conclusion of the novel, the sun stops shining and the Alphians riot. Fortunately, the king has foreseen the possibility of such a catastrophe and has invented a spectacle calculated to "instantly restore confidence to the people." First the heavens are lit with a beautiful pink, which the people know as the Ideal Dawn. Then a gigantic picture of the king is projected "on the sky" below the word "SILENCE!" in "flaming letters." The king's image tells the stunned Alphians that danger has passed and that the sun will shine tomorrow. The riot stops; the people disperse. This is but one example of the scientist-king's ability to manipulate the population with elaborate technological shows. Under normal conditions his entertainments are limited to the circus side of the bread-and-circuses philosophy of government—shows such as Ideal Dawns, musical thunder, or multicolored lightning. He evidently felt, however, that the riot called for a truly "grand effect," to borrow one of Hank Morgan's phrases.

Up to this point it could be argued that although Harben was more perceptive and more imaginative than most of the utopian authors, his criticism was basically the same as the typical utopian response to technol-ogy: machines weren't intrinsically bad; they had bad effects when controlled by the wrong people in the wrong economic and moral environment. Harben did, however, illuminate several interrelated results of technological ad-vances that suggested inherent problems associated with modern technology.

First of all, in Alpha there is practically no "natural" experience. Floors are covered with a thick, "soft carpet"; unpleasant odors are masked by artificial scents or by the "entrancing odors" from carefully planned gardens and orchards; the "rugged rocks, sharp cliffs and yawning chasms" of the unlighted portions of the cave are hidden by a huge wall; most of the machines run "noiselessly" and jarring sounds are drowned out by "seduc-tive music" or by the "monotonous hum" of a few large machines; lastly, there is no wind, no rain, no change of temperature in Alpha—the sun is cold, it is only a gorgeous ornament. This cocoon existence is a direct result of the tendency of technology to isolate man from raw experience. In spite of the comfort, order, and glitter of Alpha, this artificial environment deprives the Alphians of the many delights associated with direct contact with nature. Thus, Richard Gerber's view of existence in *Brave New World* can be applied to Alpha: "everywhere, we have the substitute instead of the real thing."[14]

Embedded within their controlled world, the Alphians develop a false sense of security that cripples the average man's capacity to react to crises. The scientist-king and the people, for example, are fond of boasting that there are no "accidents" in Alpha. Then, when the sun ceases to shine, "the populace seemed unable to grasp the situation." They respond by beating each other and destroying buildings. The king calms them with the speaking image of himself projected in the sky; but later when a real crisis is caused by a fissure in the cave, nothing can calm the terrified masses.

This final crisis reveals one of the most fundamental problems associated with technological progress: a frustrating, false sense of immediacy and power. The fissure is in a practically inaccessible part of the cave, but the Alphians can "see" the battle to save their world. They rush to the "Electric Auditorium," which is dominated by a gigantic "mirror" (a color television screen). An on-the-spot reporter appears on the screen speaking into "a cup-shaped instrument from which extended a wire to the ground." The Alphians are frantic to hear the news and to see the action, but hearing and seeing only seem to add to their anguish. The television broadens their awareness of the situation and simultaneously augments their sense of helplessness. They can hear and see all but cannot *do* anything—anything except moan and groan in their plush seats. Eventually, in desperation they flee the auditorium. Later when one of the visitors goes to see the screen, he is shocked to find that "not a soul was there save himself." Half a century before the development of television, Harben predicted how mass media would greatly enlarge the average man's consciousness and thus his sense of power, only to intensify his sense of impotency and insignificance by enabling him to hear and see but not to act.[15]

Despite Harben's perceptive glimpses of 1984 in 1894, his final vision embodied the typical utopian response to the machine. As Alpha caves in, even the scientist-king renounces his faith in technology. He hopes to lead his people in the founding of a technologically primitive, Christian society—again the assumption that a moral rather than a material change was the key to utopia. Thus, Harben's concluding stance echoes Julian West's opinion that had the technological advances of 2000 A.D. "been ten times more marvelous, they would still have impressed me with infinitely less astonishment than the moral revolution illustrated in [the] new social order."[16]

To some, this view of the future might seem naive considering the tremendous impact of technology during the twentieth century. It was only rarely, as in "With Eyes Shut," Bellamy's short story about phonographs, that an author attempted to trace in detail the full effects of a specific technological innovation. Therefore, one reaction to late nineteenth-century attempts to predict the future of technology has been to label them as simple-minded expressions of a faith that has been satirized by Orwell and Huxley, subjected to exacting examinations by historians of technology, and questioned by post-Hiroshima generations.[17]

But this criticism is unfair. It is difficult enough for scientists, anthropologists, historians, and "think tank" experts to predict how technology will affect a culture; very few of the authors had such training. Furthermore, most of the authors did see parts of both sides of the future of technology. They were aware of some of the most beneficial ways technology could be used to reshape time, space, and the individual; but they also knew that the misuse of machines could be a nightmare. And a few, especially Harben, hinted at basic problems that could profoundly affect the way people view themselves and their environment. Thus, long before Orwell's and Huxley's births, Lewis Mumford's and Daniel J. Boorstin's studies of technology, and the H-bomb, one group of American reformers had glimpses of the heavenly hell of twentieth-century technology.

After astounding the narrator with the mechanical wonders of utopia, the guide often led him away from his seat in an electric, aluminum train to a nearby school. On Milan C. Edson's Solaris Farm we find an elaborate nursery-kindergarten. Its sixty-by-two-hundred-foot learning area has an "arched decorated ceiling," brightly colored designs and pictures on the walls, plants, toys, and household objects on the floor, and a miniature railroad with swinging cribs and animal seats. Rabbi Solomon Schindler provided his utopian grade school and high school students with a "ravishing paradise": aluminum and glass schools that ringed the cities. They were "palaces" complete with gymnasiums, pools, animals, gardens, and, of course, excellent teachers. Finally, in Warren S. Rehm's "university town" college and graduate students and adults of all ages interested in self-improvement could stroll down "Greek" and "Puritan" Avenues to classes ranging from morals to landscape architecture.[18] In utopia learning became a life cycle.

As the biographical data indicate, the utopian authors were very well educated; at a time when only 1% of the population attended college, as high as 72% of the utopian authors were university men and women. It is no surprise, therefore, that they were concerned about the schools of the future.

What may be surprising is how critical they were of the schools of the present—the very institutions that helped them gain respectability. They linked nineteenth-century education with the unjust and senseless nineteenth-century economics and religion that widened the gap between the rich and the poor and perpetuated a meaningless body of knowledge. The authors pictured education, especially college, as an extravagant luxury beyond the grasp of most Americans. The tragedy of this exclusivism was that it kept the poor in a state of perpetual ignorance severely limiting their economic and social mobility and made it easy for corrupt politicians to manipulate them. (Statistical studies by Lipset, Bendix, and others support the first conclusion.)[19] The educational gap, moreover, intensified the economic and social gap to a point where meaningful dialogues between the rich and the poor were minimized. As Bellamy's Dr. Leete put it, "To educate some to the highest degree, and leave the mass wholly uncultivated, . . . made the gap between them almost like that between different species, which have no means of communication."[20] In a fragmented and diversified population education seemed to set up barriers between different types of people instead of bridging these gaps. Furthermore, education did not provide a meaningful body of knowledge that would help Americans to understand themselves and their culture; instead, like the obsolete religious creeds, the schools were out of touch with the real world. Dr. Leete even suggests that an education became one of the main forms of escapism for the wealthy: "The cultivated man in your age was like one up to the neck in a nauseous bog solacing himself with a smelling bottle."[21] Even the schooling offered to the poor seemed irrelevant. Children were made to memorize poems and lessons unrelated to their lives; the historical and literary theories taught were often outdated; there was an aversion to teaching new disciplines such as political economy and evolutionary science; a tendency to teach the type of religion the authors abhorred; and the problem of poverty was either ignored or justified as a natural result of the best possible social and economic environment. (In *President John Smith* [1897] F. U. Adams even included an illustration entitled "The teacher tells the scholar he may emulate Gould.")

Thus the utopian authors felt that an education only aggravated the sins of nineteenth-century economics and religion. To correct this, most of the authors (about 90%) recommended universal, free education usually extending through college and stressing total development rather than the rote learning of what Mortimer Leggett called "hollow intellectual" facts. Just as important was the assumption that an ideal education lasted a lifetime; it should not be confined to a few years in a classroom.[22] In the popular works and in the utopian literature in general the programs that would implement these goals were rarely outlined in detail. Nevertheless, it is possible to sketch the educational life cycle of a typical citizen of utopia.

For at least two authors, Alcanoan O. Grigsby and William Windsor, education began before birth by carefully controlling the expectant mother's physical environment and by subjecting her to an intensive learning program. Most of the authors preferred to let the child at least leave the womb before starting the first phase of education, which lasted from birth until about five or six years old. They realized the importance of these years; Addison Peale Russell even believed that by "two years old" a person's character was formed.[23] But they also realized that tampering with infants meant trespassing on the sacred ground of Motherhood. Therefore, during these early years, the child's primary teachers usually were his parents. Increased leisure time resulting from economic and technological changes, and extensive training received in school would produce ideal parent-teachers whose major responsibilities would be to cultivate cleanliness, industry, and morality, though a few authors did encourage teaching reading and writing.[24]

A small minority, composed mainly of Charles Bellamy, William Bishop, Rabbi Schindler, and Henry Olerich, challenged this view by questioning whether parents ever could or should teach their children. But the most interesting variation of the typical utopian preschool education is found in *Solaris Farm* (1900) written by a farmer and retired Civil War captain, Milan C. Edson, who predicted both the "open space" concept and the success of Sesame Street.

Edson's idea of a preschool was an original compromise to the Mother vs. nursery issue. On Solaris Farm mothers are carefully trained in "Mother's Clubs," reflecting Edson's interest in the post-Civil War Moral Education Societies influenced by doctors such as Elizabeth Blackwell.[25] Edson's clubs offer women intensive courses on enhancing the physical, mental, and moral development of their children. This program is supplemented by the previously mentioned "nursery-kindergarten" for children from one to four supervised by experts in preschool education. The two major aims of the teachers are to encourage the development of sensory perception and to make the first group school experience an enjoyable one so that learning would always be associated with enjoyable experiences: "the happy scenes of this merry kindergarten life." These two goals are achieved by alternating brief flexible periods of study, play, and rest outside and in a large room sixty by two hundred feet. "The entire floor space" of the room "is unobstructed by a partition" so that learning would not be perceived as something divided up into tidy compartments. The perimeter is encompassed by a miniature railroad track. During learning and some play sessions, the children ride around the room in brightly colored cars (swings and cribs for infants, carousel animal seats for the three- and four-year-olds) pulled by a jolly electric engine. The ceiling and all the walls are covered with colors, geometric shapes, and pictures. While the three- and four-year-olds play, the infants are taken for a ride. For three days their brief trips concentrate on various tints of one color; then they move on to other colors or to simple shapes. By the time the child is two, he can distinguish between different colors and different shapes and is exposed to his first pictures, which combine colors and shapes to form familiar sights on Solaris Farm. The three- and four-year-olds are taken on slightly longer trips designed to develop a variety of senses. Pictures sharpen visual perception; simple songs develop the voice, memory, and listening capacity; smelling flowers, plants, and household goods cultivates the sense of smell; and feeling materials of different thicknesses and temperatures develops tactile senses. Finally, toy blocks with numbers, letters, heavenly bodies, and modern historical figures are used on and off the train to help the child distinguish between different types of expression and different types of experience.[26] Edson's kindergarten is one of the best examples of how the utopian authors sought to develop the whole personality and to break down associations between learning and a classroom environment.

From about six to twelve years old the utopian child was sent to elementary school where the learning experience became more closely associated with a classroom, though the goal of developing the whole personality was still paramount. The three R's were taught, and the good habits instilled by the examples of parents were expanded to include honesty, faithfulness, sincerity, perseverance, cheerfulness, and sacrifice, which were encouraged and rewarded promptly. A sense of discipline defined as "self-denial and self-control" was also emphasized. Usually this was achieved by getting the child accustomed to a regular routine of classes and by exposing him to an extensive program in "physical culture" (hygiene, exercises, group activities).[27] For example, Schindler set up the following schedule for his live-in grade schoolers:

6:00 a.m.: rise to music, make bed, wash ("To be tidy is but a habit");
7:15: breakfast;
7:30-8:00: play or garden;
8:00-12:00: classes (conversation, reading, and models were the prime teaching methods; rote memory was not encouraged); one hour of study; half hour in the gym;
12:00: lunch;
12:30-2:00: free time;
2:00-4:00: classes;

4:00-6:00: free time;
6:00-8:00: supper;
8:00-10:00: gardening, concerts, lectures;
10:00: bed.[28]

Several authors supplemented exercise with daily periods of parade drills. Of course, the emphasis on character development, especially sacrifice and discipline, helped to prepare students for co-operative environments.

One important difference between the utopian elementary schools and their nineteenth-century counterparts, which reflected a controversial issue during the 1880s and 1890s, was that *all* students, males and females alike, received technical and manual training. In *Looking Backward*, for example, Dr. Leete explains that in the past this was impossible because "manual labor meant association with a rude, coarse, and ignorant class of people."[29] In utopia no such class existed and all trades were equally honored. Learning a technical skill thus became a respectable and a practical way of preparing for adulthood.

The academic curriculum was likewise geared towards producing useful members of society instead of pure scholars. For instance, in Fayette Stratton Giles's utopia the "first duty" of the teacher was "to teach the more useful knowledge." Useful was defined as subjects or activities that helped students to understand and to participate in the "actual world."[30] The typical curriculum consisted of modern English and American literature, simple math and science, modern history and periods in the history of the Old World most readily related to the present. Civics, practical religious principles, and a smattering of music, drawing, and modeling rounded out the curriculum and helped to develop the child's tastes. A crucial characteristic of the academic curriculum was that no course was taught as a separate entity. The interrelation of subjects was stressed, again, because in the actual world different types of behavior and different ideas were not neatly separated and categorized.

Although the utopian elementary school program was much more ambitious than anything attempted in nineteenth-century grade schools, the authors emphasized that the teachers had an easier job in utopia. They argued that in nineteenth-century America the incongruities between the classroom experience and life made the child distrust the teacher and view an education as a useless, hypocritical experience. Conversely, the ideals taught to the students in utopia were practiced by their parents and by the population in general, so learning became associated with following good examples. Thus, as with the utopian religion, the authors stressed the benefits of knowledge that made everyday life meaningful.

The primary function of the utopian high schools and colleges was to allow students to discover their particular interests and skills. If they passed the appropriate examinations, they would continue their training in a wide variety of specialized schools and universities without having to worry about the exorbitant tuition fees that kept all the poor and most of the middle classes out of college in the nineteenth century. As in the elementary schools, the emphasis was on useful knowledge. In Warren S. Rehm's model "university town," for example, male and female students could attend colleges specializing in traditional professions such as the ministry, law, and medicine or they could attend colleges leading to professions in sanitary science, food preparation, manual labor, applied morals, business, land-scaping, and even sexual science.[31]

Though many of the utopian authors' ideas about education were as old as Plato's *Republic,* their concept of formal schooling was ahead of its time. They realized that equality meant an equal distribution of learning as well as money; their emphasis on developing the whole person and on teaching useful knowledge foreshadowed John Dewey's "progressive" education; and they sought to eliminate arbitrary sexual roles and equally arbitrary barriers between static disciplines, and between learning and life. Still, the utopian schools raise some questions. A student fired by the desire for a career in engineering would thrive in utopia, but what would become of a child fascinated by Latin and Greek, or other "old-fashioned" and "impractical" studies? The utopian education, like the utopian concept of history, seemed all too ready to junk the past. Another apparent weakness was that the authors advocated a simplistic pre-Freudian Freudianism by assuming that an individual's character is determined at a very early age. After elementary school, the switch to specialized professional training suggested that just before or soon after puberty personality formation was completed; all a student had to do to attain maturity was to develop the talents he knew he had. Rabbi Schindler predicted that during the twenty-first century a ten-year-old would know himself or herself well enough to be in a special trade school. At fourteen he or she would be attending a specialized high school, which might even be geographically isolated from other types of schools.[32] The work of modern social psychologists such as the late Harry Stack Sullivan and Erik Erikson suggests how harmful these assumptions about early personality development can be.

Questions of academic freedom and early specialization raise serious doubts about the utopian education, but one basic principle stressed by the authors helped to answer both questions. An ideal education was a lifetime experience. New economics, technology, and early retirement would enable adult utopians to spend at least half their waking hours away from their specialization; and numerous libraries, theaters, art galleries, churches, and television shows insured that they would have adequate facilities to develop a wide variety of interests, even in Latin oratory. A utopian who did this might be considered eccentric, and any who became interested in anti-Christian philosophies would not be appreciated; but at least the utopians would not be limited to one occupational role for most of their lives.

Another characteristic of the authors' approach to education that helped to offset its weaknesses was their admission that educational problems could not be solved in a vacuum. Before universal, free education could be achieved, an efficient, co-operative economy had to be established to fund the schools. Furthermore, education as a total, everyday process would be sustained by the unifying daily gospel that gave meaning to the utopians' lives. Finally, even the most optimistic supporters of good education confessed that without economic and moral reform, technological advances, and changes in sex roles, the emergence of education as a diversified, lifelong experience was very doubtful.

Milan C. Edson's kindergartens were quite sophisticated; but when he attempted to portray an ideal love affair, he seemed to run amuck—or rather a-mush. Fillmore Flagg, founder of the Solaris Farm, falls in love with Fern Fenwich, an attractive heiress. She finances his community, and in a "Twentieth Century Love Letter" he expresses his appreciation and affection: "My Darling Fern: Noblest, purest and most beautiful of women!" In her "Reply" Fern gushes, "Ah, my chosen one! So manly; so noble, so true! . . . my hero . . . gallant Knight of Most Excellent Agriculture." She completes the image by crowning her future husband with a shining helmet adorned with corn-tassel plumes.[33]

Today, readers would mock these love letters as examples of the romantic bathos that pervaded nineteenth-century popular fiction. Indeed, late nineteenth-century literary critics did chastise utopian authors for diverting attention away from radical ideas with love stories and glimpses of marital bliss. To some extent this criticism was valid; even Bellamy admitted it.[34] But as Barbara C. Quissell has argued, the boy-meets-girl formula and the presence of a heroine who resembled conventional, nineteenth-century heroines helped to make the strange world of utopia more familiar and acceptable for readers.[35] (See Plates 12 and 13.) Therefore, it is not surprising that when Austyn Granville's narrator in *The Fallen Race* (1892) is ushered into the throne room of the ruler of a race descended from Australian bushmen and kangaroos (four-foot fur balls with faces and arms), he finds an "inherently well bred" beauty with "pure white skin." She's even a "latent Christian"![36] Furthermore, like Henry Adams's Virgin, the Edith Leetes of utopia often became symbols of love, harmony, and unity; they represented the highest goals of utopia and offered reassurance and comfort to the confused Julian Wests.[37]

Possibly the most interesting way of perceiving the descriptions of present and future women, love affairs, and family life, however, is as indications of the authors' attitudes about how sex roles and family structure shape the individual. These attitudes, moreover, help to illuminate an ambivalence related to the ambiguities of the utopian concept of history and similar to the apparent contradictions between advocating forward-looking economic reforms and clinging to traditional Christian beliefs.

When the utopian authors attempted to define ideal sex roles in family life, they often disagreed about the proper functions of the family. In general, three types of ideal families were pictured: the conventional, Victorian family defined in numerous marriage manuals of the period;[38] a family structure that freed women from economic dependence upon men; and a family that eliminated both economic and social functions of the family. The first model family became the framework for all discussion of sex roles and thus deserves to be described in some detail. It was defined as an essential institution that provided economic security for the wife and children, offered the best environment for procreation and child rearing, and established a socially approved context for the gratification of "spiritual" and physical love. This conventional view was defended as if it were a sacred tenet that defined "natural" sex roles: it made woman "the handmaiden of male humanity . . . as the Gods intended," and taught man his proper station, since "God had created [him] for her protection and support." Besides, all women knew that economic dependence was a "trivial matter," and that any attempt to tamper with the family would stifle the "voice of nature" by creating conditions favorable to the creation of a race of "manly" women and "effete" men.[39] Such changes would also be a threat to the "great socio-anatomical institution of the nineteenth century," the mother's knee.[40] Several of Bellamy's critics saw character building, not new economic systems or religion, as the key to an ideal future; and they maintained that the American Mother was the most important influence on character formation. For example, Richard C. Michaelis, a Chicago editor, argued that: "Nearly all our good qualities can be traced back to the influence and unfathomable love and patience of the mother. . . . Nearly all great men had good mothers."[41] Since an American utopia was to be a society of great individuals, attempts to alter the mother-child relationship would prevent the creation of an ideal civilization. (See Plate 12 for an illustration of an ideal family.)

This concept of the family was vigorously opposed by another group of utopian authors who believed that the wife's economic dependence on her husband was a remnant of the Old-World practice of stealing women from the enemy and forcing them into lives of servitude. A third group went further and declared that the nineteenth-century family was an inefficient economic unit, an inadequate environment for procreation and child rearing, and a barbaric institution that forced incompatible men and women to live together.

Which concept of the family was defended by the majority of these middle- and upper-middle-class idealists? Surprisingly enough in an era when rising divorce rates and the feminist movement made family structure an especially controversial topic, most of the utopian authors, including the popular Bellamy and the respected Howells, advocated the second form of the ideal family maintaining that women should "in no way be dependent on their husbands" for economic security.[42] Less than 10% of the authors staunchly championed the economic function of the family;[43] and the most thorough analyses of sex roles in the family were found in works written by authors who either agreed with Bellamy and Howells or went beyond them to strip the family of its child-rearing functions and to banish love from the home.

The conventional view of the family seemed barbaric to most utopian authors because it made slaves of both sexes and perverted a sacred relationship. They—like Lester Frank Ward, Charlotte Perkins Gilman, Thorstein Veblen, and many feminists[44]—felt that the typical nineteenth-century marriage was nothing more than a business partnership: women sought men who could support them instead of men they admired and loved; men sought women who would be good housekeeper-mothers, or, if they desired prestige, they looked for a housekeeper-mother with social distinction. In both cases sex roles were severely limited. The man was the brute money-maker; or as the Christian mystic Thomas Lake Harris put it, man was the "American civilizee; . . . producer, plutocrat,—prick the skin and we touch the savage still."[45] The woman was restricted to being the "homemaker" and the "social butterfly." Marriage was, in effect, a business arrangement between a featherheaded home-beauty and a money-making beast. Instead of being a union of two souls, marriage had become a form of legalized prostitution in which the woman sold herself for economic security and the man sold himself for free maid service, baby tending, and perhaps prestige.[46]

The effects of this contract spread far beyond the confines of the home. Laurence Gronlund, the economist-reformer, and several other utopian authors maintained that young men did not marry because they were afraid they would not be able to support a wife and family. This decision, though practical, failed to satisfy their instincts for sexual gratification and encouraged them to fulfill these needs outside the home in a house of prostitution. (The "social crime" was, of course, another touchy issue during the late nineteenth century, the primary target of the "purity crusade.")[47] Although in *Unveiling a Parallel* (1893), written by two women, female utopians can enjoy male whores in lavish garden settings, few authors were willing to admit that women also desired sexual gratification.[48] But the utopian authors did see part of the other side of the prostitution problem. They argued that women who lacked social distinction or domestic talents, or women who simply could not find employment because they were discriminated against, were often willing to become whores rather than starve. At least two authors went a step further, relating the economic pressures of a typical marriage to more heinous crimes than prostitution. Crawford S. Griffin, a Bostonian who supported Gronlund's and Bellamy's reform proposals, believed that rape was a direct result of postponed or "poor" marriages that forced men to reject the women they loved and marry incompatible women for convenience or money, and Rabbi Schindler maintained that economic pressures could drive parents to commit infanticide.[49]

According to the overwhelming majority of utopian authors (over 90%), the problems associated with conventional marriages could be avoided if women were not dependent upon their husbands and if they were treated as intelligent human beings instead of handmaidens. But, as with their solutions to educational problems, the authors realized that sex roles could not be changed in isolation; before this could happen fundamental changes had to occur outside the home. For instance, the new economic systems would help. In Bellamy's *Looking Backward* the state assumes the economic burdens, and everyone receives equal annual incomes. In utopian works opposing economic equality, women receive wages equal to the wages received by men engaged in the same occupations; or, if a woman prefers to be a full-time housewife and mother, the state pays her for her services as an investment in the future generation. (Recently this idea has been proposed as a "radical" alternative to day-care centers.)[50] Changes in religious attitudes and new educational programs were also recognized as important elements in the liberation of men and women. Most utopian authors believed that the best way to express love for God was to love your neighbor as yourself. Therefore, a woman deserved to be loved and respected as much as any male neighbor. In utopia women also merited respect because they could become fully educated. Women can choose to specialize in homemaking, which prepares them to be excellent wives or to get good paying jobs in co-operative kitchens, sewing shops, and laundries. They may also compete directly with men by studying farming, mechanics, politics, medicine, chemistry, and other traditionally masculine fields. The inclusion of the utopian women in the ranks of doctors and scientists is especially significant since during the late nineteenth century these were supposed to be exclusively male occupations.[51] The other side of this development is that the utopian men can become expert cooks.[52] Finally, technological advances, such as electric appliances, and even architectural changes, such as metallic floors that can be washed and drained in an instant, liberate men from their dependence on housekeepers in utopia and free women from the "dish-rag and the broom stick" creating a "housekeeper's millennium."[53]

It was predicted that several more fundamental changes in family structure and sex roles would result from the new economics, new religion, new technology, and new education. First, true parenthood would blossom. In *Equality* Bellamy argued that economically secure couples would control their "impulses of cruel animalism" better than poor people. His hypothetical proof: without the aid of birth control pills, the utopians in the year 2000 have few children, which means that they can lavish attention on each child. Bellamy and the majority of utopian authors also believed that once women became financially independent, their children were bound to improve because women would be free to select their husbands by their womanly instincts, a basis of selection that would lead to ideal parental matches. Thus, like many nineteenth-century reformers ranging from John Humphrey Noyes to Dr. Elizabeth Blackwell to Dr. John Harvey Kellogg of cereal fame, most of the utopian authors believed that "sex, purged of its dangers and channeled properly, could be converted into a force for human betterment."[54] To quote Bellamy's Dr. Leete, the "race perfection" in 2000 can be explained by "the principle of sexual selection, with its tendency to preserve and transmit the better types of the race. . . . Every generation is sifted through a little finer mesh from the last."[55] Henry F. Allen even went so far as to describe the love instinct as "an absolute science" and an "absolute law of life."[56] Hence sexual love would be simultaneously banished and cherished in an American utopia, since—as every good Victorian knew—physical love was considered to be a "crude animalism" associated with poverty whereas Platonic love was an ideal guide that inspired perfectly matched lovers to meet and, occasionally, produce ideal cherubs. Then after the children were born, their well-educated parents would be free to spend their abundant leisure time with them. Therefore, during the important preschool years, the children would be constantly exposed to excellent parent-teachers.

Economic security and increased leisure would also affect the third major function of the family, the socially accepted expression of love. Instead of having to postpone marriage and seek sexual gratification from prostitutes, a young man could marry the woman he loved without delay. After the wedding he and his wife would, moreover, have ample time to cultivate a pure and intense relationship. Thus, Rabbi Schindler could make the proponents of conventional marriages eat their self-righteous words by declaring that "only through a radical change in our social condition can . . . matrimony become a sacred institution."[57] Laurence Gronlund saw this new sacredness in relation to the ultimate religious goal of founding a society based on brotherly love. He explained that the typical American marriage forced a couple together for economic reasons and they never learned to love each other. They might be living in the same house, eating the same meals, and sleeping in the same bed; but they were still locked within their private selves. On the other hand, when men and women were free to choose one another for love and admiration and had the time to express their feelings, then "man [i.e., humanity] comes forth from his mere personality and learns to live in another while obeying his most powerful instincts."[58]

One final result of the proposed changes inside and outside the home would be that woman's influence would extend far beyond the limits of her family. Defenders of the conventional family saw woman as society's conscience, and the home as a refuge from the harsh outside world. But they pictured her role as being restricted to her moral influence on her children and husband. Even with these limitations it was doubtful whether she could prepare sons for the vicious competition of the business world. To some extent Bellamy and most of the authors respected this stereotype by suggesting that women were inherently more moral than men. (Still, a few wealthy society women, such as Howells's Mrs. Makely, demonstrated that women could be as rotten as men.) But they believed that it was wrong to limit women's influence to the home. After women realized that they did not have to bend to the will of the breadwinner, and after they were encouraged to pursue any career that interested them, they should be free to exert their influence anywhere in society. In *Looking Backward* and *Equality,* for example, Julian West is surprised by Edith Leete's intelligence and by her "serene frankness and ingenuous directness." Later he is even more shocked to find that women serve at all ranks and in all professions in the Industrial Army (Edith is a farmhand) and that there is a permanent seat for a woman on the highest council in the nation. Besides having a vote like all the other men and women on the council, she has veto power on matters specifically relating to her sex.[59] In most of the other utopian works women are encouraged or at least permitted to pursue active careers outside the home; and in at least 17 novels an inspiring woman and/or a women's movement play crucial roles in the reformation of America. In one, Dr. John McCoy's *A Prophetic Romance* (1896), a Martian visits an ideal America and is astonished to discover that a woman is president. In *The Building of the City Beautiful* (1893) Joaquin Miller's beautiful Jewess succeeds in founding a perfect city while a solitary male reformer with the same goal is a complete failure. The double standard has completely vanished in one Martian country in *Unveil-*

ing a Parallel (1893) by Alice Jones and Ella Merchant. Women not only occupy important political and financial positions, they also can "vaporize" (inhale a mixture of alcohol and pulverized valerian roots), drink, get hungover, be prizefighters, and seek sexual gratification in gardens of prostitution staffed by alluring young males. But the ultimate in freedom from men is found in Mary Lane's *Mizora* (1889). The population is ruled by a group of wise and beneficent female chemists whose experiments lead to the creation of a perfect, all-female race!

Depriving the family of its economic function and emancipating woman from the kitchen (and man from the brute, money-maker role) were two of the most radical aspects of the utopian literature. Nevertheless, the new woman was still *primarily defined in relation to her children and husband.* Two of the major results of her liberation were that she would be free to be an ideal mother and an ideal wife. Furthermore, in several of the utopian works, including *Looking Backward,* a woman's role outside the home is shaped by her role within the home. True, as revealed by Bellamy's Dr. Leete, women in 2000 A.D. participate in all occupations and have important responsibilities; but Leete makes it very clear that only wives, and preferably mothers, are eligible for the highest ranks in the Industrial Army.[60] In Dr. McCoy's utopia the Martian finds a woman president; but he also discovers that if a woman reaches the age of thirty-five without marrying, she is sent to the "Matrimonial Department" for counseling.[61] The emancipated mothers in James Cowan's *Daybreak* decide to relax their grip on child discipline. The result is a youth revolution that threatens to destroy the nation. A catastrophe is averted only because of swiftly enacted legislation protecting oppressed parents and because the liberated mothers realize that one of woman's primary duties is motherhood.[62] In an American utopia women would be liberated, but to the overwhelming majority of these reformers a liberated woman was equivalent to an emancipated mother-wife.

Thus most utopian authors simultaneously broke away from and clung to the conventional concept of the family. One important function of the family, economic security for the woman, was eliminated. But instead of predicting an entirely new form of family structure resulting from woman's new free-doms and responsibilities, the authors believed that the changes would lead to a reaffirmation and fulfillment of the two other major functions of the family, child rearing and the expression of love. One possible explanation for this ambivalent attitude has been known to anthropologists for years: it is easier to criticize and change economic practices than to alter basic assumptions about socialization, such as child rearing, and intensely personal behavior, such as the expression of love. Consciously or unconsciously most of the authors felt that the breadwinner and handmaiden sex roles had to be rejected as unjust anachronisms, but they feared that tampering with other family functions and sex roles would be unacceptable to their readers and themselves. Such changes might only lead to more instability and confusion in an already bewildering era.

Even the few authors who dared to go beyond criticisms of the economic functions of the family to challenge assumptions about child rearing argued that the changes they supported would lead to the fulfillment of traditional values. William Bishop (a Yale professor), William Windsor (a phrenologist), Rabbi Schindler, and Bellamy's brother Charles believed that even in utopia parents would not be the best qualified people to raise their children. Therefore, during preschool years, their utopians were sent to nurseries supervised by highly trained attendants. Reviewers reacted to this proposal—especially as outlined in Charles Bellamy's *An Experiment in Marriage* (1889), which advocated easy divorce—by raising the spectre of "sexual communism," "free love and free lust," and a "return to the beast."[63] But these authors maintained that eliminating the economic and child rearing functions of the family would only strengthen and sanctify marriage by eliminating all the trials and frustrations that prevent a couple from developing a rich and stable relationship, a love that was the very foundation of civilization.

One utopian author, however, seemed to challenge all the assumptions about the conventional family. In the Martian utopia described in Henry Olerich's *A Cityless and Countryless World* (1893) women are economically independent; children are raised in twenty-four hour nurseries; and each individual lives in a "splendid private apartment, to which [he or she] can retire at any moment." Every apartment complex or "big house" contains one thousand living units plus dining, educational, and recreational facilities. This community is defined as one "family." (See Plate 22.) When a woman wants to have a baby, she selects an appropriate male to "co-operate" and shares an apartment with him until she is certain that she is pregnant. During pregnancy and childbirth she lives in a large apartment with a companion to help her. (The companion is not necessarily the father or even a man.) The child is weaned at an early age and sent to a nursery. The mother is paid by her "family" for her services and promptly returns to her usual occupation. Thus, as the narrator explains, his "cityless and countryless world" is also husbandless and wifeless: "we have fathers, but no husbands; mothers, but no wives." All the "quarrels, fights and murders" associated with marriage are avoided since "both sexes are . . . completely free of each other at all times." Are the Martians lonely without spouses? Far from it, claims the narrator. Everyone is always surrounded by 999 "kind, free, cultivated, non-aggressive persons," the members of his family.

But Olerich's assaults on marriage and the family did not lead to total sexual freedom on Mars. After advocating the complete collapse of marriage and the nuclear family, the narrator justifies his culture's sexual relations by offering an argument that was common in conservative medical and marital manuals of the period:[64]

> It is a well known fact that the exercise of the sexual function is an expenditure of vital energy; and, therefore, the person who has the sexual function so adjusted that he exercises it only for the special purpose of reproduction, is the most complete person sexually; while he who exercises it the most excessively either in a marital state, as you have here in [America], or under individual freedom, is the most incomplete or licentious sexually.[65]

Why destroy the home, marriage, and the family? To ensure chastity, of course.

Edward Bellamy and the majority of the utopian writers advocated woman's economic independence primarily so that she could become an ideal mother-wife. Charles Bellamy stripped the family of its child-rearing functions so that marriage could become a stable, religious state of love. Olerich freed men and women from all traditional bonds of love so that a society built on convent-like communes could thrive.

The apparent contradictions between the reforms and the ultimate results might be explained away again by pointing to the authors' limited backgrounds: all but fourteen were men. This explanation seems quite convincing when Alice Jones's and Ella Merchant's liberated women and Mary Lane's perfect, all-female race are compared to the women in other utopian visions. But of the few authors who defended traditional sex roles, two were women (Eva Wilder McGlasson and Adelia E. Orpen); and, equally important, the changes proposed by most of the authors were fundamental and daring. During an era when Americans were hypersensitive about divorce and the feminist movement and "obsessed with family life,"[66] these reformers were willing to take a critical look at a sacred American institution and to propose a new *permanent* family structure that freed women from economic dependence. Moreover, their analysis of nineteenth-century sexual relations and their predictions about ideal relations were sophisticated on at least two interrelated levels. First, they not only realized that the nineteenth-century American woman was struggling to find a new place in society; the rejection of the male-as-breadwinner sex role domonstrates that these authors recognized that the nineteenth-century male needed liberating as much as the nineteenth-century female. Only recently have such scholars as Donald Meyer and Edward C. Kirkland stressed this.[67] Second, changes in sex roles were not perceived as isolated events. They, like most of the specific changes described in the utopian works, were seen as the results of combinations of alterations in economic and social conditions, in religious and educational principles, in technology, and even in the physical structure of the home.

Thus, rather than interpreting the ambivalence of the utopian sex roles as a simple case of radical means to achieve conservative ends or as evidence of latent male chauvinism, it might be best to view the ambivalence within the general context of the utopian concept of history. The apparent contradictions between the authors' celebration of unlimited progress and a longing for stability reflected a sincere desire for needed changes tempered by a fear of more rapid changes during a time when everything seemed to be changing too fast already. A similar tension characterized the utopian view of sex roles; only here the tension was more intense since the authors were dealing with the most sensitive area examined in the utopian works. Numerous sex manuals, marital advice books, and articles in the late nineteenth-century medical journals indicate that Americans wanted "to believe that, no matter what disorders existed in society, they could control the most intimate aspects of their experience."[68] Therefore, instead of predicting that the economic freedom of the new woman would force her to question her traditional roles as mother and wife, her economic liberation was perceived as complementary, even necessary, to the fulfillment of the mother-wife role. A radical change would thus lead to stable, understandable relations between women and children, wives and husbands, and woman, man, and society just as the Armageddon of the late nineteenth century would culminate in a stable, understandable America.

7

The Simplicity and Unity
of a Day in Utopia

It was not one evil we wanted to correct, . . . We wanted a general improvement.
—*Albert Chavannes,* The Future Commonwealth *(1892)*

If we are going to be awakened, we might as well be awakened all around and not in spots.
—*Franklin H. North,* The Awakening of Noahville *(1898)*

Consider the plight of the utopian author: If his narrator gets hungry, what should he eat? Should he drink wine? While eating and drinking, what should he wear? Would he be able to speak utopian well enough to hold up his end of the dinner conversation? When he finishes his meal and discovers the home library housing the inevitable history of The Change, won't there be other books around? What will they be like? And what about the other rooms? Would there be furniture or paintings; would there be rooms at all? And those weighty dialogues about economics and religion, might not they suggest other topics like politics? What if after the introductions to the guide's family and the visits to factories and schools, the guide wants to show the narrator some utopian nightlife? What would that tell him about utopian sex roles?

These and numerous other questions must have puzzled the authors as they led their narrators through typical days in utopia. But most of them persevered since the literary form they chose and their desire for a total change necessitated visions broad enough to suggest the day-to-day nature of an ideal American culture.

Although the daily experiences surveyed in this chapter took up less of the narrators' time than the five cultural areas already examined, they deserve attention separately and within the context of the general assumptions and tensions that influenced the authors. Separately they offer more specific examples of what infuriated and confused the authors about the late nineteenth century. Since many of these issues were controversial subjects discussed in contemporary newspapers and magazines, the utopian authors' views offer insights into attitudes shared by their contemporaries. Specific solutions advocated by the authors should also be of interest to modern readers because the problems discussed are still with us. Taken within the context of general assumptions, these comments are often ingenious, disheartening, or amusing attempts to illustrate how the utopian concepts of time, space, and the individual could direct the minutiae of everyday life. Finally, Thoreau's plea to "simplify, simplify, simplify" and Henry Adams's longing for a "universe" amidst a "multiverse" dominate the authors predictions about the details of a day in utopia, again suggesting the authors' ambivalent attitudes towards change.

The following represents a sampling of the eight most frequently mentioned topics other than economics, religion, technology, education, and sex roles. It is difficult to present such diverse subjects as government, the arts, international relations, law, food, clothing, language and mass communication, and leisure without giving the survey a "catch-all" flavor. But the diversity itself demonstrates the inclusive nature of the utopian visions, and the emphasis placed on simplicity and unity helps to link the different topics and to relate them to the longing for stability and harmony that characterize the utopian concept of history.

Charles J. Rooney, Jr.'s content analyses reveal that explicit statements about politics were second only to comments about economics and labor; and an earlier study by Margaret Thal-Larsen enumerates the many ways the utopian authors wanted to extend the powers of government.[1] Hence, government may deserve to be ranked as high as technology or even economics in the utopian concept of culture. But content analyses and concentrated surveys obscure the fact that the utopian government was similar to the utopian hero: their successes eliminated their roles. As one utopian on Mars put it, after The Change and several generations of powerful, socially responsible governments, there was "no government" because "no one . . . need[ed] governing."[2] Thus in utopia government was extended into oblivion.

Before this blissful state was achieved, however, nineteenth-century American governments had to be reformed. The authors' main complaint was a corollary to their economic criticism: government had become the servant of the wealthy few. Corrupt officials could be bought in all three branches of the government, especially in the judiciary where a few well-placed dollars could thwart the efforts of the people and the executive and legislative branches. Of course such corruption helped to widen the gap between the rich and the poor by depriving the latter of just representation. It also suggested that America was no longer a democracy. It was not quite an Old-World monarchy yet, but at best it was a "pseudodemocracy" in which the poor and the middle classes were pacified by the belief that their votes counted as much as millionaires' votes.[3]

In *Olumbia* (1893) Dr. William Von Swartwout responded to this sham democracy by advocating the immediate overthrow of the government, and a few authors, notably Donnelly in *Caesar's Column,* predicted that bloody class warfare would topple corrupt governments. But as most students of utopianism have pointed out, American utopian authors shunned the Marxist route of inevitable class warfare.[4] The overwhelming majority of the authors, including the popular Bellamy and Sheldon, felt instead that the new economics and the moral revolution combined with the effects of specific political reforms and a new attitude about the role of government was the answer. The reforms were aimed primarily at restoring political equality: for example, direct elections, recall, referendum, and initiative. These familiar Populist and Progressive measures indicated that the authors still had faith in the ballot box and in the wisdom of the majority. The change in attitude was closely related to the new religion. Government officials were to actively use their "power" to "raise the material and moral welfare of the whole body of sovereign people."[5] Specifically this meant expanding the role of government to include powers such as regulating business practices, imposing inheritance taxes and establishing limits on personal income, collecting statistics, nationalizing land and means of production, and enforcing educational and marital standards.

These functions were certainly accurate glimpses of the future, but there was one problem: the reforms and the new attitude seemed at loggerheads. The reforms expressed a faith in the will of the people, while the extended government gave a tiny portion of the population tremendous powers. How could the utopians be sure that the reforms would provide strong enough checks and balances to prevent government officials from becoming as oppressive as nineteenth-century magnates?

This question prompted a few authors, especially Richard C. Michaelis and S. Byron Welcome, to oppose extending the role of government. The rest took their places on a spectrum ranging from F. U. Adams, with his "Majority Rule Clubs," to the Boston mechanic Chauncey Thomas, who argued that the task of directing the economy required such expertise that few government officials in his utopia were "subject to the accidents of a capricious vote."[6] Most of the authors tried to strike a balance between F. U. Adams's celebration of the majority and Bellamy's "government by alumni." (To insure the objectivity of the electorate, only those retired from the Industrial Army were allowed to elect the experts who rose through the ranks and then directed the Army's activities.) But no matter which mixture of democratic and expert rule an author chose, his stance was certain to be a balancing act, not a true resolution. Thus, the utopian governments again reflected the ambivalence of these middle- and upper-middle-class reformers towards "the masses." They wanted a government that would be responsive to all the people, but they also wanted to guarantee that important administrative decisions were made by powerful, qualified officials who could impose far-reaching reforms that initially would infuriate some segments of the population—especially the rich.

The authors found a way out of this dilemma, though it may not convince modern readers. They argued that after the majority had converted to the new morality and after a few generations of constantly improving environments, conflicts over majority or expert rule would be irrelevant since there would be "little need for government."[7] Once the right economic system was implemented by the proper laws, "We [had] nothing to make laws about," explains Bellamy's Dr. Leete.[8] So much for the legislative branch of government. Moreover, the new economics combined with the religious revolution eliminated motivations for crime. So much for the judicial branch. The only branch remaining was the executive, and that was more a matter of administering established procedures than active leadership. Thus, ironically, an extended government culminated in a Jeffersonian state of anarchy with the best government ruling the least. As Henry Olerich put it, there would be "no parties, no politicians, no election frauds, no political boodle . . . no kings, queens, and presidents; no political congress, parliaments, and legislatures."[9] The only real function of government was its value as a symbol of the "unity and harmony" of the rulers and the ruled.[10]

The utopian government may seem obsolete, frightening, or evasive to modern readers depending upon whether they focus on the Populist reforms, the powerful bureaucrats, or the Marxist withering away of government. But the authors' pleas for a responsive and responsible government are still praiseworthy during times when modern governments seem too occupied with secrecy and "benign neglect." And, of course, Watergate makes their comments on the disastrous effects of money power in a democracy even more relevant.

The authors' solutions to poor government also offer more illustrations of the types of ambivalence inherent in the utopian concepts of time, space, and the individual. Again multiple changes lead to a static state, and again a sincere desire to help people exposes a distrust of the People that drifts into a vague dream of unity and harmony—a utopia where the diversity that spawns distrust has vanished.

   Although there were fewer comments about the arts than about government in the utopian works, narrators often mentioned how art flourished in utopia. But what was artistic to a narrator may seem sterile to modern readers. Geoffrey Chaucer believed that art should combine the "best sentence and moost solaas."[11] His opinion of American utopian arts would have been rather low. The utopian works abound in brief descriptions of novels, symphonies, musicals, plays, light shows, sculpture, and architecture; but the guiding concept of art was usually limited to "Art for Truth" (the motto of the Arena Publishing Company, which published several of the utopian works). Specifically this meant that the prime function of a work of art was to teach some useful lesson about how and how not to live. Only a few of the authors, notably Howells and Mary A. Tinckner, stressed the importance of the beauty or pleasure in a serious artistic creation. For the rest, the arts were supplements to the Daily Gospel. Like Franklin's *Autobiography* or Jonathan Edwards's sermons, they were supposed to provide practical guidelines that made everyday living coherent and meaningful.
   There was, however, a completely different type of art occasionally mentioned by the utopian authors, which might best be called the circus side of utopian art, a form of expression that taught nothing. Its raison d'être was that it provided spectacular entertainment for the utopians during their many leisure hours. Characteristic of this type of art was a tendency to experiment with multimedia effects, thus foreshadowing modern holography and "total experience" art forms. Different colors and intensities of light illuminated large glass spheres or pictures composed of numerous pieces of tinted glass; light and sound displays were projected on the sky; and Busby Berkeley-like musicals were enhanced by complex lights, props, and mechanical stages.[12] But the most "spectacular entertainment" in utopia was Cyrus Cole's "Electro-Camera-Lucida-Motophone" described in *The Auroraphone* (1890). It enabled Saturnians to project animated tableaux of great events to Earth. These extravaganzas clearly demonstrate the rigid division between serious and circus art in utopia. In a didactic work of art, the images of volcanic eruptions at Pompeii and Old-World battles would have been used to teach lessons about the evils of the past. But here they are presented purely as exciting combinations of movement, sound, and color.[13] Thus, the utopian artists were similar to many popular nineteenth-century American

artists: they were either preachers or P. T. Barnums, though the split was not absolute since in prefaces, afterwords, and magazine articles the authors admitted that some aesthetic appeal was necessary to attract the observers' or readers' attention to the lesson.[14]

Nevertheless, the occasional nods given to circus arts and the benefits attributed to appealing lessons were nominal compared to the emphasis placed on the purely didactic value of serious art. Even a brief survey of the utopian music, theater, fine arts, architecture, and imaginative literature should make this clear.

The utopians rarely hear performances of Old-World "classics." Instead their music celebrates America's break with the past and the glories of the present. Henry F. Allen's audiences thrill to the stirring "Melodies of Freedom" symphony, and in Ludwig Geissler's utopia a popular symphony is "Science and Labor Rule the Earth."[15] But the most didactic music is found in John Galloway's *John Harvey* (1897). He even printed the music and six verses to "The Hymn of the Nationality," a combination of songs such as "The Battle Hymn of the Republic" and "Onward Christian Soldiers," among others.

Music halls, theaters, and amphitheaters also offer inspiring and edifying performances in utopia. Henry Salisbury's *The Birth of Freedom* (1890) concludes with two of the main characters attending a musical production entitled "Birth of Freedom." The history of the world is told in a series of scenes accompanied by music. First, the suffering of the Old World is revealed in tableaux depicting slaves, serfs, and domineering priests. The New World offers man an escape from these conditions; but the "serpent," money, is contaminating the American Garden of Eden. A twentieth-century revolution vanquishes the serpent, and the final scene depicts the triumph of brotherhood, liberty, and equality while the chorus and the audience sing "freedom songs." Similar historical morality plays are found in several other utopian works; ingenious utopian directors even staged outdoor "allegorical" light shows and fireworks that cover the sky with moralistic mottos and pictures of greedy materialists falling into chasms filled with reptiles and monsters.[16]

There were few descriptions of paintings, but sculpture was mentioned fairly often, and again the emphasis was on what art could teach. In *Equality* Dr. Leete shows Julian West the most highly regarded sculpture in America, a group of statues representing the "Pioneers in the Revolt," the nineteenth-century strikers. Just to make sure that no one misses the point of why they were striking, a large placard beneath the statues proclaims, "It is better to starve than to live on the terms you give us." In other utopian works allegorical statues celebrate virtues such as equality, or they honor heroes such as James Galloway's John Harvey whose statue comes complete with a "halo of light" to remind the people of his god-like stature.[17]

Even the buildings surrounding symbolic statues teach lessons. The most beautiful buildings in every city are the public buildings emphasizing that the "social side," not the private side, is "the splendor of our lives."[18] (As the guides usually mentioned, this was in marked contrast to the late nineteenth century when the most striking buildings in a city were the mansions of millionaires.) Although the authors were often vague about the architectural style of these marvelous public buildings, they were usually neoclassic, especially neo-Greek. In a sense this was a departure from the utopian concept of history because it implied that there was something of value in the Old World. But in another sense the choice was understandable. First of all, it was argued that more than any other style, classical Greek expressed simplicity and unity.[19] Since one of the main achievements of The Change was the rejection of clutter and chaos, Greek architecture seemed an appropriate symbol of the new age. On a deeper level the evocation of Greek monumental styles was another reflection of the authors' ambivalence towards the Old World. On the one hand, in nightmarish images of an approaching worldwide cataclysm, classical ruins were used to suggest the decay of the Old World creeping into the New. (See Plate 3 and Herbert Heywood's frontispiece, "The Ruins of Paris.") But, as in the neoclassic revivals of the nineteenth century (especially in the "White City" of the 1893 Chicago Fair) Greek architecture was also used to prove that America had "arrived": it proclaimed that the grandest civilizations could thrive in the wilderness of middle America. (See plate 24.)

One architectural structure that embodied all this and more was the aqueduct-bridge designed by John Harvey and constructed out of a white miracle metal in *John Harvey*. The "Greek contours" reflect the simplicity and unity of Harvey's Confederation; the monumental proportions, the association with Roman aqueducts, and its location in the West symbolize the westward course of empire; its function stresses the usefulness of utopian art; its public nature glorifes the social side of utopia; and its purpose demonstrates man's ability to turn a wasteland into an exemplary garden.[20]

Music, theater, fine arts, and architecture were important in utopia, but fiction especially attracted the authors' attention since it was the form of expression chosen by most of the late nineteenth-century utopian authors. As their own works imply, the best novel was a "novel with a purpose," and the "true novelist" was "the champion of the worlds' helpless and oppressed millions."[21] Mrs. C. H. Stone even offered nineteenth-century readers an example of the ideal novel of the future. *One of "Berrian's" Novels* (1890) purports to be written by the most honored late twentieth-century author,

Berrian, who was mentioned briefly in *Looking Backward*. It is basically a love story set in 1997, but as in many of the utopian plays and musicals, an important theme is the final triumph of humane socialists over reactionary capitalists.

Given this concept of the ideal novel, it is not surprising that the utopian authors didn't lavish much attention on the aesthetic qualities of their own works. The novels abound in contrived manipulations that explain the narrators' presence in utopia: dreams, long sleeping spells, mesmerism, potions, cigar-shaped spaceships and submarines, and "flying chairs." In James Cowan's *Daybreak* (1896) two earthmen even hitch a ride on the moon; it falls into the South Pacific, they board, it rises and carries them to Mars! The long speeches and sermons by guides and political candidates bog down the narration. Wedding-bells endings are carried to absurd extremes. Several of the novels end in double, triple, and even quadruple marriages of "spooning couples." Many of the heroines, like conventional genteel heroines, are accomplished singers; hence the reader is forced to suffer through at least one parlor concert. When authors were confused about transitions between episodes, they often sent their characters off for a "light repast" or abruptly shift to "At this juncture. . . ." Alvarado M. Fuller even began his novel with a sentence foreshadowing the openings of Charles Schulz's budding writer, Snoopy: "It was a dark, dreary, foggy night."[22] In part these "literary offenses" can be attributed to the inexperience of the utopian authors. But their inexperience was aggravated by their belief that in the ideal novel the message was much more important than literary excellence.

An important similarity between the ideal novel, as defined by the utopian authors, and other art forms in utopia is that it is a public art. The best songs and symphonies inspire everyone, the best shows draw the largest crowds, the best statues are in a public square, the best buildings are public buildings, and the best books are popular books. In *Looking Backward* the "author of the year" is elected by a popular vote; and even Howells, who came close to embracing William Morris's view of art for beauty's sake, believed that the best literature gives "the greatest happiness to the greatest number."[23]

Literature was not just another didactic, democratic art form, however; for the utopian authors it was the most powerful means of expression. In part, they argued, this was because a novel is easier to reproduce, distribute, and interpret than a symphony or a building. But the printed word also had a revolutionary magic. *Uncle Tom's Cabin* and *Looking Backward* were presented as events that changed the course of history; and at least 22 authors described imaginary books (including utopian novels) that transformed future Americans, or they modestly hinted that their own works would do this.

Considering this faith in book power, it is easy to understand why Dr. Leete believes that the popularity of reform literature right before The Change almost "explains" the revolution or why Laurence Gronlund approached writing as a "solemn moment": "When I reflect that what remains to be said may prove [to be] the spark that . . . may turn [readers] into the Leaders of men whom we so much need, I almost tremble from the excitement that masters me."[24]

This attitude was in part an ego trip. It also exposes a bias: the assumption that novel readers compose the most important part of a population. This assumption may seem foolish from a twentieth-century viewpoint. Still, novels such as *Uncle Tom's Cabin* and *Looking Backward* did affect millions of lives, and novel reading was a much more popular pastime then than now; there were no televisions or movie houses to offer competition. The interest in the role of the new woman and the faith in the power of novel writing also suggests that the authors were especially interested in reaching the largest segment of the late nineteenth-century novel-reading audience—middle- and upper-class women. They wanted to influence these readers who would in turn influence husbands and lovers. As Virgil L. Lokke concludes, they hoped that "man may then be led, . . . through the bedroom door into utopia."[25]

To modern readers utopian art may seem an unappealing mixture of Mao's *Red Book* and Red China's revolutionary songs and plays, WPA murals, Puritan literature, and neo-Greek gauche. Moreover, the utopian authors would probably have approved of the government directed bulldozing of the Outdoor Modern Exhibition in Russia in 1974. True, the utopian arts were a democratic form of expression, but as Hank Morgan in *A Connecticut Yankee* and the scientist-king in *The Land of the Changing Sun* demonstrate, public arts can be used for undemocratic purposes. Then too, the emphasis on popularity, didacticism, and the present would certainly discourage artistic innovation and, like the utopian education, sever creative links with the rich traditions of the past.

It might even be argued that utopian art did not fit into the authors' vision of utopian unity since it was fragmented, being split into didactic and circus sides. But the fact that the authors felt that novels were more effective weapons than essays indicated that the division between "sentence" and "solaas" was not absolute. More importantly, ideal works of art were supposed to remind the utopians of the correct views of time, space, and the individual: they continually saw, heard, and read about the glorious rejection of the Old World and the superiority of the co-operative identity. This may seem stultifying, but like medieval painting, Puritan architecture, and Shaker furniture, works of art gave the utopians a concrete sense of harmony and identity. Again we see the authors' desire to give meaning and order to daily experience—even if it meant reducing all "serious" art to familiar sermons with just enough of an inspiring melody, clever lighting, or allegorical plot to attract attention to the message.

Detailed statements about international relations were as rare as celebrations of nondidactic art; this in itself is an important statement about the utopian outlook. Only a few works—especially *Looking Forward: A Dream of the United States of the Americas in 1999* (1899), written by Arthur Bird (an ex-Vice Counsul-General of America at Port-au-Prince, Haiti) and Benjamin Rush Davenport's *Anglo-Saxons, Onward!* (1898)—were completely dominated by an international viewpoint; and even these books focused not on interrelationships but on the Americanization of the world. (See Plate 15.) Only 14 authors predicted powerful world courts; a couple emphasized free trade; and 11 envisioned large-scale international ventures (missionary movements, worldwide railroads, colonization, and threatened or actual world wars). Thus, more than any other specific topic, utopian international relations revealed that the authors' visions were limited primarily to America as utopia.

And yet these visions did reach beyond America. Most, including Bellamy, predicted "a loose form of federal union of worldwide extent" with each nation adopting American customs and institutions.[26] How was America supposed to convert other nations to her point of view if even ideal Americans were not concerned with other parts of the world? Part of the answer was consistent with nineteenth-century socialistic theories. As societies became industrialized and the power of money increased, strains between capital and labor would develop. If a revolution were avoided, socialistic or "cooperative" reforms would resolve the tensions between capital and labor as they had in America.

Still, this theory of international evolution left many questions unanswered. Different countries throughout the world were experiencing very different stages of industrial development. How could it be expected that within twenty-five to two hundred years (the usual time settings) most of the countries in the world would have reached similar stages so that they could agree on similar solutions—unless there was some other powerful force besides social evolution at work?

There was: the same force that convinced one-third of the authors that America could be transformed by an exemplary community founded on virgin land. It was assumed that after the transition period in America, the example of the United States would so amaze all nations that they would change their ways and imitate America. In *Equality* Dr. Leete recalls that only two years after the "Great Revolution," the example of America "over-whelmed the world with amazement" and convinced foreigners to imitate Americans.[27] Only a few authors suggested that we would follow other countries or hinted that we owed them thanks for our triumphs.[28] Even the utopias not set in America conformed to this pattern since their histories were usually analogies for the Americanization of the world.

This view of the world exposes serious contradictions and limitations relating to the utopian concepts of space and the individual. In a *New Nation* article, "Concerning the Founding of Nationalist Colonies," Bellamy main-tained that "the world has thus far shown itself decidedly more inclined to admire than to imitate [idealistic] examples."[29] Two-thirds of the utopian authors agreed with him by advocating reform from within as opposed to reform inspired by isolated communities established on virgin land. But when their sights switched from a national to an international level, they assumed—as did the advocates of isolated communes—that outsiders would quickly renounce their heritages and emulate the Americans. Admittedly, a large example such as a nation might have more impact than a small group of saints. Nevertheless, the foreign relations predicted by most of the authors contradicted the psychology of change they defended within America. The follow-the-leader policy, moreover, embodied the same limited view of human nature expressed in the city-on-the-hill rhetoric and in the racial attitudes of the authors. Foreigners were perceived as heathen or, at best, enthusiastic copycats. Not only couldn't they solve *our* problems, we had to solve *theirs*. Americans were destined to become "the long prayed-for deliverers" who controlled the future of the "whole world."[30] After trans-forming America, the hero of Donnelly's *Golden Bottle* (1892) declares war on the corrupt Old World. Immediately Canadians clamor to enlist in the American army. The first stop is Ireland where the Irish enthusiastically greet the Americans as the "deliverers." In England the people forsake the crown and cheer the Yankees. In Germany crowds run through the streets joyously "crying 'America! America!'" The crusade continues all through Europe to Russia until the Old World is changed from a "corpse" into a free group of nations ready to follow the example of American democracy.[31] Given this view of global relations we can understand why another utopian author, the social gospeller Josiah Strong, could proclaim, "My plea is not, Save America for America's sake, but Save America for the world's sake."[32] These reformers might not have been ready to go to war to save the world for democracy, but their sincere humanism combined with their myopic view of non-Americans was certainly preparing the public for Woodrow Wilson's World War I rhetoric.

Having read about or experienced two world wars, cold wars, Korea, and

Vietnam, we may wonder at the tragic naiveté of the utopian international outlook. And yet several superficial and basic motives help to place these forecasts in a proper perspective. Like the utopian concepts of time and space, they appealed to American patriotism; this was especially the case in several works written during the Spanish-American War. (In Bird's *Looking Forward* Dewey became a utopian hero.) Again, as with the concepts of time and space, the role of international savior offered a sense of identity and importance to Americans, while helping to compensate for any inferiority feelings associated with being a young nation. Lastly, hopes for an Americanized world again indicated the desire for unity. The cluttered warehouse of cruel and senseless Old-World customs would be replaced by a world in which "art and belles-lettres, law and religion, philology, and history, [would] all become one."[33] In other words, in utopia international relations would be marvelously simplified, even nonexistent, since there would be no different nations to interrelate with. The whole world would become one vast mirror reflecting the wonderful achievements of America. The utopian authors were narcissistic missionaries.

Numerous other topics besides government, the arts, and international relations were examined by the utopian authors; these details often revealed the authors' private gripes and wishes. Several recommended cremation; others championed better barbers or prettier fishponds. Arthur Bird longed to Americanize the Western Hemisphere; he also wanted to replace kisses with pats on the cheek. To enumerate all these nuances of utopia would be an overwhelming job. Nevertheless, several of these subjects—notably law, food, clothing, language and mass communication, and leisure—did receive more attention than others. They deserve study as curious historical marginalia, as further proof of the authors' encyclopedic perspective, and as evidence of the general longings and tensions (especially the desires for change, simplicity, and unity) that informed the authors' visions of utopia.

If there was one group more despised by the utopian authors than greedy capitalists and corrupt politicians, it was the "lawyer class." Lawyers and judges were likened to the "prostitute class" because they sold themselves for money. They were "legal fogmakers" for the wealthy, their sole function being to perpetuate a system of "elaborate artificialit[ies]" used by the rich to confuse, frustrate, and oppress the poor and the middle classes.[34] The moment these unfortunates walked into a court room, they were under the yoke of "the technicalities of the *law* sustained by a strong money influence, backed by well paid legal talent."[35] The most poignant example of this effect of economic inequality is found in Charles Daniel's *Ai* (1892). After most of his career has passed, a Philadelphia judge experiences a change of heart and tries to help the poor. His attempts are frustrated by his colleagues, but he feels he can ultimately beat the law by leaving his entire fortune to the poor. After his death, a group of talented lawyers nullify the will on a technicality and all the money goes to the judge's wealthy relatives.

A few authors went beyond attacks on corrupt lawyers and judges to take on an adversary almost as sacred as Motherhood. Several years before J. Allen Smith, Algie M. Simons, and Charles A. Beard re-evaluated the Constitution, F. U. Adams, William Simpson, William Child, and Henry O. Morris were telling the American public that this revered document was written by well-to-do land owners who were primarily interested in property rights. Furthermore, the Constitution was conceived by individuals who never dreamed of locomotives, transcontinental ocean liners, trusts, and sprawling cities. Therefore, it was nothing more than a "cherished heirloom of a vanishing age, a venerable, doddering old document whose senile second childhood was taken advantage of by those of wealth and position." And it gave them a tremendous "advantage." One word, "unconstitutional," from one well-bribed judge could frustrate the combined efforts of the president, the Congress, and the people.[36]

The solutions to this problem again reflected the desire for unity and were closely related to the economic and governmental reforms. Unification was achieved by a variety of reforms: codifying and unifying local, state, and federal laws, for example, or revising the Constitution to make it simpler and more democratic. (Morris included the text of a new Constitution.) The rich gained power by hiring tricky lawyers and by bribing judges and juries—an easy problem to solve—just eliminate the lawyers, the jury, and the majority of the judges. Most authors, including Bellamy, envisioned a simplified court procedure: criminals were tried and sentenced by three to seven judges. To ensure that these judges were beyond the reach of money, they were either elected or, as in Bellamy's utopia, carefully selected and appointed by the president.

The democratization of the law and the tremendous powers given to a few judges suggests an ambivalence towards the people similar to the one inherent in the general governmental reforms. But again, the utopian authors assumed that after the economic and moral awakening, judges would have little to do: there would simply be no cases, no one to judge.

Unlike laws, food and drink were not simplified, unified, and moralized out of existence, though some utopians enjoyed liquid meals and synthesized meat made from vegetables. The authors did, nevertheless, suggest changes in diet, and these are often excellent indices to general utopian attitudes.

Food was especially related to inequality: the rich gorged themselves at Bacchanalian feasts while the poor starved in the streets. Basing his descriptions on newspaper accounts of an actual stag party at Sherry's, Henry O. Morris even provided graphic glimpses of the "sensual revels of New York's 'Four Hundred.'" Little Egypt dances on the tables, and food and wine spill on polished floors.[37] After the transition, however, the new moral attitudes, technological advances in farming, efficient and just systems of distribution, and America's marvelous fertility would provide for all, adding pounds to the poor while depriving the rich of a few excess chins.

Twenty-four authors went beyond dietary generalities to give detailed menus or specifically picture utopians as vegetarians; and these would-be chefs loaded every dish with important assumptions. In Bellamy's *Equality,* for example, being a vegetarian was just one more way of expressing faith in the Religion of Solidarity: the bonds between all living creatures were so strong that meat-eaters were considered cannibals. In other utopian works eating habits also demonstrated changes in sex roles and education. Women *and* men had more leisure time to perfect cooking skills; and if meals were prepared in communal kitchens, the chefs were usually experts who had attended a specialized cooking college. Of course, after several generations of eating delicious, scientifically-prepared meals, the human race would improve physically and mentally. Thus, if authors were clever, they could pack economics, religion, sex roles, education, and environmental conditioning into one meal.

Since prohibition was already an important issue during the late nineteenth century, we might expect that glimpses of eating habits would force the authors to express their opinions on the liquor issue. But most of the authors ignored it; and the few who did not help to explain why the others did. David H. Wheeler, a Methodist minister, and W. W. Satterlee, a "Professor of Political Science and Hygienic Philosophy [?]"—both defenders of capitalism—used a familiar argument: the poor "spent enough for liquors and tobacco to have clothed and fed the whole population comfortably." It was a few sinful habits, not a maze of senseless and cruel conditions, that caused poverty.[38] Most of the utopian authors wanted to avoid such one-dimensional explanations; hence when they did discuss alcoholism, they presented it as one of many symptoms of moral decay caused by an oppressive environment. Even the hero of Sheldon's popular *In His Steps,* who attacked liquor and saloon-keepers regularly, confessed that demon rum offered more comfort to the poor than many churches; and John Uri Lloyd, who shocked his readers with a vivid Dante-esque image of an eternal "Drunkards' Den," felt that "exhilarants could be friends" if people "could . . . be temperate."[39]

Thus, the narrators' meals not only gave their creators a chance to reiterate general principles, they again indicated the utopian authors' aversions to some of the panaceas that captivated other late nineteenth- and early twentieth-century reformers.

At least three authors (Lloyd, Dail, and Windsor) simplified clothes out of existence. (See Plate 5 and the frontispiece of Dail's *Willmoth the Wanderer*.) Nudity was too much for the other authors, but bustles, corsets, billows of petticoats, feathered hats, elaborate jewelry, tuxedos, and the like were very scarce in utopia.[40] First of all, excessive clothing was associated with the nobility and the senselessness of the Old World. Second, the outlandish fashions of the American moneyed aristocracy and the attempts by the middle classes and even the poor to imitate them proved that "it is always inequality which prompts the suppression of individuality by putting a premium on servile imitation of superiors." Thus, authors who advocated a co-operative utopia could answer charges about the monotony of socialism by claiming that with economic equality would come a new sense of individuality since no one had to worry about aping the rich. Instead utopians could express their new freedoms with a wide variety of colors, styles, and materials, including paper.[41]

Clothes especially expressed freedom from old sex roles. In William Bishop's *Garden of Eden* (1895) the heroine, appropriately named Eve, goes for a stroll with the hero. After they are in the woods, she dramatically lets her full-length skirt fall to the ground revealing a skimpy pair of knickerbockers. To her this act represents freedom from a "badge of . . . servitude" associated with the "prudish air of mystery" that kept the nineteenth-century woman on a pedestal and inhibited her active participation in numerous occupations. By implication it also liberates men from an unpleasant stereotype: "Are they babies and imbeciles that even our skirts must drag the streets as a defense against their hyena eyes and their unholy thoughts?"[42] In *A Prophetic Romance* (1896) Dr. John McCoy went even further in the cause of male liberation. In his utopia men are no longer expected to wear somber colors or wools, cottons, and tweeds. They can dress in bright colors, silks, velvets, and embroidered hose.[43]

Despite this new individuality, the trend towards simplicity and unity was still evident. The regal trappings of the Old World and the mechanical contraptions (bustles and corsets) of the New were gone; men's and women's attire was becoming similar; and—in spite of the disavowals of sameness—most of the utopians were clothed in simple shirts and shorts or skirts, or in variations of shortened Grecian gowns. Since "the favorite clothing for strange [fictional] worlds, especially utopias, is a loose-flowing garment or tunic suggestive of Greek or Roman dress,"[44] the authors' utopian fashions were quite conventional. Still, they used this fashion cliché to express their beliefs about social and sexual inequality and, again, to establish links between the few grand civilizations of the past and the glorious future of an ideal American culture.

Simplicity and unity also characterized the utopian language. Greek robes might have been stylish, but "snobbish," Old-World Greek and Latin were eliminated from utopian curricula. Several authors recommended keeping French and German; most indicated that English, or in a few cases, Volapük would unify the written and spoken languages of the world. This would facilitate the spread of American values and make the immigrants in America less "different."[45]

But before this long-range goal was reached, Americans faced a serious problem involving the misuse of the English language. According to the utopian authors, the most powerful form of late nineteenth-century mass communication had, like so many other things, become the tool of the wealthy. Many editorials and articles in newspapers were slanted in favor of the rich who controlled the papers financially. The rest of a typical news-paper was filled with sensationalistic stories, which diverted the people from real problems, and obnoxious advertisements, which fleeced them of their hard-earned money.

This problem infuriated the authors, especially since so many of them were editors and journalists. The reforms they advocated were therefore designed to alter drastically both the business organization and the contents of newspapers. Large federal grants would free papers from the grasp of financial backers; Bellamy even recommended having subscribers elect editors.[46] (Again the authors assumed that governmental support and the will of the people would be less oppressive than private money power.) The new contents reflected numerous changes in attitudes and conditions. Sheldon's editor runs the appropriately named *Christian Daily,* which excludes sen-sationalistic crime and prizefight stories and gaudy ads—especially for tobacco and liquor. Reporting is limited to objective accounts of serious problems, such as poverty, and to summaries of possible solutions. (For one week the editor of the *Topeka Capital* allowed Sheldon to run his paper according to these standards.) The newspapers read by Alvarado M. Fuller's, Henry F. Allen's, and Rabbi Solomon Schindler's utopians reveal changes in technology, social status, education, and leisure: stories from around the world are telegraphed instantly to gigantic newspaper complexes, papers contain brilliant essays and poems written by laundresses and ditch diggers, and full-length novels replace brutally condensed stories.[47]

Of course the major goal of utopian newspapers was the same as the goal of serious literature: the intellectual and moral improvement of all the people. But newspapers were not the only form of mass communication that could achieve this and also help to unify the utopians. Technological advances would lead to television (usually called the "telephone" or the "screen") and to "universal culture." Instead of being restricted to local editors, performers, teachers, and clergymen, future Americans could walk to a nearby wall, turn a few dials and learn from the greatest minds in the world. One result of this constant exposure to brilliance was an immense improvement in intelligence and ethics. To Bellamy this was important though less remarkable than the new sense of brotherhood and unity inspired by the television: it "brought mankind into a closeness of sympathetic and intellectual rapport never before imagined."[48] Thus, like the ideal language, the most advanced form of mass communication would replace the confusing diversity of the nineteenth century with a unity that would enable everyone to understand everyone else.

And utopians would have plenty of time to experience this sense of brotherhood and understanding. Early retirement and a four-hour work day meant that the utopians spent half their lives as "leisure." Considering the importance of this change, most authors paid scant attention to off hours. A quick glance at two of Bellamy's critics may explain why. The promise of less work inspired J. W. Roberts to quote Isaac Watts—"For Satan finds some mischief still / For idle hands to do"—to offer "statistics" such as "two persons use their spare time for evil purposes, to where one uses it for self-improvement or the general welfare," and to predict that an eight-hour work day would produce "a race of criminals." To avoid this disaster, the Methodist minister David H. Wheeler warned that there would be "more rather than less" work in his utopia, though "amusements" would be permitted two or three times a year.[49] This hostility to leisure may seem excessive, but it was quite typical during the late nineteenth century. Even "prominent New York reformers" reacted to their state's Saturday Half-Holiday Act (1887) with predictions that workers would spend their time "dancing, carousing, . . . rioting, shooting, and murder[ing]."[50] The scarcity of extended celebrations of increased leisure suggests that the majority of the authors were aware of such attitudes, and this awareness trapped them: they attempted to uphold the work ethic while simultaneously recommending a drastic reduction in working hours; they were forced to stress how diligently the utopians worked at leisure!

This ambivalence limited the authors' ability to explore fully new types of leisure. Nevertheless, they did at least dare to suggest that leisure could be as noble as work, since both ideally were forms of self-development; and they were perceptive enough to see that future Americans had to consciously adapt to more spare time. Otherwise lives formerly wasted by senseless toil would only be wasted in senseless boredom. Therefore, leisure became a time of active self-improvement, a task facilitated by the numerous specialized schools, libraries, concert halls, books, newspapers, art galleries, theaters, televisions, and gymnasiums of utopia. It was also a time for showering love and advice upon children, a time for nurturing intimacies between husbands and wives, and a time for travel and new experiences.

Except for the gymnasiums, these joys of utopia have already been examined. Utopian gyms are interesting again primarily because of what they tell us about general utopian attitudes. The concern with physical fitness, for instance, reflects the influence of Darwinism and the belief that an ideal education was a lifetime commitment to mental and physical improvement. Thus, in Bradford Peck's gyms, where all ages are welcome, the interior is covered by life-sized paintings of flabby nineteenth-century Americans. This didactic locker-room art reminds the utopians what can happen if the physical side of education is ignored. Bellamy used the gym as a touchstone for discussions of women's emancipation. Julian West is amazed at the "wonderful physical rebirth of woman" he sees in the gyms. (He is especially intrigued by the women's "splendid chests.") At last women were free to be as healthy and vigorous as men. Most authors were vague about the specific nature of the ideal exercises performed in the gym, but in a *Nationalist* article Robert C. Adams attacked football, baseball, even checkers and praised co-operative activities, especially dancing. Thus, the gym became a sounding board for co-operation and the social self.[51]

Of course utopian books and essays infuriated defenders of the status quo. How could they remain silent while the Almighty Dollar, the God of "Acres of Diamonds," the Breadwinner and the Handmaiden, corsets, prizefight stories, the Constitution, and even the National Pastime and an innocent game of checkers were dumped overboard?

The patterns that unified the attitudes about technology, education, and sex reappear in the cultural areas surveyed above: everyday experiences re-enforced the general concepts of time, space, and the individual. The dual view of utopia, which juxtaposed the horrors of the past and the present with the glories of the future, was maintained and especially reflected in the utopian governments, arts, laws, newspapers, and new attitudes about leisure. The follow-the-leader foreign policy suggested the immediate advantages and the long-range disadvantages of the authors' patriotism more than any other specific subject examined. Finally, the desire to enrich the minutiae of experience with significance affected the authors' views on issues as large as religion, technology, and government and as small as bustles, dinners, and checkers.

The ambivalence towards change, however, was the most persistent characteristic. Almost everything about the present had to be changed, but the ultimate goal of all change was a world without change. Governments and laws would be changeless and practically nonexistent; serious artwork would have only one function; global diversity would bow to a harmonious Americanization; men's and women's fashions would merge; and television would offer universal culture at the flip of a switch. This obsession with simplicity and unity makes these days in utopia both pathetically obsolete and surprisingly modern. It exposes the fears of a group of reformers whose terror of diversity and rapid change blinded them to the many possibilities for human enrichment swirling in the flux. Nevertheless, the utopian authors' awareness of the fragmented meaninglessness of much of modern living foreshadowed the twentieth-century arts and literatures of alienation and the absurd, as well as the dissatisfaction with shallow materialism voiced by people as different as college students, businessmen, and rank-and-file union members.

8

The "Citty upon a Hill": New Visions, Old Dreams

. . . lawns would be laid out in shrubbery, beds of flowers interspersed with statues, fountains, and beautiful works of art. Can you imagine the endless beauty of a conception like this,—a city with its thirty-six thousand buildings each a perfectly distinct and complete design, with a continuous and perfectly finished façade from every point of view, each building and avenue surrounded and bordered by an ever-changing beauty of flowers and foliage?
—*King Camp Gillette,* The Human Drift *(1894)*

From John Winthrop's "Citty upon a Hill" and Dorothy's Emerald City in the Land of Oz to modern planned communities, like Columbia, Maryland and Walt Disney's futuristic "Magic Kingdom" Americans have dreamed of the ideal city.[1] This dream seemed especially captivating and frustrating during the late nineteenth century. Reformers, bewildered by sprawling cities, sought answers in housing standards, conservation acts, settlement houses, landscape architecture, "city beautiful" projects, and "garden city" movements.[2] Thus it is not startling to discover that, like many other utopian visionaries, the late nineteenth-century American utopian authors usually set their narratives in the perfect cities of the future.

This setting, however, was not simply a matter of tradition and current interest. Descriptions of ideal cities allowed (or forced) the authors to bring together all their major assumptions about time, space, and the individual and their specific ideas about separate cultural areas. During a chaotic era, the city was the prime symbol of chaos: a "straggling and shapeless accretion of accident," a "ragged spasmodic, violently contrasting and utterly incongruous" monster.[3] Of all the places in America, cities and towns were the most contaminated with Old-World diseases. Even as far west as Kansas, Sheldon's hero was struck by the similarities between a play, "Shadows of London," and the drama of his hometown.[4] Of course it went almost without saying that the city was the worst environment for the individual. How could he improve in a place where litter covered the ground, ugly signs and horse manure debased the streets, and smoke, the "stench of . . . modern . . . pollution," and the "wail of monsters [foghorns and machines]" filled the air?[5] Furthermore, the specific evils uncovered in numerous areas of American culture thrived in the city: the many rags and few silk hats proclaimed economic inequality at its worst; grand cathedrals and "Acres of Diamonds" sermons sanctified the silk hats; acres of machines drove the workers; the workers were poorly educated; poor prostitutes, middle-class handmaidens, and wealthy social butterflies tried to capture brutal, Wall Street breadwinners; the rich captured politicians, judges, lawyers, and editors with bribes; and so on down through the layers of American culture to the "leisure," which for most meant brief moments of partial recovery before the onslaught of another twelve-hour work day.

No wonder Joaquin Miller called the city "a sin."[6] No wonder utopian visions were haunted by spectres of skylines in ruins, the Statue of Liberty overgrown with weeds, and the Brooklyn Bridge crumbling into the East River. No wonder Bellamy's Julian West expected Boston to be a "heap of moss grown ruins" by the year 2000.[7]

Considering the backgrounds of the authors—especially their migration from rural or small-town locales to urban centers—these complaints might be written off as the wailings of hicks who never adapted to the big city. And yet, unlike many nineteenth-century reformers with early rural or small-town backgrounds, the utopian authors did not simply curse the city and call for a return to rural life and agrarian values.[8] True, about one-third of them recommended leaving the cities of the East to start over in sparsely settled or virgin areas in the West. But even these authors resisted the pull toward pastoral escapism. As Joaquin Miller argued in *The Building of the City Beautiful* (1893), population trends indicated that most future Americans would live in cities. Therefore, instead of trying to avoid population concentration, instead of hoping for a return to rural life à la William Morris and John Ruskin, true reformers should plan "new cities" for "new people."[9] The remaining two-thirds of the authors agreed, but they felt that new cities could be resurrected in the midst of the old ones. During and after The Change, new funds, new man- and woman-power, and new hope could be harnessed and old cities "formed anew."[10]

The specific projections of the "new cities" varied immensely. A few utopian authors planned residential areas resembling large country towns. Others celebrated the "decay of the country village" and envisioned metropolises with triple-decked highways a thousand feet wide bordered by gigantic apartment complexes.[11] Despite these differences, one assumption and two goals guided almost all the authors. First, they assumed that the ideal city of the future would not simply repeat the present on a grander scale. It is certain, therefore, that they would have been appalled at the two-page spread entitled "New York City as It Will Be in 1999" published in the *New York World*, 30 December 1900. Except for the inclusion of a few dirigible-like airships and several automobiles, the city is pictured as an extension of the present: more Brooklyn Bridges, more steamships, more subways, more street cars, more railroads, and more and higher skyscrapers. Instead of this, the utopian authors hoped to change the American city in order to achieve two goals. First, they wanted to transform the city and the country combining the best of each. (Several urban historians have pointed out that this desire was expressed by many late nineteenth-century builders, and middle- and upper-class homeowners.)[12] The second goal was to plan a city that would embody the co-operation and especially the unity and order that the chaotic American cities lacked.

The utopian authors' specific comments about the first goal—combining the best of the city and the country—again demonstrate that they were not pastoral escapists. The two characteristics of rural life mentioned most often were loneliness and unending toil, the same grim realities frequently dramatized in the fiction of E. W. Howe and Hamlin Garland. Farmers and small-town people lived "lonely," "melancholy" lives "isolated" from each other and from the amusements of the city.[13] They had little time to enjoy nature since, in order to keep up mortgage payments to city bankers, they had to work from dawn till dusk. As a farmer's wife in Howells's *Traveler from Altruria* complains, "There's too much work in the world."[14]

Still the authors used traditional agrarian rhetoric to celebrate the fresh air and the beauties of the American countryside, especially as compared to the soot, stench, and ugliness of the city. If only the best of both worlds could be combined. The authors felt that during and after The Change, this could be accomplished (1) by utilizing expected technological advances and (2) by consciously making the city more like the country and vice versa.

After the technological monster had been tamed by the new economics and Christian management, it would radically change both country and city life. In utopia, machines make farming so easy that anyone can perform all farm tasks and city factory workers enjoy increased leisure time because of the high degree of technical efficiency in their plants. Technology also makes the city as clean as the country. Coal and other soot- and odor-producing fuels are replaced by electricity and, occasionally, solar power; the conversion of human wastes to fertilizer solves the sewage problem; subways, elevated trains, and a few electric motor cars replace the manure-producing horse; and all these changes make cities marvelously quiet. Another blessing, in this case foreshadowed by the nineteenth-century street-car suburb, is that "time and space have been practically annihilated."[15] It does not really matter where a person lives since an electric, aluminum train traveling anywhere from 100 to 200 miles per hour can whisk him to his destination in minutes. In Howells's *Traveler from Altruria* for example, most of the population prefers to live on co-operative farm villages, not unlike Howells's own boyhood town.[16] They spend three hours a day working in the fields and then can commute into the cities, which have become centers of the performing and fine arts. Conversely, in D. L. Stump's *From World to World* (1896) the entire population lives in cities ringed by co-operative farms. Each morning half the people travel to the farms by train or by "airmotor," work for a few hours, and then return to the city or remain as they please.[17]

Using advanced technology to reduce toil, make city air and water pure, and build rapid transit systems would all help to eliminate the worst of the city and the country. But this was not enough. Urban and rural environments had to be consciously recreated to enhance the best of both worlds.

To make the city more like the country a variety of minor reforms were suggested such as roof gardens, glass roofs, even placing potted flowers beside factory machines.[18] The major changes, however, were parks—parks, parks, and more parks. Depending upon the shape of the city, the parks would be either large concentric circles or grand squares and rectangles readily accessible to every citizen. In either case the effect would be to transform the city into "one great residential-park."[19]

Chauncey Thomas, King Camp Gillette, Henry Olerich, and William Bishop went beyond the concept of strategically placed parks to envision high-rise living complexes accommodating thousands while using only a small portion of the land. The most spectacular proposals of this kind were the colossal city-pyramids predicted by the master mechanic, Thomas, and the apartment complexes of "Metropolis" planned by the safety-razor magnate, Gillette.

Thomas's idea is similar to the "arcologies" designed by the modern architect Paolo Soleri. In his forty-ninth-century setting "fully organized cit[ies are] piled on end instead of being stretched lengthwise." Most of the interiors of these pyramids are filled with spacious apartments varying to suit the owners' tastes and pocketbooks. Gardens boasting flowers and trees are spread throughout so that the utopians always feel the presence of nature. Vertical and horizontal elevators carry occupants to the core of the pyramid where they find warehouses, cold storage bins, stores, schools, theaters, libraries, music halls, and restaurants—the most exciting being the "Palace of the Sun" set in a beautiful tropical garden. Of course, the entire city is heated and air conditioned, and the same elevators that take utopians to a meal or a show can whisk them to the ground floor and easy access to enormous outdoor parks.[20]

King Camp Gillette's apartment complexes are not as spectacular as Thomas's city-pyramids, but his overall plan is even more astounding. (See Plates 16-21.) His basic city plan is a huge rectangle, which from the air looks like a beehive. (Plate 16.) The major types of buildings included in Metropolis are schools and universities, food and supplies distribution centers, and apartment complexes. The apartment design is the key to Gillette's city. Each complex is

> six hundred feet in diameter, twenty-five stories in height, and consists of eighteen tiers of apartments, so arranged and connected at the back that it makes a single building in circular form, with an interior court four hundred and fifty feet in diameter, the central portion of which is occupied by a dining-room that is two hundred and fifty feet in diameter. (Plates 17 and 19.)

Using the "Chicago School" and new New York city buildings as inspirations, Gillette described these apartment complexes as being constructed

> of a steel framework that is filled in between its network of beams and girders with fire brick, which constitutes floors and walls. These floors and walls are then covered by a facing of porcelain tile in every part of the building, both inside and out. (Plate 21.)

Although the shape of each complex is basically the same (Plate 19), the designs of the exterior vary and the large interior courtyards offer a wide choice of lighting effects and "exquisite paintings." (Plate 20.)

Beneath the surface of Metropolis there are three levels: one for "sewage, water, hot and cold air, and electric systems"; one for transportation; and one for extra storage space and "facilities," and walking during bad weather. These elaborate underground systems combined with the high-rise apartment complexes permit Gillette's utopians to enjoy city life and a continuous park landscape:

> Each building is six hundred feet distant at nearest point of contact with those surrounding it. This allows for [a] . . . lawn of one hundred and fifty feet in width around each building, with a glass and porcelain walk of one hundred and fifty feet

between. These walks, being straight, would leave a triangular space between the junctions of any three roads. This triangle of about three hundred feet would be covered, in part, with glass, in dome shape, to give light to the walks and chamber below the upper pavement. These walks below would correspond with the walks above, while the triangular space below the glass dome in the upper chamber would be a park or conservatory of flowers. . . . Here flowers would bloom at every season of the year. There would also be trees and urns of flowers distributed at regular intervals along both sides and through the centre of every walk in the city, both on the upper platform and in the chamber below. (Plates 16 and 19.)

This urban landscape of steel, brick, porcelain, glass and endless parks was, however, only part of Gillette's vision. He hoped that during the twentieth century his Metropolis would grow into a megalopolis with thirty-six thousand apartment complexes housing sixty million Americans (the approximate population of the United States during the late nineteenth century). As the population grew, "accomodations would always keep a little in advance of actual requirements." In other words, Gillette assumed that eventually all Americans would live in one city-park, which would be connected to the rest of the country by rapid transit systems that bring raw materials to Metropolis and facilitate vacations beyond the city limits. In Gillette's utopia much of the urban landscape would be parklike and almost all the rest of America would be parks, farms, and natural wilderness; thus his utopians enjoy the comforts and sophistication of city life and the beauties of nature.[21]

Gillette was the only utopian author to advocate a one-city America. Nevertheless, the other authors, including Bellamy, agreed with him that changes in the urban landscape would mean changes in the country. Therefore the other side of obtaining the best of both worlds consisted of a variety of suggestions about reshaping rural America. As a reflection of the economic changes, for example, small farms are organized into large co-operative-farm communities enabling farmers to take advantage of large-scale production and to tear down the stone fences that isolated them from one another. Each community has its own libraries, theaters, restaurants, gymnasiums, and schools. These might not be as large as similar facilities in areas of greater population density, but they are adequate complements to the larger facilities, which could be reached in minutes, and to the television programs broadcast into each home. Finally, the utopian authors advocated reforming the land itself. In part this meant the efficient use of "every inch of [farm] land." Crawford S. Griffin even suggested arranging the land "hothouse fashion, [so] that a dozen crops [could] be grown in tiers, one above the other, all the time."[22] But reshaping the countryside also meant changing land not used for crops. Some of this would be left in a natural state forming grand national preserves. The rest would realize the dreams of the most visionary landscape architect. As Bellamy's Julian West gazes out over the countryside in 2000 A.D., he is struck by the fact that

> every natural feature appeared to have been idealized and all its latent meaning brought out by the loving skill of some consummate landscape artist, the work of man blending with the force of Nature in perfect harmony.[23]

The ultimate result of all the technological changes and all the reshaping of the city and the country would be a glorious blend of the best of two worlds: a final fulfillment of the original promise of America's virgin land. Vast urban parks would merge with the civilized contours of nature. The entire country would be one enormous garden city proving that the city sickness of the Old World could be replaced by a new, efficient, and orderly Garden of Eden.

The second major goal these amateur city planners agreed upon was the fulfillment of another dream that helped shape their views on time, space, the individual, and almost all the specific cultural areas: a totally integrated and coherent American civilization. Specifically this meant that the ideal city was founded upon *co-operation* and *order*: the two qualities which, according to most of the authors, were seldom discovered in the chaotic cities of nineteenth-century America.

For William Dean Howells and several others the "White City" at the 1893 Chicago Fair had already proved that diverse groups could co-operate and build an ideal city. In a letter to the illustrator Howard Pyle, sent while Howells was writing his Altrurian romances, Howells lauded the co-operative spirit of the "White City": "the New Jerusalem . . . a direct leading of the Lord toward 'the wonder that shall be,' when men all work in harmony, and not in rivalry."[24] Howells's Altrurian, Mr. Homos, singled out the same city as the only spot in America that resembled his native land: it was an "Altrurian miracle" that illustrated how architects, landscape artists, businessmen, drainage engineers, and government officials could work together.[25] Authors who did not allude to the "White City" also agreed that co-operation was the key to a perfect city. To mention just a few examples, in *The Golden Bottle* (1892) Ignatius Donnelly's model Populist city was actually named Co-operation; Joaquin Miller's City Beautiful was an attempt to recapture the co-operative spirit of American Indians; the foundation of Henry Olerich's cities was "practical co-operative individualism"; and Chauncey Thomas and King Camp Gillette predicted a time when thousands could live in harmony under one roof.

The utopian authors placed the most concrete symbol of their faith in co-operation at the heart of their cities: the glorious cluster of central buildings that Bellamy's Dr. Leete called the "splendor of our lives."[26] This complex usually included an administration building housing representatives of the major industrial and agricultural departments as well as educational and religious leaders. (See Plate 25.) A simple church, a library, a university, a theater, an art gallery, an observatory, and a gymnasium often completed the cluster. The grandeur of the buildings proclaimed the greatness of American civilization, and the harmonious style of architecture (again, usually neoclassic) symbolized the triumph of co-operation over "the old egotistical conditions."[27]

But these marvelous co-operative enterprises didn't just happen. Without order, co-operative city life might simply be a more brotherly kind of chaos than the chaos of nineteenth-century city life. Only total planning could turn "a conglomerate mass of heterogeneous, nondescript dwellings into a harmonious and beautiful whole."[28] In Clark Edmund Persinger's *New America* (1900), for example, whenever a group decides to build a community, they must hire a professional architect to help plan the town; and in William Simpson's Martian utopia, potential city sites must be approved by "sanitary and civil engineers" to insure proper drainage and to prevent any future ecological imbalance.[29]

Not all the authors were as strict as Persinger and Simpson, but the majority agreed that the ideal city imposed order on the urban landscape. No characteristic of the utopian city plans emphasized this more than their shapes. Several authors envisioned rectangular cities: more predicted perfectly square cities. (See Plates 16, 22, and 23.) But the typical utopian city took the form of the geometric figure which, more than any other shape, symbolizes order and unity—the circle.

In *New Era* (1897) Charles W. Caryl, a Denver businessman, offered the most interesting and most detailed plan for a circular utopian city. (See Plates 25 and 26.) As usual, at the center of his "beautiful white city" is a monumental, neoclassic administration building with tiers of columns rising to a dome similar to the dome of the Capitol. It is encircled by a beautiful park, a man-made stream, and yet another, larger park. The next concentric circle is filled with a continuous exposition-building–department-store inspired by the Chicago Fair. Rings 9 through 17 contain libraries, a university, parks, gymnasiums, and amusement parks. Then comes another ring of water followed by a circle of hotels with enormous roof gardens. The rest of the rings out to number 222 alternate between residential areas and parks. Reversing the trend of nineteenth-century suburbs, the large homes nearest the center are reserved for the highest ranks in the industrial army (called the New Era Union), and each residential circle beyond is filled with separate ranks, the lower the rank the farther away from the center. Beyond ring 222 are factories, warehouses, farms, hospitals, a cemetery, a railroad depot, and still another park. In other words, what Caryl envisioned was a self-contained microcosm of the utopian civilization in the vicinity of Denver, Colorado.[30]

Although Caryl's rigid hierarchical zoning was not typical of most utopian cities, his desire for harmony, order, and unity was; and it again reflects the yearning for unity and coherence that permeated the utopian literature. Everywhere they looked, the authors saw irrationality and chaos. Late nineteenth-century history was chaotic; the settlement and cultivation of American soil seemed haphazard; and the population was becoming a confusing, heterogeneous mixture of seemingly incompatible individuals. Economic systems, religions, educational programs, family relations, governments, laws, and many other areas of American culture were a hodgepodge of cruel and confusing relics. The culmination of these layers of chaos was the American city; and the authors' reaction to this crisis, more than their response to any other specific problem, demonstrated their desire for order and unity. Thus their ideal cities were designed to bring together their abstract concepts of time, space, and the individual and their more concrete views of an ideal culture to create one glorious vision of a unified and understandable existence. Or, as Henry Olerich declared, the ultimate goal of the utopian city was "the exact correspondence between the subjective conceptions and the objective order of the relations among things."[31]

This preoccupation with unity and coherence gave the utopian cities a forward-backward looking character. The new cities were supposed to represent the most striking examples of America's ability to escape the evils of the Old World. (The name of Caryl's city was "New Era.") Furthermore, the emphasis on orderly patterns is characteristic of reactions to modern cities: according to William Irwin Thompson, "When the megalopolis is too vast to be perceived meaningfully, the individual projects, against the chaos of his world, a new mythopoeic simplification."[32] Whether it be King Camp Gillette's beehive grids and Charles Caryl's concentric circles in the 1890s or the image of a transistor radio's printed circuit projected by Thomas Pynchon's Oedipa Maas onto Southern California in the 1960s,[33] the psychological response is basically the same. Still, in spite of what the utopian authors thought their cities represented, in spite of the reflections of modern psychological reactions, and in spite of the many genuinely progressive elements of the utopian cities—if the aluminum, electric railroads and other technological advances are stripped away from the utopian cities, what remains? Orderly residential areas where everyone knows his place, large public parks, and—instead of centerless suburbs—central clusters of buildings symbolizing the grandeur and unity of American culture. In essence these utopian cities of the future are idealized medieval or baroque cities complete with people who know their places and updated versions of the commons, the cathedral, and the castle.

In Harold Frederic's *Gloria Mundi* (1898) an aristocrat actually tries to recreate a medieval community. He fails, indicating that Frederic recognized the serious problems inherent in the ambivalence of the utopian city. But the unconscious ambivalence of most of the authors should come as no surprise. It is simply another—possibly the most dramatic—example of the underlying paradox of late nineteenth-century American utopianism—a desire for rapid, multiple innovations coupled with a longing for security and changelessness. The ideal city thus became the abode of strange bedfellows: Henry Adams's dynamo and Virgin (or at least an updated Mont-Saint-Michel) met head-on in the streets of utopia.

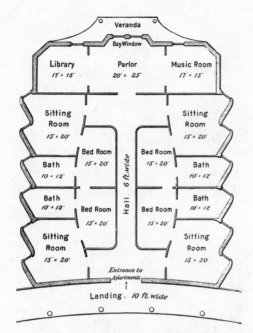

Plate 18: "Floor Plan of a Single Apartment." King Camp Gillette, *The Human Drift*.

Plate 16: "Plan of Distribution of Buildings." A = educational facilities; B = amusement parks; C = food storage. King Camp Gillette, *The Human Drift*.

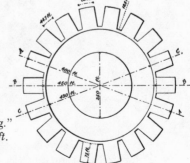

Plate 17: "Plan of Apartment Building." King Camp Gillette, *The Human Drift*.

Plate 19: Completed Apartment. King Camp Gillette, *The Human Drift*.

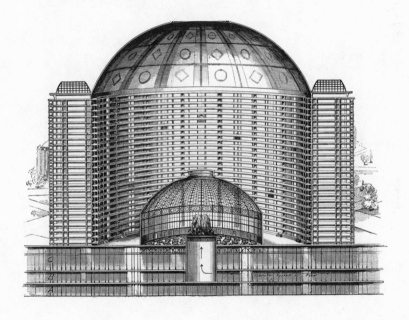

Plate 20: "Side Elevation of Apartment Building, Showing Interior Court, Dining-room&c." A = water pipes, sewage, air conditioning, electrical equipment: B = transportation; C = storage and walkway. King Camp Gillette, *The Human Drift*.

Plate 21: Single Tier in Process of Construction. King Camp Gillette, *The Human Drift.*

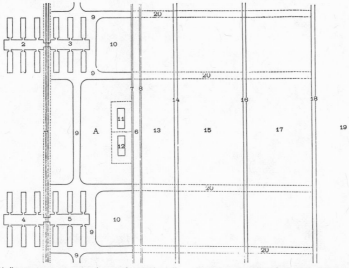

This diagram represents a cross-section, somewhat more than half mile wide, and extending across from the motor-line to the field.

A is a park one-fourth mile wide, extending from the motor-line to the boulevard all around the community.

1 represents a double track motor-line.

2, 3, 4 and 5 represent "big-houses."

6 represents a hundred-foot wide boulevard.

7 and 8 represent foot-paths.

9 represents a hundred-foot walk leading through and around the "big-houses" from one to the other.

10 are two outdoor nurseries for little children.

11 and 12 are two artificial lakes for bathing and swimming.

13 represents a 500-foot wide conservatory and green-house.

14 represents a walk between the green-house and garden.

15 represents a 1000-foot wide garden.

16 represents a walk between the garden and the orchard.

17 represents a 1000-foot wide orchard.

18 represents a walk between the orchard and field.

19 represents the field, extending clear across to the opposite side of the orchard.

20 represent walks extending across park, green-house, garden etc., from the "big-houses" to the field.

Plate 22: A "Big-House" Community. Henry Olerich, *A Cityless and Country-less World*. Reproduced from Arno Press Inc. reprint (1971) with permission.

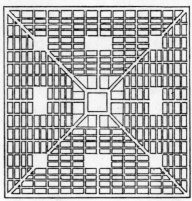

Plate 23: Neuropolis. James M. Galloway, *John Harvey*.

Plate 24: Street Scene. William R. Bradshaw, *The Goddess of Atvatabar*.

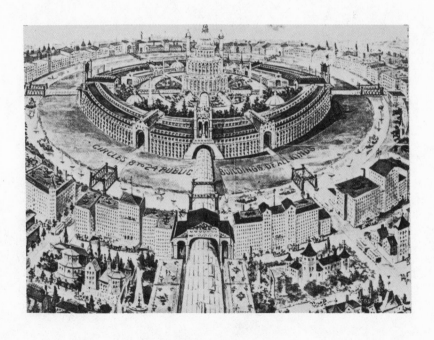

Plate 25: "Sketch of the Center of New Era Model City." Charles W. Caryl, *New Era*. Reproduced from Arno Press Inc. reprint (1971) with permission.

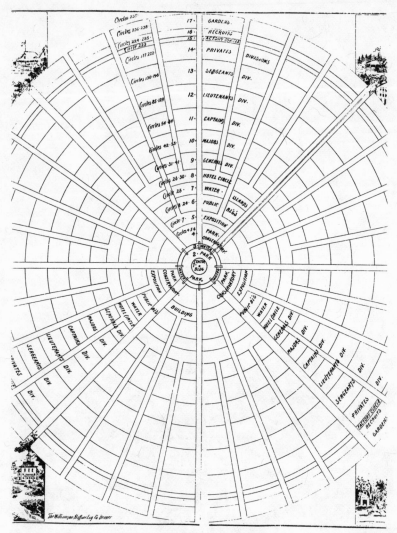

OUTLINE OF PLAN FOR NEW ERA MODEL CITY.

Plate 26: "Outline of Plan for New Era Model City." Charles W. Caryl, *New Era*.
Reproduced from Arno Press Inc. reprint (1971) with permission.

9

The Obsolete Necessity:
America as Utopia

As in the case of reactions to so many symbols and images undermined by new historical forces, there is confusion and ambivalence rather than full rejection or genuine replacement.
—Robert Jay Lifton, Home From War *(1973)*

One generation's utopia can become another generation's dystopia.
—Peyton E. Richter, Utopias *(1971)*

We can never reach the points of the compass [the utopian poles]; and so no doubt we shall never live in utopia; but without the magnetic needle we should not be able to travel intelligently at all.
—Lewis Mumford, The Story of Utopias *(1922)*

Old wine in new bottles might do, but a more recent phenomenon, the soybean chicken, is a better analogy. It may seem ridiculous to doctor up soybeans to look, smell, and taste like familiar foods, but soybean wholesalers know that if they marketed some totally new kind of food, say edible chairs, no one would buy. We have learned that food comes in certain forms, and chairs are not one of them. Thus, even though it would be entirely possible to make a soybean chair, such an innovation will probably never be considered—it would violate too many assumptions. Like the soybean wizards, the utopian authors often had the makings of completely new customs and beliefs—the utopian sex roles testify to that. And yet the utopian family, like most products of the authors' speculations, was a soybean chicken: a revolutionary change presented in a familiar form.

Such mixtures of the old and the new were the offspring of the utopian authors' confusion—their hopes and fears about past, present, and future America. It is this conglomerate of anachronisms and futuristic visions that makes late nineteenth-century American utopian works such fascinating reflections of late nineteenth-century culture and such interesting guides to the potential uses or uselessness of utopian speculation today.

As an index to late nineteenth-century American culture, the utopian works suggest the intensity of the future shock experienced by Americans and indicate how they reacted to this trauma. The utopian authors' view of their times might best be described by borrowing the title of William O'Neill's *Coming Apart*—coming apart in several ways. First of all, American culture and the American population were changing so fast and in so many ways that it seemed impossible for anyone—even authors lucky enough to have college educations and relative social and economic security—to keep up with all the changes. Furthermore, different cultural areas didn't re-enforce or clarify each other. To name just two types of incongruities singled out by the authors, religious advice often contradicted economic realities, and technology, instead of creating more leisure time, either imposed unwanted leisure (unemployment) or meant longer work days. If there were any coherence in American culture, it was an immoral or amoral pattern of inequality stretching from economics, religion, and sex roles to meals, clothing, and leisure. Finally, American culture was coming apart because the traditional perspectives and values preached by magnates, ministers, authors, teachers, government officials, and parents seemed to be out of touch with the day-to-day realities of the chaos of rapid change and the inequalities experienced by many Americans.

What made this frightening interpretation of the eighties and nineties even more frightening was that the authors believed that the late nineteenth century represented the last chance to put American culture back together; and if Americans failed, all mankind would suffer. To again quote Bellamy's "Letter to the People's Party," America was the

> great experiment, on which the last hopes of the race depends, . . . if it be a failure, it will be a final failure. There can be no more new worlds to be discovered, no fresh continents to offer virgin fields for new ventures.[1]

Faced with this view of their era, the utopian authors decided that pre-Civil War tenets about life in America weren't the answers to the future. The criticisms of popular maxims about self-made men, poverty, otherworldly Christianity, breadwinners and handmaidens, and Satan's claims to idle hands made this clear. Nevertheless, they were understandably fearful about "letting go"; they certainly weren't ready to consider modern relativistic, existential, or nihilistic assumptions about relative morality, amorality, or the meaninglessness of existence. Instead they hoped to offer enough old and "new" attitudes to reassure their readers and to prepare them for the future.

Specific examples of these combinations and the degree to which the average, the popular, and the most perceptive authors agreed about them often reveal which parts of American culture the authors valued most; these blends of the familiar and the unfamiliar also support Frank E. Manuel's contention that a utopian vision "may well be a sensitive indicator of where the sharpest anguish of an age lies."[2] The utopian authors' concept of history, for instance, was a mixture of Puritanism, evolutionary theories, and a longing for a nirvana-like stability. Since the overwhelming majority of the authors emphasized the importance of placing late nineteenth-century America within the context of this historical framework, it is evident that, according to them, the present was understandable and significant only if it were juxtaposed against the backdrop of a grand historical drama, a divine crusade. Even Twain's agonized attempts to contrast an Old-World nadir and a nineteenth-century civilization imply a preoccupation with historical perspectives. This orientation suggests the continuing reverberations of the unique event associated with American history (the discovery of a New World), the sustained influence of early American messianic hopes, and the tendency of a young nation to seek legitimacy and respectability by creating instant historical traditions. The last trend is especially obvious. European and Oriental nations could point to centuries of heritage. By 1888, Americans could only point to a bit over one hundred years of national existence. But this insecurity, or "anguish" to use Manuel's term, could be overcome by linking American history with Divine Providence, thus stretching a century into a timeless historical drama.

The unwillingness of the most perceptive authors, the popular Bellamy and Sheldon, and two-thirds of the utopian authors to accept the traditional faith in virgin land indicates that a specific geographical orientation or condition was less important to the authors than a dramatic historical perspective. Of course the American landscape was still significant; when the authors said utopia, they usually meant America as utopia. Furthermore, one of the most inspiring episodes in the history of America was the discovery of a green and virgin continent where mankind could escape the contamination of the Old World. But the utopian authors found it difficult to maintain a simplistic faith in the promise of virgin land when confronted with the numerous failures of nineteenth-century utopian communities and the corruption of once virgin territory by Americans in the East, the Mid-West, and even the Far West—one of Joaquin Miller's heroes is debased by San

Francisco. To resolve this dilemma most of the authors advocated reform from within, focusing on corrupt cities, while still championing the inspirational value of the original promise of America's virgin land.

Whether the utopian hero lit out for open spaces or stayed at home to do battle with urban magnates and politicians, the real keys to the climactic drama of American history were the actors—individuals. In their attempts to predict how typical Americans would react to the rapid changes of the late nineteenth century, the utopian authors achieved their greatest successess and worst failures. They realized that a combination of religious, psychological, biological, and environmental stimuli were needed if average citizens were to become utopians. Popular authors, like Bellamy and Sheldon, were especially adept at blending moving descriptions of conversion experiences with forecasts of controlled environmental conditioning. Still, in spite of this complex view of human nature, the authors' projections of ideal individuals were all-too-often polished mirror images that directly or indirectly insulted or ignored Americans who were not white, native American, Protestant and middle or upper-middle class. This blindness exposed what was for the utopian authors one of the most painful and confusing characteristics of the late nineteenth century—the increasing diversity of the American population.

As the authors attempted to flesh out their hypotheses about time, space, and the individual with glimpses of many different aspects of utopia, they continued to combine the old and the new and to expose painful and confusing questions, some of them as baffling as the diversity of Americans. Plans to centralize, computerize, and equalize methods of production and distribution were justified with traditional Christian ethics; government bureaucracies were given tremendous powers so that utopians could eventually enjoy an idealized Jeffersonian anarchy. But it was the more personal dilemmas, such as changing sex roles, and the more inclusive problems, such as the modern city, that pushed the utopian authors to the limits of their abilities to provide forward-looking yet familiar advice about the present and the future. In these areas the ambivalence becomes more pronounced: descriptions of new occupational alternatives for women mingle with conventional accolades to Motherhood, Wifehood, and the inherent moral and spiritual superiority of women; mass transit systems and glass and steel arcologies can't conceal an almost medieval longing for order and unity. And, of course, these two examples are only striking illustrations of the ambivalence that pervades the narrators' tours—a sincere desire for multiple, fundamental changes coupled with a fear of continual change.

Despite the popularity, numbers, and influence of late nineteenth-century utopian works, it would be foolish to assume that all Americans or even "typical" Americans were as concerned about historical perspectives, the role of the individual, sexual stereotypes, cities, and the possibilities and nightmares of change as were the utopian authors. It is not likely that devotees of Andrew Carnegie's "gospel" or Horatio Alger fans would have agreed that American culture was coming apart. Nevertheless, with the exception of a few important issues (most notably prohibition), the specific problems that aggravated the utopian authors were the same issues that concerned contemporary reformers as well as "average" citizens: depressions, social and economic inequality, unions, irrelevant theology, conflicts between science and religion, technological unemployment, manual vs. academic education, child rearing, changing sex roles, prostitution, corrupt politicians, lawyers, judges, and editors, and the whole question of whether men and women were given the "privilege of living in order that they may work"—especially if a life of work meant toiling from twelve to fourteen hours a day in a factory, a sweatshop, or on a farm.[3] Then too, the ambivalent nature of many of the utopian reforms related to these issues should help us to understand the forward-backward-looking character of many late nineteenth-century reform movements—including purity crusades, social gospelism, feminist reforms, Populism, and Progressivism—since they were in many cases led by middle- and upper-middle-class, white, middle-aged Protestants. An awareness of the ambivalent attitudes expressed in the utopian works should at least encourage modern historians not to label such movements with one-dimensional "conservative" or "radical" tags—terms which are often inappropriate when applied to American reform movements. Finally, the longings for simplicity, unity, and order that permeate the utopian literature are characteristic of late nineteenth-century America. They are found in "aristocratic" books such as *The Education of Henry Adams,* in popular historical novels, in the beginnings of urban planning, in the move to the suburbs, in the desire for simplified religions, and in the push for unionism among workers; hence it seems logical for a modern historian like Robert H. Wiebe to choose *The Search for Order* as the title for a study surveying 1877 to 1920. An understanding of the utopian authors' yearnings for simplicity, unity, and order and the instances when they were forced to advocate complexity, disunity, and disorder (i.e., multiple changes) to achieve these goals should therefore illuminate some of the most basic hopes and fears of late nineteenth-century Americans.

Late nineteenth-century utopian works are, however, more than interesting reflections of a specific era. Modern Americans are still concerned about the United States' role in history; ecological problems have charged America's virgin resources with new meanings; the impersonality of urbanized-industrialized-bureaucratic society and the civil rights movement have intensified questions about the role of the individual and the diversity of the American population; and many of the specific problems examined by the authors—especially the economy, technology, sex roles, and the city—are as controversial today as they were in the 1890s. Furthermore, as writers as diverse as Alvin Toffler and Erich Fromm argue convincingly, rapid, multidimensional change accompanied by a desire for simplicity, unity, and order are, if anything, more characteristic of the twentieth than of the nineteenth century. Therefore, late nineteenth-century utopian works should provide insights into the roots of modern problems and into psychological reactions to these problems.

Probably Bellamy, certainly obscure authors such as Sutton E. Griggs and Henry Olerich, would have been flattered to know that seventy-five years after the publication of their utopian works, some Americans would consider their ideas fascinating guides to an important period and provocative hints about modern conditions and attitudes. But they would have also been very disappointed. The utopian authors hoped that twentieth-century Americans would look back upon their books as the beginnings of The Change—pleas that would "turn the very stones into revolutionaries."[4] As Bellamy's Dr. Leete recalled,

> The figures that have come down to us of the amazing circulation of some of the books devoted to the advocacy of a radical social reorganization are almost enough in themselves to explain the revolution.[5]

The utopian works were supposed to help Americans cope with problems in the present and the future, which raises an obvious question. Can these nineteenth-century prophesies help Americans to solve the problems of the twentieth or twenty-first centuries or are they simply obsolete dreams that deserve to yellow on the shelves or, at best, find new life as reprints used by students and scholars as indices to nineteenth- and twentieth-century American culture? Of course some of the specific predictions such as blimp voyages to the North Pole or female chemists can easily be classified as outdated or as directly applicable to modern situations. But what about the general usefulness of the brand of utopianism popularized during the late nineteenth century?

Clearly, several elements of this utopian perspective are ridiculously, even cruelly, obsolete, though they still persist, especially in political rhetoric. For example, contrary to the Bard's pronouncement, these utopian authors did not believe that "all the world's a stage." When they spoke of the grand historical drama, they meant American history with an American cast and an American setting. Such nationalistic utopianism no doubt appealed to a nation on the threshold of world power. But it helped to maintain a distorted view of international relations in 1890 and viewing non-Americans as inferior beings certainly makes no sense today.

Foreigners weren't the only inferior beings according to the utopian authors. For immigrants, Indians, and blacks the image of the "barred gate of the future," used by the Rev. Mr. Barton in *Looking Backward,* had a rather disheartening meaning: unless they were "refined" or invisible, they weren't allowed in. This limitation of the utopian view of human nature emphasizes the dangers of allowing a homogeneous group to establish ideals for an extremely diversified population, even if the idealists are sincerely devoted to helping mankind, as were the late nineteenth-century utopian authors.

The tendency to see reality in terms of black and white characterized the authors' views of time as well as the perfect individual. The Armageddon concept of history charged their works with a sense of urgency. The role of a prophet in an all-or-nothing crusade also must have been very appealing to middle-aged men who had "missed out" on the Civil War and who felt threatened by the amassed wealth of those "above" them and the volcanic frustrations of the masses "below" them. But even in the 1890s this outlook raised false hopes and fears, made short-range predictions vulnerable, undercut dedication to long-term reform commitments, and popularized a simplistic view of history. Today some forms of all-or-nothing absolutism may be compelling means of arousing interest in critical issues such as nuclear arms limitations or ecological crises. In general, however, Armageddon jeremiads seem less effective now than seventy-five years ago, in part because Americans hear so many of them, but also because the "all" side of the all-or-nothing formula seems even more distant today than during Bellamy's lifetime.

The faith in man's ability to obtain the all—the literal belief in utopia as an attainable goal—is perhaps the most outmoded characteristic of late nineteenth-century American utopian works. Even as early as 1905 in *A Modern Utopia,* H. G. Wells was satirizing this attitude:

> There is a common notion that the reading of a Utopia should end with a swelling of the heart and clear resolves, with lists of names, formation of committees, and even the commencement of subscriptions.[6]

American utopian works were the obvious targets of these barbs. The Postscript to the second edition of *Looking Backward* announced that the novel was "intended, in all seriousness, as a forecast"; William Bishop entitled his Appendix "Why Not an Eden?"; F. U. Adams's final note "To the Reader" asked him to "kindly consider the feasibility of forming a Majority Rule Club in your vicinity"; King Camp Gillette bound a Certificate of Membership for the United People's Party into *The Human Drift*; John Uri

Lloyd concluded *Etidorhpa* with a well-padded list of over a thousand subscribers and would-be subscribers; and Charles W. Caryl presented multimillionaires with a cookbook recipe for one of his New Era cities: "secure a block of land as near the centre of the largest city in the state as it is possible to get; build on this block the most complete modern building for hotel, offices and department store and emporium. . . ," etc., etc. As if this weren't enough, Caryl also offered a prize to the person who sold the most copies of *New Era* and another for anyone who, in 150 words or less, could pick out and describe the most important section of the book.[7]

As the numerous Nationalist Clubs demonstrated, such appeals certainly gave the utopian works a feeling of immediacy and their readers a spur to action. Nevertheless, these explicit pleas robbed utopian literature of much of its magic by reducing idealism to a blueprint or, even worse, a sales pitch. From a twentieth-century viewpoint this "realistic" utopianism also seems a bit frightening and pathetically naive. Orwell's and Huxley's satires come to mind as do memories of Stalin's blueprints for a perfect society and Hitler's literal-minded plans for a "pure blood" race. And when we pick up one of these volumes, which usually hasn't been checked out in years, and come across blank membership forms, phony subscription lists, or appeals that were never heeded, it is almost impossible not to pity the utopian authors, just as Washington Irving in "The Mutability of Literature" pitied the "voice" of the obsolete "little quarto" buried in an old abbey library.

Still, it would be wrong to conclude with a requiem for the late nineteenth-century American utopia. In spite of a narrow nationalism, a tendency to ignore or whitewash "different" people, an all-or-nothing outlook, and a literal-minded optimism, these utopian writings have much to offer modern Americans—or anyone living in industrialized, urbanized societies. First of all, the utopian authors may have been naive and limited, but their utopias weren't limited to naive optimism. Like Howells, most of the authors had "touches of nightmares" while creating their utopias. Often this was expressed in volcanic imagery or in warnings about or descriptions of future strife; occasionally it appeared in the anguish of a conversion experience (Bellamy's Julian West, Howells's Eve) or in dramatic combinations of utopianism and anti-utopianism (Harben's *Land of the Changing Sun,* Donnelly's *Caesar's Column,* Twain's *Connecticut Yankee*). In any case, the implications were that there were real dangers in the present that were potential catastrophes in the future. Furthermore, as the most perceptive authors, including the popular Bellamy, intimated, the changes that would help Americans to avoid these catastrophes would force them to view reality in new ways. The rewards would be substantial, but as Julian West could testify, shedding an old way of seeing things wasn't easy.

The descriptions of the horrors of the present and the potential disasters and joys of the future reveal another way that late nineteenth-century utopian literature can be useful today. Like some of the best literature, Thoreau's *Walden* for example, it confronts readers with a dual perspective: visions of utopia allow them to escape to a better world, but flashbacks to the present and implicit contrasts with the present from a utopian perspective encourage readers to face the shortcomings of their environment. This is especially so in novels, like Sheldon's *In His Steps,* that focus on the transition period or in retrospective episodes, like the nightmare sequence near the conclusion of *Looking Backward.* But even in an adventure story such as Harben's *Land of the Changing Sun,* nineteenth-century readers could escape into an exciting world of beautiful Alphians, color televisions, kaleidoscopic sunlight, and winter parks on summer days while the Frankenstein-Ancient Mariner, the TV scanner, and the collapse of Alpha introduced readers to some of the catastrophic possibilities of nineteenth-century technology.

The many combinations of the old and the new in the utopian works suggest that tempting readers to escape from and face reality simultaneously is not the only dual function of utopian writings. The echoes from sentimental novels, drama, speeches, and sermons and the use of traditional Christian images (Resurrection), figures (Moses, Jesus), experiences (conversions), goals (heavenlike stability), and ethics (brotherly love) helped to make startling predictions about the future familiar and reassuring. In essence this type of utopian speculation is similar to the peyote cult so popular with twentieth-century Indians "caught between two worlds." There are enough traditional elements in the peyote ceremony—the mention of ancient holy beings, visions for Plains Indians—to preserve a sense of Indianness. Yet the behavioral code of the Native American Church, with its emphasis on a Protestant work ethic, is geared to preparing Indians for future experiences in the white world.

Pinpointing the catastrophic trends in the present, allowing readers to escape while confronting reality, and simultaneously reassuring and preparing readers during times of rapid change—these are all important aims of utopian literature. There are, nevertheless, other varieties of speculation—futuristic predictions hatched in think tanks or good science fiction—that fulfill these functions. The unique value of the best utopian fiction is the ability to create humane, inclusive visions of the day-to-day lives of people motivated by ideals—ideals that are often familiar to the reader but rarely experienced or observed during his everyday life.

Nineteenth-century utopian authors, like many of their contemporaries, were blind to the humanities of immigrants, Indians and blacks, and their immediate solutions to short-range problems were sometimes overly dependent upon economic means. But the traditions and format of utopian literature encouraged these middle- and upper-middle-class prophets to imagine how life could be improved for millions of people who had not been as fortunate as they had been and encouraged them to explore how pet schemes would affect as many aspects of modern life as they could imagine. Furthermore, the conventional assumption that utopias were supposed to be ideal worlds forced the authors to give direction to their predictions about alternate ways of living. To quote Bellamy,

> Until we have a clear idea of what we want and are sure we want it, . . . it would be a waste of time to discuss how we get it.[8]

This idealistic, futuristic orientation may be a relic of a nineteenth-century world view. It may also be crucial to our survival. If we don't carefully plot the probabilities of the future, if we refuse to speculate about what we really want, we could be caught up in a torrent whose only guidelines are points of minimum resistance.

If this sounds a bit too much like the doomsday rhetoric of the utopian works, at least consider the day-to-day value of utopian writings. As the late nineteenth-century American utopian authors sensed, one of the most perplexing problems of modern civilization is that the combination of specialized occupations and the sheer variety of experience available often renders everyday life meaningless or at least incoherent. Admittedly, utopian authors weren't the first or the last to discover this. Thoreau and Henry Adams were fully aware of the emptiness of the lives of industrious farmers and urban merchants and the incoherence of the dynamo's multiverse, while T. S. Eliot's hollow men and thousands of other modern fictional characters attest to twentieth-century analyses of meaninglessness and fragmentation. Still, the brand of humane and inclusive utopianism preached during the late nineteenth century challenged idealists to consciously explore the possibilities of endowing history, space, individuality, God, the boss, the machine, a spouse, children, even language, clothing, and leisure with significance and wholeness.

Of course, speculating about bringing the good life to everyone and ideals that make daily existence meaningful is a frustrating—"utopian"—venture. Moreover, today it calls for a pluralistic idealism quite foreign to late nineteenth-century utopianism. But consider the alternative: drifting from expedient to ad hoc buoyed only by piecemeal reforms and fragmented values that are out of touch with much of our everyday experience. Some ingredients of utopianism are ridiculously, even cruelly, obsolete; but now, more than ever, discovering utopia is a necessity.

BIBLIOGRAPHIES

The following resumés and annotated listings represent a substantial expansion of bibliographies first published in *American Literary Realism* 4 (Summer 1971): 227-54. The annotated listings are divided into three sections: bibliographies, primary sources, and secondary sources. *Since the primary sources are arranged chronologically, not alphabetically, the quickest way to locate a specific book is to find the final page reference after the author's name (or the book if the author wrote more than one utopian work) in the index.*

The first section is an annotated listing of bibliographies that were very useful to me in compiling my sample of utopian works. Besides these titles, other helpful bibliographical tools are: (1) bibliographies focusing on specific authors, especially Sylvia E. Bowman's "Bibliography," appended to *The Year 2000: A Critical Biography of Edward Bellamy* (1958) and her "Edward Bellamy (1850-1898)," *American Literary Realism* No. 1 (Fall 1967):7-12; (2) the special-collection and subject card catalogue listings at Duke University Library (special collection), Pennsylvania State University Library (special collection), the Library of Congress, the New York Public Library, Widner Library, Yale University Library, the Newberry Library, and Columbia University Library; (3) book reviews and advertisements in reform journals such as *The Nationalist, The New Nation,* and *The New Time;* and (4) general bibliographies such as Gorman Beauchamp's "An Annotated Guide to Utopia" (paper delivered at the Ninetieth Annual Meeting of the Modern Language Association, December 1975) or the general listings mentioned in the annotations for Negley and Lewis. The general bibliographies and the more specific bibliographies of non-American works, such as I. F. Clarke's *The Tale of the Future* (2nd ed.; 1972) or the bibliography appended to Richard Gerber's *Utopian Fantasy* (2nd ed.; 1973), are excellent touchstones for comparative studies.

The annotated listings of primary sources follow the bibliography of bibliographies. They include separate descriptions of the 160 works that constitute the sample of utopian literature examined in this study. Several annotations, for instance Ramsey (1891), Olerich (1893), and Howells (1893), mention other published or unpublished utopian works or short stories by that author. Other annotations, Stockton (1889), McDougall (1891), and Welcome (1894) for example, list works similar to the major entry—works representing types of novels (such as futuristic war fiction, lost tribe stories, or Symmesian center-of-the-earth tales) that exhibit many characteristics of utopian speculation. The major and secondary entries together total over 200 titles. Though over 50 important reviews are noted in the annotations, the primary source bibliography does not offer a comprehensive survey of reviews for the years 1888 to 1900. (Many reviews appeared in the above-mentioned magazines as well as in *Arena* and *The Literary World*. For listings of reviews see Clayton L. Eichelberger's *A Guide to Critical Reviews of United States Fiction, 1870-1910* [1971], Volume II [1974].) Since I have included works other than fictionalized visions of more perfect worlds, the following abbreviations in parentheses placed before certain annotations should clarify the nature of each entry: (NF) = nonfictional; (A) = anti-utopian; (P) = partially utopian. The bibliography of utopian works is followed by a brief, short-title list of intentional omissions: books sometimes incorrectly listed as American or works previously listed but containing little utopian content.

To locate libraries where specific works are available, check Lyle H. Wright's *American Fiction, 1876-1900* (1972) and *The National Union Catalogue; Pre-1956 Imprints* (1968-) where most of the books are listed. The microfilm collection of Wright's bibliography is very useful to scholars who do not have access to extensive interlibrary loan services or who find it inconvenient to travel to the libraries with special utopian collections. (The few works I was not able to obtain are listed with the source of the annotation in brackets following the annotation, for example [Rooney].)

The third section is a highly selective list of secondary sources. I have included only books, dissertations, and articles that focus on late nineteenth-century American utopian literature. (Articles on several of the lesser-known works are mentioned in the annotations.) Other types of useful secondary sources include: (1) studies of well-known authors, especially John L. Thomas, Joseph Schiffman, Arthur E. Morgan, and Sylvia E. Bowman on Bellamy; Howard Baetzhold, Henry Nash Smith, and Roger B. Salomon on Twain's *Connecticut Yankee;* Clara W. and Rudolf Kirk on Howells's Altrurian romances; and Alexander Saxon and Walter B. Rideout on Donnelly's *Caesar's Column*; (2) general literary histories of the period, especially Jay Martin's *Harvests of Change* (1967); (3) general historical or cultural studies dealing with reform or millennial traditions, for instance Daniel Aaron's *Men of Good Hope* (1951), Richard Hofstadter's *The Age of Reform* (1955), Frederic C. Jaher's *Doubters and Dissenters* (1964), Michael Kammen's *People of Paradox* (1972), Perry Miller's *Errand into the Wilderness* (1964), *Passport to Utopia*, eds., Arthur and Lita Weinberg (1968), Charles L. Sanford's *The Quest for Paradise* (1961), Henry Nash Smith's *Virgin Land* (1950), Ernest Lee Tuveson's *Redeemer Nation* (1968), and Robert H. Wiebe's *The Search for Order* (1967); (4) articles in science-fiction journals such as *Extrapolation*; and (5) general studies of utopian literature and some surveys of science fiction, for example W. H. G. Armytage's *Yesterday's Tomorrows* (1968), "Aspects of Utopian Fiction," a special issue of *Studies in the Literary Imagination* 6 (Fall 1973), *Aware of Utopia*, ed., David W. Plath (1971), J. O. Bailey's *Pilgrims Through Space and Time* (1947), Marie Louise Berneri's *Journey Through Utopia* (1950), Ernst Bloch's *A Philosophy of the Future*, tr. John Cumming (1970), Paul Bloomfield's *Imaginary Worlds* (1932), Robert C. Elliott's *The Shape of Utopia* (1970), Nell Eurich's *Science in Utopia* (1967), Bruce H. Franklin's *Future Perfect* (1966), J. C. Garrett's *Utopias in Literature*

since the Romantic Period (1968), Richard Gerber's *Utopian Fantasy* (1955),
Joyce Oramel Hertzler's *The History of Utopian Thought* (1923), George Kateb's
Utopia and Its Enemies (1963), David Ketterer's *New Worlds for Old* (1974), Karl
Mannheim's *Ideology and Utopia* (1936), Thomas Molnar's *Utopia: The Per-
ennial Heresy* (1967), Arthur E. Morgan's *Nowhere Was Somewhere* (1946), Lewis
Mumford's *The Story of Utopias* (1922), Glenn Negley's and J. Max Patrick's *The
Quest for Utopia* (1952),Martin G.Plattel's *Utopian and Critical Thinking* (1972),
Howard Ozmund's *Utopias and Education* (1969), Harold V.Rhodes's *Utopia in
American Political Thought* (1967), "Utopian Social Thought," a special issue of
Comparative Literature Studies, 10 (December 1973); *Utopias,* ed. Peyton E.
Richter (1971). *Utopias and Utopian Thought,* ed. Frank E. Manuel (1967),
Edward Wagenknecht's *Utopia Americana* (1929), and Chad Walsh's *From Utopia
to Nightmare* (1967); and (6) studies of communes such as Michael Fellman's *The
Unbound Frame* (1973).

A. Selected Bibliographies

Bailey, J. O. "Bibliography," appended to *Pilgrims Through Space and Time:
Trends and Patterns in Scientific and Utopian Fiction.* New York: Argus
Books, 1947. Pp. 325-33.
General listing of American, English, and European utopian and science fiction.
Bentley, Wilder, I. *Bibliography. The Communication of Utopian Thought; Its
History, Forms, and Use.* San Francisco: San Francisco State College
Bookstore, 1959.
A general listing of primary and secondary sources organized around a course
syllabus. It is based on an examination of secondary sources, especially Buell G.
Gallager's *Utopias; A Bibliography.* Berkeley, 1946.
Bleiler, Everett Franklin. *The Checklist of Fantastic Literature; A Bibliography
of Fantasy, Weird and Science Fiction Books Published in the English
Language.* Chicago: Shasta, 1948.
Science-fiction, partially utopian, and utopian titles.
Boggs, W. Arthur. "Bibliography," appended to *"Looking Backward* at the Utopian
Novel, 1888-1900." *Bulletin of the New York Public Library* 64:335-36.
Lists 55 titles.
Burt, Donald C. "Bibliography," appended to "Utopia and the Agrarian Tradition in
America, 1865-1900." Ph.D. dissertation, University of New Mexico, 1973. Pp.
248-55.
Lists 95 American works, 10 European, and 90 secondary sources (most of these
deal with social, economic, and political history rather than utopian literature).
Clareson, Thomas C. "An Annotated Checklist of American Science-Fiction: 1880-
1915," *Extrapolation* 1:5-20.
Useful for finding utopian works with extraterrestrial settings.
Dupont, V. *L'Utopie et le Roman Utopique dans la Littérature Anglaise.* Cahors:
A. Coueslant, 1941. (Also Paris: Librairie M. Didier, 1941.)
"Appendice III" (789-822) provides a very selective listing of novels in the form of
a book-by-book discussion; "Appendice IV" (823-25) lists British and European
collections and secondary sources often ignored in American bibliographies.
Flory, Claude R. *Economic Criticism in American Fiction, 1792-1900.* Philadel-
phia: University of Pennsylvania, 1936.

Ch. II, ii, and Ch. III, iii, mention pre-1900 utopian titles, and an appended bibliography lists utopian works published in the twentieth century (258-61).

Forbes, Allyn B. "Bibliography of American Utopias, 1884-1900," appended to "The Literary Quest for Utopia, 1800-1900." *Social Forces* 6:188-89.

Lists 47 titles between 1888-1900 found mainly at the Library of Congress.

Lewis, Arthur Orcutt, Jr. "Utopian Literature." New York: Arno Press, 1971.

Twelve-page booklet lists the 41 titles in the Arno Press reprints of American utopian literature. Good annotations. Lewis is compiling an extensive bibliography of utopian literature in part based on the collection at Penn State. See also Lewis's "The Anti-Utopian Novel: Preliminary Notes and a Checklist," *Extrapolation 2*: 27-32.

Negley, Glenn. *Utopia Collection of the Duke University Library*. Durham: Friends of Duke University Library, 1965.

General list of utopias; a mimeographed supplement (1967) is also available. Negley also has forthcoming a comprehensive bibliography of worldwide utopian writings.

————, and J. Max Patrick. "Selected List of Utopian Works, 1850-1950," in *The Quest for Utopia; An Anthology of Imaginary Societies*. New York: Henry Schuman, 1952. Pp. 19-22.

Includes American, English, French, and German works.

Normano, J. F. "Bibliography," appended to "Social Utopias in American Literature." *International Review for Social History* 3:296-300.

Nineteenth- and twentieth-century utopias; contains several inaccurate listings.

Parrington, Vernon Louis, Jr. "Bibliography," appended to *American Dreams: A Study of American Utopias*. Providence: Brown University Press, 1947. Pp. 219-29.

Includes secondary sources and some annotations; covers 1659-1946.

Pfaelzer, Jean. "Bibliography," appended to "Utopian Fiction in America 1880-1900: The Impact of Political Theory on Literary Forms." Ph. D. dissertation, University College, University of London, [expected acceptance date: June 1975].

Lists over 100 titles for this period. [I have not seen the bibliography.]

Pratter, Frederick Earl. "Speculative Fiction, Part I," appended to "The Uses of Utopia: An Analysis of American Speculative Fiction 1880-1960." Ph. D. dissertation, University of Iowa, 1973. Pp. 342-61.

Covers 1880-1909. Lists about 200 works divided into the following categories: "Near Future Anticipations," "Future Wars," "The Realizable Future," "The Far Future," "Present Time Alternatives," and "Past Time Alternative Worlds." Part II covers 1947-1959. Also a good secondary sources listing.

Quissell, Barbara C. "The Sentimental and Utopian Novels of Nineteenth Century America: Romance and Social Issues." Ph.D. dissertation, University of Utah, 1973. Pp. 299-305.

One or two page "Bibliographic Notes" focusing primarily on secondary sources follow each chapter, e.g., Ch. V. "The Minor Utopian Writers, 1865-1900," Ch. VI. "Edward Bellamy." A final bibliography of "Literature Cited" deals mainly with the late nineteenth century.

Ransom, Ellene. "Bibliography," appended to "Utopus Discovers America; or Critical Realism in American Utopian Fiction, 1798-1900." Ph.D. dissertation, Vanderbilt University, 1946. Pp. 535-46. (Published by Folcroft Press, Folcroft, Pa., 1970.)

Includes 81 American utopian, partially utopian, and fantastic stories between 1888 and 1900; also secondary sources.

Roemer, Kenneth M. "American Utopian Literature (1888-1900): An Annotated Bibliography." *American Literary Realism* 4:227-54.
Lists 150 works plus several bibliographies and secondary sources.

_____. "Annotated Bibliography," appended to "America as Utopia, 1889-1900: New Visions, Old Dreams." Ph.D. dissertation, University of Pennsylvania, 1971. Pp. xvii-xlvi.
Besides utopian works published between 1888 and 1900, this includes earlier and later works, reviews, contemporary essays, and modern secondary sources.

_____. "Edward Bellamy," *American Literary Realism* 8: (191-98). A critical bibliographical resumé of 22 American and European Ph.D. dissertations containing extended discussions of Bellamy and late nineteenth-century American utopian literature. Also mentions several masters theses.

Rooney, Charles J., Jr. "Primary Bibliography," appended to "Utopian Literature as a Reflection of Social Forces in America, 1865-1917." Ph.D. dissertation, George Washington University, 1968. Pp. 264-88.
Excellent critical bibliography includes 63 works, 1888-1900, which fit the "classical" definition of utopia: "a literary work which describes a fictional state or society that is intended to be ideal and is set in some distant place and time." Utilizing the Rose bibliography, Rooney also provides an extensive listing of reform literature, antireform literature and anti-utopias, religious literature, science fiction, foreign works, and instructional literature, 1865-1917; also secondary sources.

Rose, Lisle A. "A Bibliographical Survey of Economic and Political Writings, 1865-1900." *American Literature* 15:381-410.
Lists utopian titles not found in Flory or Taylor. See also unpublished supplements: I (28 April 1944) and II (1 October 1944), Houghton, Mich.; III (5 October 1949) and IV (1949-1951), Urbana, Ill.

Russell, Frances Theresa. "Classified Lists," in *Touring Utopia: The Realm of Constructive Humanism*. New York: Dial, 1932. Pp. 27-37.
Includes "Classical," "Modern" (1516-1932), Satires, Non-Fiction, and Partial Utopias.

Shurter, Robert L. "A Critical Bibliography of American Utopias, 1865-1900" appended to "The Utopian Novel in America, 1865-1900." Ph.D. dissertation, Case Western Reserve, 1936. Pp. 286-95.
An excellent bibliography lists one German and 85 American utopian, partially utopian, and possible utopian works between 1888 and 1900.

Stupple, A. James. "Primary Materials—Utopian Novels," appended to "Utopian Humanism in America, 1888-1900." Ph.D. dissertation, Northwestern University, 1971. Pp. 230-32.
Lists 36 works; also secondary sources and "Other Primary Materials."

Taylor, Walter. "Bibliography," appended to *The Economic Novel in America*. Chapel Hill: University of North Carolina, 1949. Pp. 341-64.
Contains many utopian works mentioned in the text. Also, 141n (106) and a paragraph listing (206) specifically mention utopian titles.

Thal-Larsen, Margaret. "Bibliography," appended to "Political and Economic Ideas in American Utopian Fiction, 1868-1914." Ph.D. dissertation, University of California, Berkeley, 1941. Pp. 229-36.

Includes 2 German and 49 American utopian titles, 1888-1900; also secondary sources.

"United States Library of Congress Division of Bibliography, List of References on Utopia." A mimeographed list (1922).

General list of books and articles; supplements were compiled in 1926 and 1940.

B. Primary Sources

1. Selected Annotated Bibliography of American Utopian, Anti-Utopian, and Partially Utopian Writings, 1888-1900

Abbreviations Relating to Reviews

Ar = *Arena*	*Natl* = *The Nationalist*
Atl = *The Atlantic Monthly*	*NN* = *The New Nation*
F = *Forum*	*NT* = *The New Time*
LW = *The Literary World*	R = review(s)

1888

Bellamy, Edward. *Looking Backward, 2000-1887*. Boston: Ticknor.
The most famous American utopian work utilizes long dialogues between Dr. Leete, a retired twentieth-century M.D., and Julian West, a wealthy nineteenth-century Bostonian, to describe twentieth-century America under Nationalism. Concludes with West converted to the new life style and to the concept of the social self. R: *Atl* 65: 248-62; *LW* 19: 85-86; *F* 8: 199-208. Some contemporaries claimed that Bellamy plagiarized John Macnie's *The Diothas* (1883), but Morgan dispelled that criticism in *Plagiarism in Utopia* (1944).

[De Mille, James.] *A Strange Manuscript Found in a Copper Cylinder*. New York: Harper & Brothers.
(A) Anti-utopian adventure story mocks antimaterialism by depicting a society in which the poorest, ugliest, and filthiest are the elite and self-hatred and self-destruction are eulogized.

Hale, Edward Everett. *How They Lived in Hampton: A Study of Practical Christianity Applied in the Manufacture of Woollens*. Boston: J. Stillman Smith. (Arno reprint, 1971.)
Describes the growth and success of a New England town organized around a profit-sharing venture similar to the whaling, lay system. R: *Natl* 3:53-54; *LW* 19:254. See also Hale's *Sybaris* (1869).

1889

Bellamy, Charles J[oseph]. *An Experiment in Marriage. A Romance*. Albany: Albany Book.
Two Easterners visit an isolated, Nationalistic community where marriage depends only on the duration of a passionate, religious love. Received very unfavorable reviews. R: *Unitarian Review* 34: 60.

Bunce, Oliver Bell. *The Story of Happinolande and Other Legends.* New York: Appleton.

The title story describes the failure of an egalitarian society made possible by the discovery of vast amounts of gold, which the government distributed to all the people. Despite the criticism of egalitarianism, extensions of government services for everyone is advocated. Another story, "The City Beautiful," contrasts Manhattan's filth, chaos, noise, "vulgar ostentation," and "riotous outbreaks of signs" to an immaculate, orderly, quiet, and tasteful ideal city.

Clemens, Samuel L. [Mark Twain]. *A Connecticut Yankee in King Arthur's Court.* New York: Charles L. Webster.

(A) Twain imagined a nineteenth-century mechanical genius who attempted to create a democratic, technological utopia in the midst of an alien tribe of Arthurians. The vision becomes catastrophic when Hank finds that he has failed to convert the tribe and tries to change them by annihilating thousands of knights with his efficient weapons. R: *LW* 21: 52-53. See also Twain's "The Curious Republic of Gondour," *Alt* 36: 461-63.

Griffin, Crawford S. *Nationalism.* Boston: C. S. Griffin.

(NF) Series of essays defends Bellamy and Gronlund by summarizing their ideas, noting precedents (e.g., post office) and criticizing the competitive system.

Heywood, D. Herbert. *The Twentieth Century. A Prophecy of the Coming Age.* Boston: F. B. Heywood.

Light satire of the entire utopian genre in the form of a book prospectus that includes lists of super inventions, irrelevant illustrations, and "Ballads of the Rockies." Wild rhetoric.

[Lane, Mary E.] *Mizora: A Prophecy.* . . . New York: G. W. Dillingham. (Evidently first serialized in the *Cincinnati Commercial,* 1880-1881.)

Describes an idyllic, education-oriented land beneath the North Pole where men are extinct and a race of blond women thrives.

Mitchell, John Ames. *The Last American:* . . . New York: Frederick A. Stokes & Brother.

(A) Satiric, anti-utopian: thirtieth-century Persians visit America—a barren wilderness destroyed by greed, imitation of Europe, poor climate, and the Irish "Murfey Dynasty."

Petersilea, Carlyle [Ernst von Himmel]. *The Discovered Country.* Boston: Ernst von Himmel.

One of the few spiritualist utopias. After death, the narrator discovers that instead of heaven and hell there is one heaven; the dead evolve from spirits to angels to archangels. The Second Commandment and several Beatitudes are the ruling wisdom of heaven, and the ideal marriage is a Socratic unity of two soul mates. (See Petersilea's *Oceanides* [1890].) Angels can visit Earth and other planets, especially Jupiter where an advanced civilization foreshadows America's future: a technologically primitive country where the utopians live a thousand years and are as mature as a twelve year old at three days old. (Possible source for Shaw's *Back to Methuselah?*) For other spiritualist utopias see Elizabeth Stuart Phelps's *Gates Ajar* (1868) and Fiske (1891).

Stockton, Frank R[ichard]. *The Great War Syndicate.* New York: Dodd, Mead. (Also P. F. Collier.)

(P) Science-fiction, war story in which a private syndicate develops fantastic naval weapons used to defeat England and to ensure a reign of peace, Anglo-American

power, and prosperity. R: *LW* 21: 143. Other futuristic war stories described in this
bibliography include Vinton (1890), Waterloo (1898), and Newcomb (1900).
Shurter mentions Oto Mundo's [pseud.?] *The Recovered Country* (1898); Pratter
lists James Barnes's *The Unpardonable War* (1900) [L of C says 1904], Samuel
Barton's *The Battle of the Swash* . . . (1888), S. W. Odell's *The Last War*
(1898), and King Wallace's *The Next War* (1892) [not listed in Wright or L of C].

[Woods, Katharine Pearson.] *Metzerott, Shoemaker*. New York: Crowell.
(P) Narrates the successes and failures of a co-op community in a slum district.
Advocates Christian socialism with the emphasis on the Christianity. R: *Lippin-
cott's Magazine* 45: 883-88.

1890

[Bachelder, John.] *A.D. 2050. Electrical Development at Atlantis*. San Francisco:
Bancroft.
Disjoint anti-utopian, utopian novel, narrates the decay of Bellamy's utopia, a
Chinese invasion, and the world's salvation achieved by the efforts of an exclusive
island nation of American technocrats and businessmen who have powerful
weapons and advocate modified competition.

Cole, Cyrus. *The Auroraphone: A Romance*. Chicago: Charles H. Kerr.
A miraculous invention establishes communication with a Saturnian who describes
the history of his nation, which mirrors America until a religious hero appears and
proves the "transmigration" of all experience. The population is reformed, and
progress is interrupted only by a war between robots and man: a fearful result of an
overdependence on technology. (See Fuson in "Secondary Sources.") Besides the
many other contact-with-advanced-worlds novels listed in this bibliography, Pratter notes: Robert D. Braine's *Messages from Mars* (1892), Garrett Putnam
Serviss's *The Moon Metal* (1900) and "Edison's Conquest of Mars," New York
Evening Journal (1896), F. M. Clarke's *A Maiden of Mars* (1892), and Alfred
Smythe's *Von Hoff; or, The New Planet* (1897) [L of C lists the subtitle as *The
New Faust*].

Dail, C[harles] C[urtis]. *Willmoth the Wanderer; or The Man from Saturn*.
[Atchison, Kans.: Haskell.]
(P) Mostly the narrative of a Saturnian who uses a flying armchair to visit strange
lands on Saturn, Venus, and prehistoric Earth; the lands often represent different
stages in man's evolution. The book does, however, open with a description of an
ideal city on Saturn. Unlike most utopian authors, Dail defended the delights and
"purity of sexual intercourse." (See Fuson, "Secondary Sources.")

Donnelly, Ignatius [Edmund Boisgilbert]. *Caesar's Column: A Story of the Twentieth Century*. Chicago: F. J. Schulte.
(A) Vivid anti-utopian, utopian history opens with the expected technological
wonderland, penetrates to the "rotten" core of the "gorgeous shell," and predicts
that if the masses remain oppressed, a bloody revolution led by a gigantic brute and
his secret cult will destroy America. Concludes with the establishment of an
isolated, pastoral-Populist community in Africa. R: *Ar* 6: lxiii; 9: [ad section]; *LW*
21: 240.

Fuller, Alvarado M. *A.D. 2000*. Chicago: Laird & Lee. (Arno reprint, 1971.)
A lieutenant-inventor sleeps for 100 years, awakes and is guided through a

gadget-filled America extending over all of North America. The transition period involved a providential flood that drowned the greedy and paved the way for a Nationalistic system and the invention of a powerful explosive used by a strong army to defeat our enemies. (See Fuson in "Secondary Sources.")

Gilpin, William. *The Cosmopolitan Railway Compacting and Fusing Together All the World's Continents*. San Francisco: History.

(NF,P) Series of essays maintains that the geographical characteristics of America provide a perfect environment for the development of an ideal "Aryan" race whose "Mission" is to build an intercontinental railroad that will make the deserts bloom and spread American civilization around the globe.

Gronlund, Laurence. *Our Destiny. The Influence of Nationalism on Morals and Religion*. Boston: Lee & Shepard. (First appeared in *The Nationalist*, March-September 1890.)

(NF) Series of essays argues that Nationalism is the "carry[ing] out of God's thoughts" because it helps to develop sympathy and love for others and provides salvation through a regenerated society. (A revised edition of *The Coöperative Commonwealth* [London: S. Sonnenschein] also appeared in 1890.)

Leggett, Mortimer Dormer. *A Dream of a Modest Prophet*. Philadelphia: Lippincott.

Visitor-guide dialogues describe a Martian country transformed by a "small book" which proved that "true Christianity," uncorrupted by Judaism and the Church, was the universal panacea. An educational program emphasizing industry and thrift also helped to mold a new, noble race.

Longley, Alcander. *What is Communism? A Narrative of the Relief Community. . . .* St. Louis: Altruist Community.

(NF) A lengthy description of the "principles, organization and practical details of community homes," common property and co-op labor. Predicts that such communities will spread over America, consolidate, and transform the nation. R: *Natl* 3: 428-29; 570-71.

Michaelis, Richard C. *Looking Further Forward, An Answer to Looking Backward by Edward Bellamy*. Chicago and New York: Rand, McNally. (Arno reprint. 1971.)

(A) Anti-utopian novel in which a demoted professor reveals to Julian West that human nature did not change in Bellamy's utopia; the new system only encouraged corruption and favoritism while undermining initiative and motherhood. Advocates modified competition. R: *LW* 21: 283.

Pittock, Mrs. M. A. (Weeks). *The God of Civilization. A Romance*. Chicago: Eureka.

(P) A party of Americans shipwrecked on a Pacific isle intermarry with the natives, adopt their customs and dress, and live an idyllic life free from the "god of civilization," money. R: *Overland Monthly* 17 (2d ser): 659.

Porter, Linn Boyd [Albert Ross]. *Speaking of Ellen*. New York: G. W. Dillingham.

(P) Story of a New England mill hand who leads the workers, converts a lawyer to her cause, inherits a fortune, triumphs over capitalists and anarchists, and helps to plan a profit-sharing, socialistic community.

Salisbury, Henry Barnard. *The Birth of Freedom, A Socialist Novel*. New York: Humbolt. (First published in *The Nationalist*, November, 1890–March-April, 1891. One later edition was entitled *Miss Worden's Hero*.)

The competitive system culminates in a bloody revolution that purges the land.

During a 25-year transition period, America follows the example of Europe (very rare in American utopias) and adopts "voluntary" Nationalism and a suburban style of living. See also Salisbury's "Saved by Nationalism," *Natl* 3: 145-58.

Satterlee, W. W. *Looking Backward and What I Saw*. Minneapolis: Harrison & Smith. (Arno reprint, 1971.)

Critique of Bellamy and single-tax programs in the form of an allegorical dream narrative set in the decaying Nationalistic America of 2101. Supports some land, tax, and voting reforms; attacks drinking, immigrants, and the decline of religion; and parodies (plagiarizes?) Bellamy's water tank parable and Hawthorne's "Celestial Railroad" in dream-within-a-dream sections.

Stone, Mrs. C. H. *One of "Berrian's" Novels*. New York: Welch, Fracker.

A defense of Bellamy in the form of a novel of the future written by an imaginary author, Berrian, briefly mentioned by Dr. Leete in *Looking Backward*. Set in 1997, it is mostly a trite love-seduction story involving a love-sick, male relic of the nineteenth century, a "modern" woman, and a handsome hero. Also pictures the last futile revolt against Nationalism and speculates about "ego development" and "psychic treatment." R: *Overland Monthly* 17 (2d ser): 659.

Vinton, Arthur Dudley. *Looking Further Backward*. . . . Albany: Albany Book. (Arno reprint, 1971.)

(A) Utilizing Julian West's diary, a Chinese professor describes how Nationalism undermined initiative, racial purity, chastity, motherhood, and manliness, and opened the way for a successful Chinese invasion. R: *LW* 22: 43.

Worley, Frederick U. [Benefice]. *Three Thousand Dollars a Year*. . . . Washington, D. C.: J. P. Wright.

Unoriginal description of the gradual evolution of Bellamy's utopia from local co-ops to Nationalization. But unlike Bellamy, Worley stressed the gradual disappearance of racial segregation.

1891

Allen, Henry Francis [Pruning Knife]. *A Strange Voyage. A Revision of the Key of Industrial Co-operative Government*. . . . St. Louis: Monitor.

Narrative of a tour of Venus emphasizes the importance of statistics, makes some excellent predictions (e.g., Polaroid cameras), and offers a superficial catalogue of Nationalistic reforms, which Allen claims to have advocated as early as 1874.

Bartlett, Mrs. Alice Elinor (Bowen) [Birch Arnold]. *A New Aristocracy*. New York and Detroit: Bartlett.

(P) The influence of a fiancée sympathetic to the poor and the example of a model workers' community in Paris inspire an aristocrat to create an ideal, profit-sharing community supported by a shoe factory. The "Society of Universal Brotherhood," a movement guided by Christ's example, also furthers the cause of reform.

Fiske, Amos K[idder]. *Beyond the Bourn, Reports of a Traveller Returned from "The Undiscovered Country," Submitted to the World*. New York: Fords, Howard & Hulbert.

Spiritualist romance pictures a planet where the individual has been transformed by careful childhood training, birth control (abstinence), and a scientific religion. Since everyone is good, there is little need of external regulations except for "voluntary cooperation." R: *LW* 22: 210.

Fitch, Thomas and Anna M. *Better Days, or A Millionaire of To-morrow*. San Francisco: Better Days.
(P) Dedicated to millionaires who help workers. Narrates the history of a gold mine owner who uses his money to increase the money supply, to start co-op and urban renewal projects, and to develop powerful weapons to enforce peace. Contains many anti-Semitic and anti-Indian passages. R: *Ar* 6: lxiv.

Geissler, Ludwig A. *Looking Beyond; A Sequel to "Looking Backward," by Edward Bellamy, and An Answer to "Looking Further Forward," by Richard Michaelis*. New Orleans: L. Graham & Son. (Arno reprint, 1971.)
Answers the criticisms posed by Michaelis's demoted professor with statistics and rather poor logic. Also, questions Bellamy's concept of alumni rule. R: *NN* 1: 683.

Harris, Thomas Lake. *The New Republic: A Discourse of the Prospects, Dangers, Duties and Safeties of the Times*. Santa Rosa, Calif.: Fountaingrove Press.
Evangelical treatise warns of an "impending calamity" that will lead either to a millennial age guided by a wise minority or to a cataclysm. Describes capitalism as a primitive "survival" and develops a concept of "social personality" similar to Bellamy's. See also *The Brotherhood of the New Life. Its Fact, Law, Method and Purpose*. London: E. W. Allen, 1891. A long letter describing a California commune and a system of "Divine breathing."

Houston, Benjamin F. *The Rice Mills of Port Mystery*. Chicago: Charles H. Kerr.
(P) Detailed factual and fictional history of the Northwest; free trade is the key to an ideal future. [Ransom.]

McDougall, Walter H[ugh]. *The Hidden City*. New York: Cassell.
(P) Adventure, intrigue story in which a white god (a Yankee mechanic) falls from the Arizona skies (from a balloon), discovers a primitive lost race in a canyon, and transforms their settlement into a mechanical wonderland that will eventually be run by a joint stock company financed by a gold mine. R: *LW* 22: 440. Other lost-tribe tales listed by Pratter are: Thomas Allibone Janvier's *The Aztec Treasure-House* (1890), [James Otis Kaler's] *The Search for the Silver City* (1893), Frank Aubrey's *The Devil-Tree of El Dorado* (1897) and *A Queen of Atlantis* (1900), Charles Sumner Seeley's *The Lost Canyons of the Toltecs* (1893) [not listed in L of C or Wright], and Mrs. Mary B. M. Toland's *Atlina, Queen of the Floating Isle* (1893).

McGlasson, Eva Wilder (Brodhead). *Diana's Livery*. New York: Harper & Brothers.
(A) Narrative of an imaginary, Kentucky Shaker community; praises the attempt to practice ideals, but abhors the "unnatural" restrictions on family ties. R: *LW* 22: 72.

Ramsey, Milton Worth. *Six Thousand Years Hence*. Minneapolis: [Alfred Roper].
(P) Bizarre interplanetary tale describes America in 7902 A.D. as a highly specialized, mechanized, competitive culture from which the hero escapes to a primitive, polar island (warmed by a volcano) where all the natives live happy lives without books or machines. See also Ramsey's *Future Dark Ages* (1900) and *Two Billions of Miles* (1900).

Simpson, William [Thomas Blot]. *The Man From Mars: His Morals, Politics and Religion*. San Francisco: Bacon.
A Martian visits a California hermit and describes Mars as a slowly evolved utopia where a homogeneous race is motivated by scientific Christianity. Land is govern-

ment owned (single tax), statistics balance the economy, and the cities are carefully planned.

Thomas, Chauncey. *The Crystal Button, or, Adventures of Paul Prognosis in the Forty-Ninth Century.* Ed. George Houghton. Boston and New York: Houghton Mifflin.

Engineer's utopia complete with technological marvels and ingenious pyramid-shaped living complexes housing thousands. The transition was inspired by a religious hero who preached a vague gospel of "Truth" after a retreat into the wilderness among the Indians. R: *NN* 1: 19.

[Walker, Samuel.] *The Reign of Selfishness. A Story of Concentrated Wealth.* New York: M. K. Pelletreau. (Published in 1899 as *Dry Bread* by G. W. Dillingham.)

(P) Fictional history narrates the collapse of a corrupt, all powerful trust as a result of an economic depression and an avenging plague. Society is regenerated under the guidance of a businessman who redistributes the population to small villages and restores "friendly" competition.

1892

[Austen, Edward J.] *The Lost Island.* Conclusion by William Lloyd Garrison. [New York: G. M. Vescelius, c. 1892.] (Also published with Louise Vescelius Sheldon in *The Cosmopolitan,* January 1893, pp. 365-84.)

(A) Anti-utopian, effectively satirizes private land ownership by describing the experiences of a shipwrecked crew on an idyllic island. A mate discovers he owns the island (old Spanish title) and insists that the crew pay rent for Nature's gifts.

Bradshaw, William R. *The Goddess of Atvatabar Being the History of the Discovery of the Interior World and the Conquest of Atvatabar.* New York: J. F. Douthitt. (Laudatory introduction by Julian Hawthorne.)

At first Atvatabar seems to be a luxurious ideal society where the human soul is worshipped as expressed in invention, art, and spirituality. But the civilization is founded upon the "unnatural" worship of celibacy. One of the visitors sparks a revolt, marries the Goddess, and founds a society where invention, art, and spirituality are still admired; but marriage replaces celibacy and Christianity will replace the human soul religion. Also satirizes technological advances: for example, the mechanical ostrich is the primary means of transportation.

Chavannes, Albert. *The Future Commonwealth, or, What Samuel Balcom Saw in Socioland.* New York: True Nationalist. (Arno reprint, 1971.)

Antireligious utopian novel (rare) describes an African colony established by a group of "sociologists" who advocate a mixed economy (Nationalism and small scale capitalism), an elaborate apprentice system, and secular "happiness" as life's only goal.

Crocker, Samuel [Theodore Oceanic Islet]. *That Island.* Oklahoma City: C. E. Streeter. (Also Kansas City: Sidney F. Woody.)

Dull, detailed account of an island nation's transition from oppressive capitalism to Populist programs. The masses were mobilized in a "single day" by reading a book written by a wealthy genius who is the leader of a secret reform group.

Daniel, Charles S. *Ai. A Social Vision.* Philadelphia: Miller. (Arno reprint, 1971.)

(P) Lighthearted and confusing narrative focuses on an Episcopal bishop's regeneration of Philadelphia and alternately recommends the renovation of Revolutionary (1776) homes, mixing Christianity, Judaism, Islam and Buddhism, urban renewal, law reform, kindness to animals, and the reform spirit of society belles. R: *Ar* 9: [ad section].

Donnelly, Ignatius. *The Golden Bottle, or, The Story of Ephram Benezet of Kansas*. New York: D. D. Merrill.
A farm-boy dreams he is given a liquid that enables him to make gold. He uses his wealth to support a secret organization (Populist-Christian-co-op) and to finance low interest loans. His policies save America, and America saves the masses of the world.

Doughty, Francis Worcester. *Mirrikh; or A Woman from Mars; A Tale of Occult Adventure*. New York: Burleigh & Johnston.
(P) Mostly a spiritualist story (bastardized Swedenborg) about the soul's ability to travel outside the body. A Martian enables the souls of two New Yorkers to visit Mars. The Martians worship one god, abhor religious ritual, encourage advanced mechanical and spiritual sciences, and practice mental telepathy. One of the visitors returns to Earth with an ideal Martian woman for his "soul mate."

Everett, Henry L. *The People's Program. The Twentieth Century Is Theirs. A Romance of the Expectations of the Present Generation*. New York: Workingmen's Publishing Co. (Foreword indicates prior serial publication in Utah.)
An opportunistic student-editor organizes a secret, co-ed youth movement that advocates Christianity, city planning, and "variation of labor" (profession varies with age and season). Various parts of the program are attempted in Europe, in a religious camp in California, and in a mining colony in Kansas.

Granville, Austyn. *The Fallen Race*. New York and Chicago: F. T. Neely.
(P) A doctor-scientist and his faithful bushman companion discover a new race in an Australian desert—a cross between a lost tribe of bushmen and some pugnacious kangaroos! These four-foot fur balls are ruled by a white woman who had been stranded among them as a child. Like Twain's Hank Morgan, the doctor revolutionizes the native culture with mechanical wonders. The final result is a technologically sophisticated land where governments, judges, lawyers, and police are unnecessary because of the new morality inspired by the doctor's explosives and ideals. The hero marries the white woman, of course.

Grimshaw, Robert. *Fifty Years Hence: or What May Be in 1943. . . .* New York: Practical.
(P) An engineer narrator utilizes a scientific, "graphic method" which, based on past and present historical patterns, predicts an Electric Age by cataloging clusters of inventions. R: *Ar* 7: [ad section].

Harben, Will[iam] N[athanial]. "In the Year Ten Thousand." *Arena* 6: 743-49.
A 600-year-old man reveals the history of the world since 2000 A.D. There were two fundamental changes: In 2320 a colony of Americans advocated vegetarianism, which led to the physical perfection of humanity. In 4051 mental telepathy was discovered, which led to the purification of thought and action (all evil ideas were exposed by mind reading) and worldwide brotherhood. See also Bellamy (1898).

Kinnear, Dr. Beverley O[liver]. *Impending Judgments on the Earth; or "Who May Abide the Day of His Coming."* New York: James Huggins.
(P,NF) Utilizes biblical prophesy and chronology combined with mathematical "proofs" to demonstrate that the imminent collapse of mammonism and corruption

will herald a Kingdom of God on earth. Kinnear pinpoints the location of Armageddon (map included) and predicts that the final struggles will begin in September 1896. R: Boston *Evening Transcript* 9 December 1893, p. 7. See also Fishbough (1899) and J. B. Newbrough's *Oahspe* (1882).

McCowan, Archibald [Luke A. Hedd]. *Philip Meyer's Scheme. A Story of Trades Unionism.* New York: J. S. Ogilvie.
   A journeyman, inspired by *Looking Backward,* writes a short treatise advocating a universal federation of labor. After several confrontations between capital and labor, the federation, led by the journeyman and Abraham Lincoln Homeborn, unite the workers. By 1910 America is well on the road towards the Nationalistic state envisioned by Bellamy.

[Moore, M. Louise.] *Al-Modad; or, Life Scenes Beyond the Polar Circumflex. A Religio-Scientific Solution of the Problems of Present and Future Life.* Shell Bank, Cameron Parish, La.: M. Louise Moore & M. Beauchamp.
   Pictures a co-operative, communal, vegetarian utopia beneath the North Pole. Burdened by long chemistry "lectures" that "prove" the scientific validity of the Bible. Enlivened by humorous typos, e.g., "in those boobs [books] of travel."

Schwahn, John George. *The Tableau; or, Heaven as a Republic.* Los Angeles: Franklin.
   (P) In a bizarre panoramic history Reason guides Humanity from ancient Israel to the future America where Christianity, the main deterrent to Progress, has died out; and the true "Saviour," steam, and the true religion, Science, have led to an ideal, "godless" society that thrives especially in California.

Stockwell, Lucius A. *The Earthquake. A Story of To-Day.* Indianapolis: Non-con[f]ormist.
   (P) Mixture of historical fact and fiction narrates the rise of railroads, money power, and oppression especially in Indiana. A revolution is avoided and a just society established when speculative land holdings are distributed to the landless and when the Morgan estate is willingly donated to provide "happy little homes" for five million Americans.

Tibbles, T[homas] H[enry], and Beattie, Elia M. *The American Peasant.* Chicago: F. J. Schulte.
   An ancient Christian manuscript is the law of an arctic community where the common good is more important than the individual. [Rooney.]

Tinckner, Mary Agnes. *San Salvador.* Boston and New York: Houghton Mifflin.
   An orphan visits a secret mountain community in Europe where Christ is worshipped as the King, a wise, hereditary ruler watches over secular affairs, agriculture and hand crafts are preserved, and missionaries are sent out annually. R: *Atl* 69: 19.

1893

The Beginning, a Romance of Chicago as It Might Be. Chicago: Charles H. Kerr.
   Disjoint, boring story of a lover who trys to impress his love by writing about an ideal America. The masses are elevated by the creation of free, national boarding schools where children are disciplined with military vigor and subjected to periodic examinations that determine their future occupations.

Howells, W[illiam] D[ean]. *Letters of an Altrurian Traveller*. *The Cosmopolitan*, November 1893–September 1894. (Parts of Letters I-V revised for *Impressions and Experiences* [1896]; Letters VI-XI revised as Pt. I of *Through the Eye of the Needle* [1907].
Sequel to *A Traveler from Altruria*. Mr. Homos compares competitive NYC unfavorably and the co-operative "White City" (Chicago Fair) favorably with Altruria. See also Howells (1894) and Howells's *Three Villages* (1884) and *New Leat Mills* (1913).

[Jones, Alice Ilgenfritz, and Merchant, Ella.] *Unveiling a Parallel. A Romance*. Boston: Arena.
A male narrator visits two Martian countries. In the first women have absolute equality: they can be ambitious businesswomen or successful professionals, can vote, belong to secret clubs, box, drink, inhale valerian root, and frequent brothels run by male whores. In the other country the sexes are still equal, but the "selfish" and "vulgar" drives of both have been replaced by a brotherly (and sisterly) love that pervades their physical, moral, and spiritual lives.

Miller, Joaquin. *The Building of the City Beautiful*. Cambridge & Chicago: Stone & Kimball.
Chaotic fantasy describes two utopian projects: a mysterious Jewess succeeds in creating a technologically sophisticated and religiously inspiring city in a desert, while a solitary American fails to build a city on a barren mountain overlooking "sinful" San Francisco. R: *Ar* 8: xxiii.

Niswonger, Charles Elliot. *The Isle of Femine*. Little Rock, Ark.: Brown.
(A) Trite, antifeminist fantasy pictures an isle completely dominated by women. The immortal queen dies when she falls in love with the narrator (immortality bars all passion), and the visitor leaves with a maid who accepts him as her protector.

Olerich, Henry. *A Cityless and Countryless World: An Outline of Practical Co-operative Individualism*. Holstein, Iowa: Gilmore & Olerich. (Arno reprint, 1971.)
A Martian visits an American family and describes his planet's civilization, which is organized around huge communal, living complexes housing a thousand persons, each in his own room (the nuclear family has disappeared). One hundred and twenty of these "families" interspersed with factories and warehouses are distributed around the circumference of a 24 by 6 mile rectangle, which is divided into co-op farms, parks, etc. These "communities" form national districts. See also Olerich's *Modern Paradise* (1915) and *The Story of the World a Thousand Years Hence* (1923).

Roberts, J. W. *Looking Within. The Misleading Tendencies of "Looking Backward" Made Manifest*. New York: A. S. Barnes. (Arno reprint, 1971.)
(A) A bitter, contradictory, anti-utopian novel utilizes a sleeper who awakes in 1927 (K vs. L war), 2000 (Bellamy's utopia encourages sin and laziness, human nature cannot be changed), and 2025 (a return to a slightly modified nineteenth-century civilization instantly transforms America into a virtuous, prosperous land). R: New York *Times* 23 March 1895, p. 3; *LW* 24: 293.

Russell, Addison Peale. *Sub-Coelum: A Sky-Built Human World*. Boston: Houghton Mifflin.
(NF) Chaotic catalogue of observations about a utopia that embodies "tasteful" diversity and individuality (e.g., "Worship," "Fish-Ponds," "Ideal Manhood," "The Sub-Coelum Oyster"). R: *LW* 25:44.

Strong, Rev. Josiah. *The New Era; or, The Coming Kingdom*. New York: Baker & Taylor.

(NF,P) A millennial appeal to churches to aid in the reform of America, so that the "greatest race" (American Anglo-Saxons) can fulfill its mission: Anglo-Saxon unity and a reformed world that combines individuality and social organization.

Swift, Morrison I[ssac]. *A League of Justice, or, Is It Right to Rob the Robbers?* Boston: Commonwealth Society.

A secret organization of clerks systematically steals from trusts and supports unions and co-ops. The capitalists react violently but surrender when revolution is threatened. The rise of co-ops and the elimination of lawyers, judges, and professors follows.

Von Swartwout, Dr. William H. *Olumbia; or Utopia Made Practical*. New York: New Columbia University Press.

(NF,P) Wild pamphlet declares that the government is unconstitutional because it is not representative; hence, it is legal to overthrow it and to establish a utopia in which the labor force dominates and money is abolished.

1894

Astor, John Jacob. *A Journey in Other Worlds. A Romance of the Future*. New York: Appleton. (Also London: Longmans, Green.)

Adventure, science-fiction story offers three utopias: the Earth in 2000 A.D., a haven for technologists, expansionists, and competitors; Jupiter, a virgin paradise of raw materials; and Saturn, a simplistic, Christian heaven.

Brooks, Byron A[lden]. *Earth Revisited*. Boston: Arena.

Awkward mixture of romance and spiritualism in which a sleeper awakes in 1992 to find that "applied Christianity" and co-op trusts have changed Brooklyn into a suburban paradise where the city owns most of the land and inventors are eulogized (poets and novelists are extinct). R: *Ar* 9: [ad section].

Browne, Walter. *"2894"; or, The Fossil Man. (A Mid-Winter Night's Dream.)* New York: G. W. Dillingham.

[Listed as utopian by Allyn B. Forbes: "Bibliography of American Utopias, 1884-1900," appended to "The Literary Quest for Utopia, 1880-1900." See Bibliographies.]

Chamberlain, H[enry] R[ichardson]. *6,000 Tons of Gold*. Meadville, Pa.: Flood and Vincent.

(A) An attempt to "benefit all mankind" by putting vast amounts of newly discovered gold into circulation results in a disastrous inflation, which is finally relieved after most of the gold is sunk. Satirizes the American financial system and the easy-money utopian reformers. See Bunce (1889) and Donnelly (1892).

Flower, B[enjamin] O[range]. *The New Time: A Plea for the Union of the Moral Forces for Practical Progress*. Boston: Arena.

(NF) Series of essays maintains that it is the duty of "thoughtful people" to aid movements that advocate social reform (especially educational) during this confusing transition period, which will end in a cataclysm or a Christian utopia depending upon how people respond to the crisis.

Giles, Fayette Stratton. *Shadows Before; or, A Century Onward*. New York: Humbolt.

In 1993 a 130-year-old professor explains to a Japanese visitor that the "Science of Natural Law" dictated an evolution of "voluntary competitive cooperation," technological progress, eugenics, and racial limitations (inferiors are competent servants) instead of the utopia predicted by Bellamy.

Gillette, King C[amp]. *The Human Drift*. Boston: New Era.

(NF) The inventor of the safety razor advocates the founding of a mammoth, co-operative, joint stock company that will eventually control all America's production and distribution. The company, located near Niagara, will be surrounded by a gigantic city that will depopulate the rest of the country and possibly the world. Includes detailed, full-page illustrations of city plans and duplicate, high-rise apartments. See also Gillette's *The Ballot Box* (1897), *"World Corporation"* (1910), and *The People's Corporation* (1924).

Harben, Will[iam] N[athanial]. *The Land of the Changing Sun*. New York: Merriam.

(A) Orwellian, anti-utopian story begins with glowing descriptions of a suboceanic, artificial world, only to reveal that the people are slaves to scientists who are experts in psychological torture, banish the unfit, and maintain a powerful police force complete with TV scanning devices. A devasting flood convinces even the ruler that it is blasphemy to imitate God's Creation with technology. (See Roemer, Kenneth M. "1984 in 1894: Harben's *Land of the Changing Sun*," *Mississippi Quarterly* 26: 29-42.)

Howells, W[illiam] D[ean]. *A Traveler from Altruria. A Romance*. New York: Harper & Bros. (First published in *The Cosmopolitan*, November 1892–October 1893.)

One of the few American utopian works similar to William Morris's *News from Nowhere*. A visitor from an ideal country, shocked by the social and economic inequality in America, describes his unhurried land where the ballot box toppled the Age of Accumulation and replaced it with a form of Christian Socialism. The population lives in small towns using rapid transit to commute to cities where machinery is limited to drudgery eliminators. The ideal individual is the artist-craftsman. R: *LW* 25: 201.

Pomeroy, William C. *The Lords of Misrule. A Tale of Gods and Men*. Chicago: Laird & Lee.

(A) Fictional history, narrated by Greek gods, describes the Age of Mammon (overthrown in 1910), the Socialistic Republic (ambition dies and America divides into five nations), and the re-establishment of a glorious American Republic after New England (a hotbed of socialism) has been ravaged by anarchy.

Pope, Gustavus W. *Journey to Mars. The Wonderful World: Its Beauty and Splendor; Its Mighty Races and Kingdoms; Its Final Doom*. New York: G. W. Dillingham.

(P) Mostly an interplanetary adventure story, but Ch. 36 describes an advanced yellow race—the result of generations of selective breeding. Includes glimpses of solar and geothermal energy production, Polaroid cameras, TV's, dictaphones, and a Fountain of Youth. See also Pope's *Journey to Venus* (1895).

Rosewater, Frank. *'96; A Romance of Utopia. Presenting a Solution of the Labor Problem, a New God and a New Religion*. Omaha: Utopia. (Also published in 1897 by F. T. Neely, London, as *Utopia: A Romance of Today*. Arno reprint, 1971.)

Confusing fantasy of two African nations: one (in the East) worships gold, is dominated by a capitalist-prince, and eventually succumbs to the other nation (in the West) where the people have adopted the "American" system: in America a labor party victory in 1896 insured government ownership of the land and an ethical administration of justice by industrial departments. See also Rosewater's *The Social Problem Solved* (1917).

Schindler, Solomon. *Young West: A Sequel to Edward Bellamy's Celebrated Novel "Looking Backward."* Boston: Arena. (Arno reprint, 1971.)

Julian West's son's biography provides a detailed account of the life cycle in Bellamy's utopia (especially education). Emphasizes that fundamental change comes only with the gradual internalization of new values over several generations. R: *Ar* 13: 123-25. See also Schindler's "Dr. Leete's Letter to Julian West," *Natl* 3: 81-86.

Welcome, S. Byron. *From Earth's Centre, a Polar Gateway Message.* Chicago: Charles H. Kerr.

Describes a single-tax nation beneath the North Pole where all industries and institutions are automatically guided by competition (e.g., teachers compete for students). Besides the numerous other interior-of-the-earth narratives described in this bibliography, see Frank Cowan's *Revi-Lona* (188?) and two works listed by Pratter: Charles Aikin's *Forty Years with the Damned* (1895) and Duffield Osborne's *The Secret of the Crater* (1900: first published in *Lippincott's* as *A Mountain Moloch* in 1897).

1895

Bishop, William H[enry]. *The Garden of Eden, U.S.A. A Very Possible Story.* Chicago: Charles H. Kerr.

A millionaire establishes a model co-op community in North Carolina settled by select individuals and organized around huge apartment complexes offering a combination of privacy and social life. R: *NT* 1: ii.

Call, Henry L[aurens]. *The Coming Revolution.* Boston: Arena.

(NF) Series of essays outlines five major injustices contributing to the suffering of the 1890s: inheritance, land monopoly, bank interest, transportation costs, and unregulated trusts. Recommends Populist solutions and predicts a glorious New Republic, which avoids the "extremes" of socialism and the inhumanity of the status quo.

Chavannes, Albert. *In Brighter Climes, or Life in Socioland. A Realistic Novel.* Knoxville, Tenn. Chavannes.

Focuses on "rational" attitudes about marriage, immigration restrictions, careful town planning, and the preservation of an independent, farm life.

Davenport, Benjamin Rush. *"Uncle Sam's" Cabins. A Story of American Life Looking Forward a Century.* New York: Mascot.

(A) Anti-utopian, utopian; predicts the culmination of nineteenth-century land monopolies in serfdom. Fortunately, an avenging plague purges the land and a "fighting Parson" inherits his father's estate, frees the serfs, leases the land, and supports competition and free trade. The result is a yeoman's utopia.

Fitzpatrick, Earnest Hugh [Hugo Barnaby]. *The Marshal Duke of Denver; or, The Labor Revolution of 1920. A Novel.* Chicago: Donohue & Henneberry.

(P) Oppressed labor organizes a secret army led by a military genius who seizes control after a bloody revolution and establishes a provisional triumvirate who advocate income tax, land-based money, and a Labor Bureau. Concludes as the "peoples'" hero receives the title of Duke.

Haedicke, Paul. *The Equalities of Para-Para*. Chicago: Schuldt-Gathmann.

(A) Satire narrates the history of a lost civilization that peaked under the wise rulership of hereditary despots and then suffered through a civil war. Next a cruel competitive era (characterized by a monument to "Man Chest") led to an age of equality imposed by physical mutilation and strictly enforced mental norms. For a similar satire see Oliver Wendell Holmes's "Over the Teacups." *Atl* 65: 232-43.

Holford, Castello N. *Aristopia. A Romance-History of the New World*. Boston: Arena.

American history as it could have been if a wise and wealthy settler had created a heterogeneous colony in the "virgin world" of Virginia and Ohio. Advocates communal ownership of land and means of production. R: *Ar* 13: 338-47.

Howard, Albert Waldo [M. Auburré Hovorrè]. *The Milltillionaire*. Boston: [Author]. (Arno reprint, 1971.)

Wild catalogue of visions describes a world controlled by a beneficent monarch and 26 departmental "bards." All work for a few hours a day, cities have triple-deck highways, the young "love naturally" before marriage, and polygamy is permitted.

Lease, Mary Elizabeth (Clyens). *The Problem of Civilization Solved*. Chicago: Laird & Lee.

(NF) Series of essays argues that American poverty and urban overcrowding can be eliminated by a huge colonization project in South America where millions of "Caucasian" families will train the "inferior" races (Negro, Chinese, Indian) to be independent farmers. This combined with an American Federation (N. & S. America), international arbitration, and Populist reforms will usher in a utopian age.

Lloyd, John Uri. *Etidorhpa or the End of Earth. . . .* Cincinnati: John Uri Lloyd.

(P) Mixture of chemistry and occult sciences, fact and fiction; narrates the journey of a stone mason through a subterranean world of wonders and temptations (drink, drugs, sirens) to a vague land of noble love (title is Aphrodite backwards). The main guide represents the result of a future controlled evolution: a being whose entire body is a sensory receptor. R: *Ar* 16: 855-57.

Mitchell, W[illis]. *The Inhabitants of Mars; Their Manners and Advancement in Civilization and Their Opinion of Us*. Malden, Mass.: C. E. Spofford.

(P) Mitchell, an inventor-evangelist, narrates the observations of Ego, who travels to Mars in hyponotic trances. Predigested foods have improved the race, all homes are electrified, and marriage is regulated by physical, mental, and moral exams. The last half of the book attacks religious theories based on poor translations of the Bible.

Smith, Titus K[eipler]. *Altruria*. New York: Altruria. (Arno reprint, 1971.)

Loose narrative of a Spartan community in Iowa based on Christian "voluntary co-operation," which will eventually dominate America. People live in prefabricated steel and terra-cotta homes and commute from the city to work in the country.

Walker, John Brisben [Sir Robert Harton]. *A Brief History of Altruria. The Cosmopolitan*, November 1895–March 1896.

An English explorer finds Howells's utopia and is told the story of a beneficent iron mine owner who financed a co-op experiment that caused the downfall of competition and the rise of a co-op system modeled on Christian love and the comradeship of private clubs.

Wheeler, David H[ilton]. *Our Industrial Utopia and Its Unhappy Citizens.* Chicago: A. C. McClurg.

(NF) Series of essays maintains that late nineteenth-century America is utopia; people fail to see this because they lack "character" and desire "superfluities." Poverty exists, but it is either character building or a just punishment for laziness. R: *LW* 27: 199.

1896

Blair, Thomas Stewart. *Human Progress: What Can Man Do to Further It?* New York: W. R. Jenkins.

(NF,P) Long philosophical-economic treatise "proves" that the "Want-Principle" ("satisfied wants" generate "elevated wants") is the key to an ideal future. "Proves" that wants can best be satisfied by developing a "Concrete Science of Progress" that will reveal to the public the common wants of capital and labor, and "prove" that labor should dominate America.

Burnham, Elcy. *Modern Fairyland.* Boston: Arena.

(P) Children's story about a princess who introduces clothes, useful work, and technology to the fairies. Result: Fairyland becomes an ideal, modern Fairyland. (For more on children's literature and utopianism see Baum, [1900].)

Chambers, [James] Julius. *"In Sargasso." Missing. A Romance.* New York, London: Transatlantic.

(P,A) A silly adventure-love story about a captain whose ship is hijacked to a nation of ship dwellers in the Sargasso Sea. Near the end the narrative turns into a satire on feminism: a movement to liberate women and create a better society fails. Consequently the leader concludes that she would rather have the narrator (a male) think for her.

Cowan, James. *Daybreak; A Romance of an Old World.* New York: George H. Richmond. (Arno reprint, 1971.)

Vague fantasy describes how "a radical change in [individual] character," which accompanied a rebirth of Christian brotherhood, led to a utopia in which property is neither private nor public—people simply use things temporarily. Also, the invention of the airplane has caused wars to cease. R: *LW* 27: 366.

[Emmens, Stephen Henry.] *The Sixteenth Amendment.* New York: G. W. Dillingham.

Detailed proposal for the elimination of poverty by establishing racially segregated, Nationalistic "Districts" run by the Legion of Labor (an industrial army). The Districts will peacefully co-exist with private industry as a "safety-valve" for unemployment. Emmens promises a sequel, *In District No. 1;* evidently it was never published.

Giles, Fayette Stratton. *The Industrial Army.* New York: Baker & Taylor.

(NF) Series of essays describes a practical application and modification of Bellamy's Industrial Army: a gigantic profit-sharing enterprise requiring only five years of service.

Lockwood, Ingersoll.—*1900—or, The Last President.* New York: American News.

(A) Narrates the disastrous results of Bryan's election and the implementation of a Populist utopia: inflation, rising taxes, mob rule, depression, and "rampant paternalism." Praises Northern Republicans; vilifies Southerners and Westerners. See also John Lockwood's *Hi-Li, The Moon Man; or, Free-Silver in America* (1896).

[McCoy, Dr. John.] *A Prophetic Romance, Mars to Earth.* Boston: Arena.

Reverses the usual Martian formula by having a Martian visit an American utopia: a semi-Populist republic guided initially by women reformers. A woman president rules over an extended, consolidated America where all political candidates must attend "statecraft" schools.

Man or Dollar, Which? A Novel. Chicago: Charles H. Kerr.

A backward glance by a government historian in 1983 surveys American history from 1861 to 1976. A gradual evolution from oppressive capitalism to socialism, guided by the Golden Rule, was achieved by a universal strike, the efforts of a pro-labor millionnaire, fiat money, and government ownership legislation. The novel ends happily: the historian's lover is permitted to marry him because an operation removing excess ribs has enabled her to expand her chest measurement enough to pass the physical requirements for marriage!

Phelps, Corwin. *An Ideal Republic or Way Out of the Fog.* Chicago: W. L. Raynolds.

An American miner discovers a gold mine. This enables him to triumph over a conspiring group of English aristocrats and Jewish bankers and to establish an African colony. The currency is the greenback and all companies valued over $100,000 are government controlled. R: *Ar* 16: 514-15.

Stump, D. L. *From World to World. A Novel.* Asbury, Mo.: World to World.

Describes a nation without money or private property where the entire population lives in cities and half the population commutes daily to work on the public farms surrounding each city. Stump promises a sequel, *A Romance of Two Planets*; evidently it was never published.

1897

Adams, F[rederick] U[pham]. *President John Smith.* Chicago: Charles H. Kerr. (Arno reprint, 1971.)

Mixture of real and fictional history describes how a Boston judge, turned Nationalist, becomes president. He supports a new constitution that insures the "right to work," by creating a government trust, and guarantees "majority rule," by instituting recall, initiative, etc. The Senate is eliminated. R: *NT* 1: 409. See also Adams's "From John Smith's Standpoint," *NT* 1: 61.

Bellamy, Edward. *Equality.* New York: Appleton.

Bellamy answers his critics with a dry, detailed forecast about the transition to Nationalism: after the people fully understood the flaws of competition, Nationalist candidates were elected and the government organized trusts that crushed all competitors. The whole transition was accompanied by a profound religious awakening that prepared Americans for the new era. R: *Ar* 18: 517-34; *Atl* 82: 253-56; *LW* 28: 251-52.

[Caryl, Charles W.] *New Era.* Denver: New Era Union. (Arno reprint, 1971.)

Caryl, a Colorado businessman-miner, utilizes a stilted, autobiographical play form (cast includes: Bellamy, Tolstoy, and Jay Gould) to deliver a personal plea for the establishment of a co-op, union city near Denver. Comes complete with elaborate illustrations of a rigidly zoned, hierarchical city (privates to generals) and the announcement of several contests, e.g., in 150 words or less, what is the "most important" part of the book? R: *NT* 2: xv-xvi.

Colburn, Frona Eunice Wait. *Yermah the Dorado*. San Francisco: William Doxey.
(P) Mythic tale of "Pre-historic America" describes the trials of "the Ideal Man of all time": a blue-eyed, blond-haired, pure "Aryan" who journeys from Atlantis to an Atlantian colony in California (aqueducts, public hospitals, etc.) during the waning years of his race when an earthquake drives the Aryans from America.

Flower, Benjamin O[range]. *Equality and Brotherhood, the Dreams of the Ancient World, Become the Realities of Today.* . . . Boston: Arena.
(NF) Short essay eulogizes Bellamy's *Equality* as an accurate denunciation of the nineteenth century and a useful guide to the twentieth-century commonwealth foreshadowed by present conditions. Similar to "The Latest Social Vision," *Ar* 18: 517-34.

Galloway, James M. [Anon Moore]. *John Harvey: A Tale of the Twentieth Century*. Chicago: Charles H. Kerr.
An English aristocrat narrates the history of a colonization movement begun by a mineralogist who discovers a gold mine and two miracle metals. He uses his riches to form a secret brotherhood and to establish the Nationality Confederation in the Midwest and Southwest. After his death, the Confederation peacefully spreads over America. The hero's disciples honor him with elaborate oaths and rituals. R: *NT* 1: 293-95.

Harris, George. *Inequality and Progress*. Boston and New York: Houghton Mifflin. (c. 1897; published 1899.)
(NF,A) Series of essays marred by Harris's disregard of poverty and his persistent use of a strawman: the assumption that Bellamy and other utopian reformers wanted absolute economic, social, physical, and mental equality. Nevertheless, he realized that higher standards of living increased the variety of types of people rather than producing an upward leveling.

Morris, Henry O. *Waiting for the Signal. A Novel*. Chicago: Schulte.
(P) Muckraking history of actual and fictional misdeeds by the wealthy. The response to these acts is a relatively peaceful overthrow of the government by a secret organization, complete with "mystic" signals. A Populist constitution is written. R: *LW* 29: 370.

Orpen, Mrs. Adel (Elizabeth Richards). *Perfection City*. New York: Appleton.
(A) Sympathetic narrative of the failure of a communistic community on the Kansas prairie plagued by the physical environment and, more importantly, by the flaws of human nature, especially eccentricity (an obnoxious man-hating neighbor) and jealousy (a love triangle involving the founder). R: *LW* 28: 278-80.

Sheldon, Charles M[onroe]. *In His Steps. "What Would Jesus Do?"* Chicago: Advance. (First published in *The Advance* in 1896).
(P) Extremely popular story of a small town where an "awakened" minister shows that fundamental change can only occur when individuals voluntarily convert to a new standard of behavior (Christ) and faithfully practice this standard in everyday life. R: *LW* 29: 172.

Windsor, William. *Loma; A Citizen of Venus*. St. Paul, Minn.: Windsor & Lewis.
Long narrative based on a cosmic germ theory of evolution. A Venusian comes to Earth to educate the male fetus of an unwed mother so that the fetus will become the apostle of Venus's ideal culture. On Venus clothes are considered ugly and

unsanitary, all human faculties are developed and "balanced," and social status is determined by a network of interpersonal relations among strangers, acquaintances, associates, brothers and sisters, lovers, and consorts—the more of the latter three, the higher the status. The visitor also reveals that Christ's ascension was accomplished by Venusian astronauts.

1898

Albertson, Ralph. *The Social Incarnation; Studies in the Faith of Practice.* Commonwealth, Ga.: Christian Commonwealth.
    (NF) A collection of essays originally published in two social-gospel magazines. Albertson advocates "applied" Christianity: common property, self-sacrifice, and "the Law of Love." The last essay outlines the aims of a Christian community in Georgia, and the third attacks isolated utopian communities that limit membership or strive only for material rewards. Rose suggests that Albertson's unpublished novel, *The Passion that Left the Ground,* is also utopian.
Athey, Henry and A. H[erbert] Bowers. *With Gyves of Gold. A Novel.* New York: G. W. Dillingham.
    In a trance a young man travels to a spiritually and materially "regenerated" planet where a reform group, led by a philanthropist, built a model city and supported companies injured by corrupt trusts. The result was a heaven of free competition and religious piety.
Bellamy, Edward. *The Blindman's World and Other Stories.* Boston and New York: Houghton Mifflin.
    In the title story the narrator visits Mars in a dream. There is no uncertainty or chance on Mars because people can foresee the future. "With Eyes Shut" details the numerous changes caused by the sound revolution of the future (radio, phonograph, tape recorders, dictaphones). "To Whom This May Come" offers a glimpse of an island of mind readers. The ability to "read" evil thoughts has abolished crime and guilt, and everyone has the satisfaction of being "understood" immediately. R: *LW* 29: 434. For Bellamy's other short works including "Women in the Year 2000" and "Christmas in the Year 2000" see Bowman's excellent bibliography appended to *The Year 2000.*
[Child, William Stanley.] *The Legal Revolution of 1902.* Chicago: Charles H. Kerr. (Often attributed to Bert J. Wellman. Arno reprint, 1971.)
    Narrates the creation of a new majority-rule constitution that legalizes the confiscation of all fortunes over half a million dollars. After a war provoked by English bankers, the government establishes public trusts and farms. Everyone prospers except for small farmers and middlemen, the "wasteful relics" of competition.
Clarke, F. H. [Zebina Forbush]. *The Co-opolitan; a Story of the Co-operative Commonwealth of Idaho.* Chicago: Charles H. Kerr.
    History of the success of an imaginary Nationalistic community, which inspires the establishment of similar communities. Eventually the idealists control Idaho and several Western states. A utopian novel attracts worldwide attention to the colonies. R: *Ar* 21: 681.
Craig, Alexander. *Ionia; Land of Wise Men and Fair Women.* Chicago: E. A. Weeks. (Arno reprint, 1971.)
    A young English philanthropist visits a hidden country in the Himalayas where a

race descended from the Greeks and the Danes have solved humanity's problems by practicing principles proclaimed by a warrior-king long ago: common land, limited inheritance, and eugenics with a vengeance (Jews and the slightly deformed cannot marry and all criminals are either sterilized or executed).

Davenport, Benjamin Rush. *Anglo-Saxons, Onward! A Romance of the Future.* Cleveland: Hubbell.

(P) Deplores the "[e]ffeminating inaction" of nineteenth-century America by describing a virile twentieth-century America. "Petty" disputes about the economy and poverty are forgotten as Americans unite in a "New Crusade" to liberate Palestine, to crush Russia, and to preserve and spread "the Civilization, Commerce and Christianity" of "the Anglo-Saxons of the universe."

Farnell, George. *Rev. Josiah Hilton, the Apostle of the New Age.* Providence, R. I.: Journal of Commerce.

(P) During a series of boring discussions, a conservative Reverend is converted to a Nationalistic view of society and dedicates his life to educating the masses about the benefits of government trusts, which pay their employees in "labor notes" based on "labor performed."

Frederic, Harold. *Gloria Mundi. A Novel.* Chicago and New York: Herbert S. Stone.

(P) Analyzes the responsibilities of and psychological reactions to receiving title and inheritance suddenly. Includes descriptions of a Jewish-British aristocrat's futile attempt to create an exemplary medieval village that revives the stable interpersonal relationships of feudalism.

North, Franklin H. *The Awakening of Noahville.* New York: New York.

(A) A humorous satire recounts the exploits of two Yankees in a sleepy medieval country where they introduce nineteenth-century technology. At first the standard of living improves and class lines weaken; but eventually a new moneyed class establishes trusts, aliens and laborers agitate, and a gigantic tunnel project miscarries flooding the entire country. (See Roemer, Kenneth M. "The Yankee(s) in Noahville." *American Literature* 45: 434-37.)

Rehm, Warren S. [Omen Nemo]. *The Practical City. A Future City Romance, or, A Study in Environment.* Lancaster, Pa.: Lancaster County Magazine.

Describes a totally planned community supervised by three councilmen. Specialized schools dominate the town: e.g., "sanitary sciences," "food preparation," "landscaping," "sexual science."

[Reynolds, Walter Doty]. *Mr. Jonnemacher's Machine. The Port to which we Drifted.* Philadelphia: Knickerbocker Book.

Traces the history of America from the 1870s to 2016. Focuses on 1997-1998 in Philadelphia: after generations of political corruption and the misuse of technological innovations, over two-thirds of the workers are unemployed. The invention of a gigantic machine, which converts raw wool into finished products thus replacing thousands of workers, touches off a revolution accompanied by a flood of "aerial liquid," a substance similar to Kurt Vonnegut, Jr.'s deadly ice IX. After the revolution and flood, a benign socialistic form of government is established and the use of technology is regulated so as to raise everyone's standard of living without the threat of technological unemployment. Contains crude satiric portraits: for example, Jonnemacher is Wanamaker, Theo. Rosewet is Roosevelt, and William Stunning Tryon is Bryan.

The Rise and Fall of the United States. A Thin Leaf from History, A.D. 2060. New York: Neeley, Popular Library.

(A) [Listed in Pratter; not in Wright or L of C.] See also *The Fall of the Great Republic* (1885).

Sanders, George A. *Reality: or Law and Order vs. Anarchy and Socialism, A Reply to Edward Bellamy's Looking Backward and Equality.* Cleveland: Burrows Brothers.

(NF, A) Long series of essays criticizes Bellamy by cataloguing Divine Laws, e.g., inequality, self-maintenance, survival of the fittest. Statistically "proves" that farmers and laborers are prosperous and criticizes Bellamy for assuming that material necessities, instead of noble ideas, motivate progress.

Sullivan, J[ames] W[illiam]. "A Modern Co-operative Colony" in *So the World Goes.* Chicago: Charles H. Kerr. Pp. 213-33.

A visit to a commuter's utopia established by a clerk who wanted the city's "high pay" and the country's low prices. He started a joint stock company, bought land near New York City, built an inclined gravity railroad, and insured low prices by requiring that all professions and trades conduct business by charging annual, average fees.

Waterloo, Stanley. *Armageddon; A Tale of Love, War, and Invention.* Chicago and New York: Rand, McNally.

(P) Mostly a science-fiction, war story about a global confrontation between an "Anglo-Saxon" alliance and the Germans, Slavs, and Latins. The war unifies Americans, vanquishing racial and ethnic diversity; a Nicaraguan canal promises prosperity for America and the end of famine in the world; and the invention of a dirigible bomber by an American insures an Anglo-Saxon victory and an end to all wars.

1899

Beale, Charles Willing. *The Secret of the Earth.* London and New York: F. Tennyson Neely.

(P) Adventure narrative based on Symmes's theory about temperate regions inside the Earth. An airship carries two brothers beneath the North Pole to the original Garden of Eden. The soil is laced with precious metals, and it is so fertile that no "work" is necessary: it is a "world of dreams, of poetry, rest, beauty and contentment."

Bird, Arthur. *Looking Forward: A Dream of the United States of the Americas in 1999.* Utica, N.Y.: L. C. Childs & Son. (Arno reprint, 1971).

A white-man's-burden utopia. Rambling account of an America that includes all the Western Hemisphere while England lords over Africa and India. Airplanes have made total war so terrifying that no country dares to start a war, and the utopians are surrounded by numerous mechanical gadgets.

Bond, Daniel. *Uncle Sam in Business.* Chicago: Charles H. Kerr.

Letters from a twentieth-century American to an Englishman explain how America solved her economic problems and elevated the people's morals by establishing huge government "exchanges" where federal certificates were given in return for deposits of goods, services, and currency. R: *Ar* 21: iii.

Fishbough, William. *The End of the Ages; with Forecasts of the approaching Political, Social and Religious Reconstruction of America and the World.* New York: Continental. (Rooney lists an 1898 edition.)

(NF) An elaborate mathematical theory of historical cycles "proves" that the late nineteenth century will witness the end of the "old-world" cycle and the birth of a new epoch. American Anglo-Saxons will lead the world by establishing a government based on seven "organic" interests ("raw materials" to "spiritual") represented by seven guilds.

Franklin, A[braham] B[enjamin]. *The Light of Reason, Showing the First Step the Nation Should Take toward a Social Order Based on Justice.* Chicago: Charles H. Kerr.

(P) A wealthy youth writes a treatise advocating nationalization of land and natural monopolies combined with social experiments in the Spanish-American War territories. The book and hard times inspire a movement that transforms America. R: *Ar* 21: iii.

Griggs, Sutton E. *Imperium in Imperio: A Study of the Negro Race Problem: A Novel.* Cincinnati: Editor. (Arno reprint, 1969; Introd., Hugh M. Gloster.)

(P) Written by a black Baptist minister. Fictional biographies of two black leaders who help to organize a secret society guided by visions of freedom and a perfect government. The society is torn by a disagreement between two factions: one advocates peaceful coexistence (a separate black state, Texas); the other advocates revolution. The revolutionaries triumph, and the novel ends with a warning to white America.

Mendes, H[enry] Pereira. *Looking Ahead. Twentieth Century Happenings.* London: F. Tennyson Neely. (Arno reprint, 1971.)

Confusing history predicts wars, an Anglo-Saxon confederation (which keeps the peace), the writing of a "perfect document" (which includes the delegation of important powers to a Board of Pastors who evaluate school and employment standards), and the establishment of a Jewish State (which will make Palestine the arbitration and cultural center of the world). R: *LW* 30: 343.

Merrill, Albert Adams. *The Great Awakening; The Story of the Twenty-Second Century.* Boston: George Book.

The example of an African colony advocating equal distribution of money and currency based on national wealth helps to foster revolutions in America and the rest of the world. By 2199 man has adjusted to these changes, and private planes have eliminated the need for cities.

Michels, Nicholas [Nicolai Mikalowitch]. *The Godhood of Man; His Religious, Political and Economic Development and the Sources of Social Inequality.* Chicago: Author.

(P) Vague discursive history of Mars told by a Martian to a priest. Describes the evil effects of the priesthood and a personal concept of God. Martians became "gods" when priests were abolished, land and monopolies were state owned, and scientific selection and birth control improved the race.

1900

Baum, [Lyman] Frank. *The Wonderful Wizard of Oz.* Chicago: G. M. Hill.

(P) Oz can be interpreted as a fanciful American pastoral utopia. (See

Wagenknecht, Edward. *Utopia Americana*. Seattle: University of Washington Bookstore, 1929; Erisman, Fred. "L. Frank Baum and the Progressive Dilemma." *American Quarterly* 20:616-23; Sackett, S. J. "The Utopia of Oz." *Georgia Review* 14: 275-91; Indick, Ben. "Utopia, Allegory and Nightmare." *Baum Bugle* 18: 14-19.)

Bayne, Charles J[oseph]. *The Fall of Utopia*. Boston: Eastern.

(A) Incoherent narrative includes an old utopian's description of the decay of Thomas More's Utopia because of its inherent impracticality, alien immigration, jealousy, and an obsessive love of fictional tales.

[Caswell, Edward A.] *Toil and Self*. Chicago: Rand, McNally.

(A) In 2400 A.D. a Yale professor delivers a series of lectures that trace the failure of every utopian movement until "selfishness" was accepted and strict birth control was achieved by scientifically favoring the birth of males.

Edson, Milan C. *Solaris Farm: A Story of the Twentieth Century*. Washington, D.C.: Author. (Arno reprint, 1971.)

An engineer-agriculturist and an heiress establish a co-op farm community. It ennobles rural life and farming and inspires similar co-ops throughout America. Novel features of the co-op are: human stirpiculture, nursery schools that develop all the senses, elaborate conservation projects, and the automobile, not the railroad, as the main form of transportation.

Grigsby, Alcanoan O. [Jack Adams]. *Nequa; or, The Problem of the Ages*. Topeka, Kans.: Equity.

Long shipwreck-love story; narrates the discovery of a land beneath the North Pole where a consumers' movement, a women's reform movement, labor colonies, improved schools, and a religious revival hastened a peaceful revolution to a technological utopia of communal homes. The future character of fetuses is "predisposed" by pregnant mothers who live in controlled environments during pregnancy.

Lubin, David. *Let There Be Light; The Story of a Workingmen's Club, . . . Its Plan for the Amelioration of Existing Evils*. New York: G. P. Putnam's Sons.

(P) A series of laborers' debates led by Ezra, a Jewish worker. Concludes that America's salvation depends upon the union of the wealthy and the workers. This will lead to collectivism and racial harmony. The new era will be guided by a scientific religion developed by Ezra: God is worshipped by studying humanity and Nature.

Mason, Caroline A[twater]. *A Woman of Yesterday*. New York: Doubleday, Page.

(A) Book III describes the establishment of a stern Christian community dominated by an evangelical reformer. Isolation, stark living standards, jealousy, and the leader's selfish dedication to the cause precipitate failure. R: *Nation* 71: 410.

Myers, Cortland. *Would Christ Belong to a Labor Union? or, Henry Fielding's Dream*. New York: Street & Smith. (Republished as *Henry Fielding's Dream*.)

(P) Other "If Christ Came" tracts mentioned by Rose include Edward Everett Hale's *If Jesus Came to Boston* (1895), A. J. Gordon's *How Christ Came to Church* (1895), and Mrs. I. D. Alden's *Yesterday Framed in Today* (1899).

Newcomb, Simon. *His Wisdom the Defender*. New York and London: Harper & Brothers.

(P) A Harvard professor of molecular physics develops antigravity air ships ("motes") that enable him to dictate a "Golden Age" of world peace. In 1946 his Proclamation establishes his world government, which allows countries to determine their form of government but bans armies and navies.

Peck, Bradford. *The World a Department Store: A Story of Life Under a Coöperative System*. Lewiston, Me.: Bradford Peck. (Arno reprint, 1971.)
Describes a businessman's utopia based on efficient distribution by co-op department stores—a "practical" application of Christianity. Peck actually tried this experiment. (See Davies, Wallace E. "A Collectivist Experiment Down East. . . ." *New England Quarterly* 20: 471-91.)

Persinger, Clark Edmund. *Letters from New America; or, An Attempt at Practical Socialism*. Chicago: Charles H. Kerr.
A constitutional convention and government's entry into industry pave the way to socialism. Cities must be approved by federal architects and mothers receive stipends for raising every child up to three children.

Wilson, [John] Grosvenor. *The Monarch of Millions; or the Rise and Fall of the American Empire*. New York, Chicago, and London: Neely.
(A) Humorous satire of money power and the typical utopian hero. In 1950 America is ruled by a multimillionaire and the national symbol is a cute, golden pig. An earnest Alaskan hunter arouses the public with platitude-ridden speeches; there is a general strike and the Republic is restored.

Wright, W[illiam] H[enry]. *The Great Bread Trust*. New York, London, and Montreal: Abbey Press.
(A) Short, anti-utopian novel predicts the end result of money power protected by the Constitution: a secret group of five billionaires corner the grain market. America collapses and the leader of the group is crowned King of America.

2. Selected Short Title List of Intentional Omissions, 1888-1900
(See also Rose, Shurter, and the comprehensive listings in Rooney.)
i. Foreign Works Sometimes Listed as American
England
    Berens, Lewis Henry and Ignatius Singer. *The Story of My Dictatorship* (1894).
    Besant, Walter. *The Inner House* (1888).
    [Coste, Frank.] *Towards Utopia* (1894).
    Reynolds, Thomas. *Prefaces and Notes* (1890).
    Shipley, Mrs. Marie A. *The True Author of Looking Backward* (1890).
    Tracy, Louis. *An American Emperor* (1897).

France
    [Grousset, Paschal.] *The Crystal City* (tr. L. A. Smith, 1896).

Germany and Austria
    Herizka, Theodore. *Freeland* (tr. Arthur Ransom, 1891).
    Müller, Ernst. *My Afterdream* (tr., 1900).
    Richter, Eugen. *Pictures of the Future* (tr. Amos Nungesser, 1894).
    Wilbrant, Conrad. *Mr. East's Experiences* (tr. Mary J. Safford, 1891).

New Zealand
    Looking Upwards (1890).
ii. Previously Listed, Little Utopian Content
    Ballou, William H. *Bachelor Girl* (1890).
    Barnes, Willis, *Dame Fortune Smiled* (1896).
    Bouton, J. B. *The Enchanted* (1891).

Bouvé, Edward T. *Centuries Apart* (1894).
[Michels, Nicholas.] *Numa's Vision* (1899).
Millspaugh, C. S. *Plantae Utowanae* (1900). Listed by Normano as *Utowana Yacht.*
Williams, F. H. *Âtman* (1891).

C. Selected Secondary Sources

Bailey, J. O. "To the Islands of the Blest: Scientific Fiction, 1871-1894," in *Pilgrims Through Space and Time: Trends and Patterns in Scientific and Utopian Fiction.* New York: Argus Books, 1947. Pp. 51-78.
Claims that utopian and anti-utopian writing dominated science fiction during this period.

Bleich, David. "Utopia: The Psychology of a Cultural Fantasy." Ph. D. dissertation, New York University, 1968.
Focuses on American and English utopian literature, 1870-1914. Defines the social and political conditions most conducive to utopian speculation; analyzes the "childhoods, adolescences, and mature identities" of leading utopian authors including Bellamy; and surveys the "utopian and artistic" literature of the period. [DA: 30: 4935-A.]

Boggs, W. Arthur. "Looking Backward at the Utopian Novel, 1888-1900." *Bulletin of the New York Public Library* 64: 329-36.
Brief survey emphasizes the influence of Bellamy on the genre and delineates six types of utopian novels: the pro- or anti-Bellamy novel, the industrial novel, the religious novel, the fantastic romance, the proletarian novel, and the quasi-fictional economic novel.

Burt, Donald C. "Utopia and the Agrarian Tradition in America, 1865-1900." Ph.D. dissertation, University of New Mexico, 1973.
Presents the utopian authors as heirs of a pre-Civil War agrarian tradition who realized that they had to compromise between their nostalgia for the past and the terrors and rewards of the urbanized, industrialized future. For example Burt examines attitudes about co-operative farms, the garden city, publically owned land, humane technological advances, centralized governments, and equality.

Dupont, V. *L'Utopie et le Roman Utopique dans la Littérature Anglaise.* Cahors: A. Coueslant, 1941. (Also Paris: Librairie M. Didier, 1941. Originally a thesis for the University of Lyon.)
"Appendice II" offers an interesting analysis of Julian West's psychological traumas. (See also John L. Thomas's "Introduction" to the Belknap Press edition of *Looking Backward* [1967] and Tom H. Towers's "The Insomnia of Julian West," *American Literature* 47: 52-63.) "Appendice III" is a book-by-book survey (1836-1900) with specific sections on Howells and on responses to Bellamy; it concludes with a discussion of *Caesar's Column.*

Eddy, H. H. "The Utopian Element in American Literature." (See Russell.) Flory, Claude R. *Economic Criticism in American Fiction, 1792-1900.* Philadelphia: University of Pennsylvania Press, 1936.
Ch. II, ii, concludes a book-by-book survey by listing four utopian approaches: change human nature, adopt national communism, modify socialism (co-ops), and preserve competition. Ch. III, iii, concludes that the utopian works have little

210 The Obsolete Necessity

literary merit but that they encouraged literary realism by focusing on contemporary problems.

Forbes, Allyn B. "The Literary Quest for Utopia, 1880-1900." *Social Forces* 6: 179-89.

Offers a brief description of several utopian works and maintains that they were a reaction to industrialization, urbanization, and the closing of the frontier.

Fuson, Ben. "Three Kansas Utopian Novels of 1890." *Extrapolation* 12: 7-20. (See also *Kansas Quarterly* 5: 63-77.)

Mostly plot summaries of Cole's *Auroraphone*, Dail's *Willmoth*, and Fuller's *A.D. 2000*.

Ketterer, David. "Utopian Fantasy as Millennial Motive and Science-Fiction Motif," in *New Worlds for Old; The Apocalyptic Imagination, Science Fiction, and American Literature*. Bloomington & London: Indiana University Press, 1974. Pp. 96-122. (First published in *Studies in the Literary Imagination* 6: 105-20, along with several other interesting articles on utopian fiction.)

Mostly a standard interpretation of *Looking Backward*, though Ketterer does make several interesting comments about the tensions between Bellamy's explicit arguments and the implications of his metaphors.

Lewis, Arthur Orcutt, Jr. "Introductions" to the Arno Press "Utopian Literature" collection. New York: Arno Press, 1971.

Mostly brief biographical notes and summaries of the major proposals in specific books, e.g., see Satterlee's *Looking Backward and What I Saw*. Not all of the 41 Arno reprints have introductions. Lewis is also working on a full-length study, *The Fall of Utopia*.

Lokke, Virgil L. "The American Utopian Anti-Novel," in *Frontiers of American Culture*, eds. Ray B. Browne, et al. [Lafayette, Ind.]: Purdue University Studies, 1968. Pp. 123-53.

Emphasizes the nonliterary, propagandistic character of late nineteenth-century utopian fiction. Also establishes the "oral conventions of the pulpit, the lecture platform, and the stage" as important influences on American utopian literature (141).

Martin, Jay. "Paradises (To Be) Regained," in *Harvests of Change. American Literature, 1865-1914*. Englewood Cliffs, N.J.: Prentice-Hall, 1967. Pp. 202-39.

Basing his comments on the works discussed by Parrington, Jr., Martin characterizes post-Civil War utopian contributions as a reaction to rapid change and as an attempt to fill the resulting values vacuum. Martin and Alexander Saxton ("*Caesar's Column*: The Dialogue of Utopia and Catastrophe," *American Quarterly* 19, Pt. 2: 224-38) are really the only two scholars who have emphasized the blend of catastrophism and utopianism found in utopian fiction, although Frederic C. Jaher's study of cataclysmic thought, 1885-1918, obviously implies such a mixture. See *Doubters and Dissenters* (1964).

Negley, Glenn. "Modern Utopias, 1850-1950," in *The Quest for Utopia; An Anthology of Imaginary Societies*, ed. Glenn Negley and J. Max Patrick. New York: Henry Schuman, 1952. Pp. 12-19.

Emphasizes the differences between early and modern utopias: economic rather than religious, more emphasis on centralization, and the realization that national, institutional reforms must replace isolated experiments.

Normano, J. F. "Social Utopias in American Literature." *International Review for Social History* 3: 286-300.

Characterizes American utopian works as valuable, untouched sources of social attitudes. Compared to classical and European utopian contributions, however, they are dull, "wasteland[s]" obsessed with practicality.

Nydahl, Joel Mellin. "Utopian Americana: Early American Utopian Fiction, 1790-1864." Ph.D. dissertation, University of Michigan, 1974.

Focuses on early utopian writings, but the contrasts and similarities discussed between early and late nineteenth-century works—for example, the decline in satire and the continuation of a forward-backward-looking stance—help to define the nature of the later utopian speculation.

Parrington, Vernon Louis. "The Quest of Utopia," in *Main Currents of American Thought,* 3 vols. New York: Harcourt, Brace, 1930, 3: 301-15.

Primarily a pro-Bellamy discussion of the merits of economic democracy as it was presented in the late nineteenth-century utopian works.

Parrington, Vernon Louis, Jr. *American Dreams: A Study of American Utopias.* Providence: Brown University Press, 1947. (Originally written as a dissertation [1942]; a new edition with a postscript was published in 1964 [New York: Russell & Russell].)

Besides Ransom's published dissertation, this is still the only full-length, published study of American literary utopias. Parrington gives a chronological, book-by-book survey from 1689 through 1888, then continues to 1946 (1963 in the new edition) with book-by-book subject and thematic discussions, e.g., "The Utopia of Escape," "Mars and Utopia," "Utopia Now."

Pfaelzer, Jean. "Utopian Fiction in America 1880-1900: The Impact of Political Theory on Literary Forms." Ph.D. dissertation, University College, University of London [excepted acceptance date: June 1975].

I was not able to see a copy of this study before submitting my book for publication. A section of it was, however, delivered at the Eighty-ninth Annual Meeting of the Modern Language Association. New York, December 1974. In this paper Ms. Pfaelzer depicts the utopian fiction as being shaped by middle-class reactions to the struggles of laborers, farmers, and women. She describes the literary form as an "apologue" divided into "manifestoes" (interpretations of contemporary and improved institutions) and "fables" (the action part of the narrative). This theory offers provocative hints about the mixtures of realism and romanticism in utopian fiction. Ms. Pfaelzer has an article on women in utopian fiction forthcoming in the *Journal of Women's Studies;* she is also working on several other articles.

Pratter, Frederick Earl. "The Uses of Utopia: An Analysis of American Speculative Fiction 1880-1960." Ph.D. dissertation, University of Iowa, 1973.

Utilizing the concept of formula fiction, specifically speculative fiction (narratives involving imaginary or displaced settings), Pratter compares novels written from 1880-1909 to modern social science fiction, 1947-1960. He concludes that in both periods the primary function of speculative fiction was to lessen anxieties about the future. Nevertheless, the earlier novels focused more on economic insecurities, while the modern works emphasized psychological problems and the threat of global holocaust. Though Pratter's contrasts sometimes obscure the psychological analyses and the pessimism of the earlier works, his comparative approach is useful and his views on the psychological functions of utopian fiction are provocative (70-78).

Quissell, Barbara C. "The Sentimental and Utopian Novels of Nineteenth Century America: Romance and Social Issues." Ph.D. dissertation, University of Utah, 1973.

One of the few literary analyses; focuses mainly on the period 1888–1907 (*Looking Backward–The Iron Heel*). Argues convincingly that the utopian authors utilized the traditions of the popular, sentimental reform novel—a blend of "message, realistic descriptions, and emotional appeals"—to gain acceptance. Includes a perceptive chapter on the use of the "sentimental heroine" and individual chapters on Bellamy, Howells, and London.

Ransom, Ellene. "Utopus Discovers America or Critical Realism in American Utopian Fiction, 1798-1900." Ph.D. dissertation, Vanderbilt University, 1946. (Published by Folcroft Press, Folcroft, Pa., 1970.)

Offers a long, book-by-book description of utopian fiction (40-165) plus historical background and discussion of specific economic and social criticism. Also includes a detailed literary analysis of American utopian works as "missing links" between early nineteenth-century romanticism and late nineteenth- and early twentieth-century realism and muckraking.

Roemer, Kenneth M. "America as Utopia, 1888-1900: New Visions, Old Dreams." Ph.D. dissertation, University of Pennsylvania, 1971.

Composite study utilizing literary, historical, and anthropological methods to analyze attitudes about cultural change and the ideal American culture. After an introduction and a detailed biographical profile of the authors, Pt. II focuses on attitudes about historical change, on whether change should start from within or in virgin territory, and on how to transform the individual. Pt. III treats the utopian visions as projections of entire cultures (e.g., earning a living, religion, the home, sexual relations.) See also articles listed under Harben and North in the bibliography of primary sources.

————. "Eyewitness to Utopia: Illustrations in Utopian Literature, 1888-1900." Paper delivered at the Fifth Biennial National Convention of the American Studies Association, San Antonio, October 1975.

Surveys the sometimes humorous, often revealing, results of the clash between nineteenth-century publishers' inclination for detailed illustrations and the traditionally vague descriptions in utopian literature. Places emphasis on tensions suggested by illustrations of machines, women, cities, and catastrophies (especially the battles in *A Connecticut Yankee*).

————. "The Heavenly City of the Late 19th-Century Utopians." *Journal of the American Studies Association of Texas* 4: 5-17.

The utopian authors offered a wide variety of futuristic cities loaded with technological advances. Still these predictions were basically expressions of a desire for a unity and order not unlike the unity and order of medieval cities.

————. "Sex Roles, Utopia and Change: The Family in Late Nineteenth-Century Utopian Literature." *American Studies* 13: 33-49.

Most utopian authors wanted to abolish the economic functions of the family; some even opposed child rearing and the expression of love in a family context. Nevertheless, almost all changes were justified as returns to traditional roles (wife, mother) or values (spiritual purity).

————. "Utopia and Methodology: Uses of Fiction in American Studies." *Rocky Mountain Social Science Journal* 12: 21-28.

Calls for an integration of statistical surveys, best-seller studies, and the humanist's preference for complex works of art. Most examples are drawn from late nineteenth-century utopian literature.

————. "'Utopia Made Practical': Compulsive Realism." *American Literary Realism* 7: 273-76.

Outlines possible causes for the ambivalent mixtures of realism and romanticism in American utopian fiction. Suggests that this ambivalence should be of interest to literary historians and students of American culture.

Rooney, Charles J., Jr. "Utopian Literature as a Reflection of Social Forces in America, 1865-1917." Ph.D. dissertation, George Washington University, 1968. Comprehensive composite survey of the intellectual sources of American utopian thought (Enlightenment, Christianity, Evolution, Socialism); the specific problems, solutions, and values delineated (quantitative survey); and the various types of utopias (e.g., individualist, legal, socialist).

Russell, Frances Theresa. *Touring Utopia; The Realm of Constructive Humanism.* New York: Dial, 1932.
The "Prospectus" offers one of the most persuasive overviews of utopianism. Ch. X surveys the reactions to Bellamy, especially German responses; mostly well-written plot summaries. In the "Bibliographical Note" Russell mentions a "forthcoming" dissertation, H. H. Eddy's "The Utopian Element in American Literature." Stanford, where Russell taught, has no record of it, and an administrative assistant informed me that it probably was never completed.

Shurter, Robert L. "The Utopian Novel in America, 1865-1900." Ph.D. dissertation, Case Western Reserve University, 1936.
After an examination of nineteenth-century English utopias and pre-Civil War American utopianism, Shurter concludes that late nineteenth-century American utopian concepts were not greatly influenced by either of these sources. Instead they were responses to contemporary social and economic problems and the closing of the frontier. The study includes a fairly detailed discussion of Bellamy and his immediate predecessors, and a chronological book-by-book survey, 1888-1900. See also Walter Taylor's *The Economic Novel in America* [1942 and 1964] and James D. Koerner's "The Triumph of the Dinosaurs." Ph.D. dissertation, University of Washington [St. Louis], 1952.

————. "The Utopian Novel in America, 1888-1900." *South Atlantic Quarterly* 34: 137-44.
See above. Singles out Howells's *A Traveler from Altruria* as the "best" utopian novel; examines its frontier ethics and Howells's celebration of the family as a model for national brotherhood. Concludes by stating that for "a decade the utopian novel was perhaps the most widely read type of literature in America" (143).

Stupple, A. James. "Utopian Humanism in America, 1888-1900." Ph.D. dissertation, Northwestern University, 1971.
Argues convincingly that the utopian authors were not materialists but humanists who were primarily concerned with ideal worlds where each individual could develop fully. Stupple offers provocative theories about Bellamy's Edith Leete and Twain's Hank Morgan, but his tendency to divide authors into opposing camps—supporters and critics of modernization—often obscures complex, ambivalent attitudes.

Thal-Larsen, Margaret. "Political and Economic Ideas in American Utopian Fiction, 1868-1914." Ph.D. dissertation, University of California, Berkeley, 1941.
Mostly a book-by-book survey of economic and government reforms; however, two brief sections discuss the historical perspective (11-30) and attitudes about home, education, religion, and the physical environment (214-23). Concludes that most authors desired either partial or complete socialism achieved by extending the powers of a democratic, centralized government.

NOTES

Chapter 1

1. Ernest Lee Tuveson, *Redeemer Nation* (Chicago: University of Chicago Press, 1968), p. 165.
2. See Michael Kammen, *People of Paradox: An Inquiry Concerning the Origins of American Civilization* (New York: Knopf, 1972).
3. Frank Luther Mott, *Golden Multitudes; The Story of Best Sellers in the United States* (New York: R. R. Bowker, 1960), p. 169; Everett Mac Nair, *Edward Bellamy and the Nationalist Movement 1889 to 1894* (Milwaukee: Fitzgerald, 1957), p. 7. The American Supply Company distributed 25,000 copies of this issue for free.
4. Robert L. Shurter, "The Utopian Novel in America, 1865-1900" (Ph.D. diss., Case Western Reserve University, 1936), 160-61.
5. Hamilton W. Mabie, "The Most Popular Novels in America," *Forum* 16 (December 1893): 508-10.
6. Robert L. Shurter, "Introduction" to Edward Bellamy, *Looking Backward, 2000-1887* (New York: Modern Library, 1951), p. xv.
7. Alice Payne Hackett, *70 Years of Best Sellers, 1895-1965* (New York and London: R. R. Bowker, 1967), p. 12.
8. A. James Stupple, "Utopian Humanism in America, 1888-1900" (Ph.D. diss., Northwestern University, 1971), p. 2.
9. Robert L. Shurter, "The Utopian Novel in America, 1888-1900," *South Atlantic Quarterly* 34 (April 1935): 143.
10. Mac Nair, *Bellamy and the Nationalist Movement,* pp. 148-96, 319.
11. Except for the discussion of periodization, the following is a revised version of Kenneth M. Roemer, "Utopia and Methodology: Uses of Fiction in American Studies," *Rocky Mountain Social Science Journal* 12 (January 1975): 21-28.
12. See "Bibliographies" in the secondary sources listings. Nydahl discovered the early utopian work (1715) after his dissertation was accepted.
13. James D. Hart, *The Popular Book in America; A History of America's*

Literary Taste (Berkeley and Los Angeles: University of California Press. 1961), p. 180.

14. Edward Bellamy, *Looking Backward, 2000-1887* (Cambridge: Belknap Press of Harvard University Press, 1967), p. 144. All quotes from *Looking Backward* will be taken from this edition.

15. Barbara C. Quissell, "The Sentimental and Utopian Novels of Nineteenth Century America: Romance and Social Issues" (Ph.D. diss., University of Utah, 1973); Virgil L. Lokke, "The American Utopian Anti-Novel" in *Frontiers of American Culture,* eds., Ray B. Browne et al. ([Lafayette, Inc.]: Purdue University Studies, 1968), p. 141; Jean Pfaelzer, "Utopian Fiction in America 1888-1900: The Impact of Political Theory on Literary Forms" (paper delivered at the Eighty-ninth Annual Meeting of the Modern Language Association of America, New York, December 27, 1974), p. 3.

16. Quissell, "Sentimental and Utopian Novels," pp. 79-80.

17. "Bi-Millennial Literature," *The Literary World,* 19 July 1890, p. 240. Also in *The Literary World* see the reviews dated 20 June 1891, p. 210; 9 September 1893, p. 293; 17 November 1895, p. 392.

18. Mac Nair, *Bellamy and the Nationalist Movement,* pp. 148-96.

19. See Kenneth M. Roemer, "American Utopian Literature (1888-1900): An Annotated Bibliography," *American Literary Realism* 4 (Summer 1971): 227-54.

20. J. F. Normano, "Social Utopias in American Literature," *International Review for Social History* 3 (1938): 290; and Allyn B. Forbes, "The Literary Quest for Utopia, 1880-1900," *Social Forces* 6 (December 1927): 188.

21. *Statistical Abstracts of the United States* (Washington, D.C.: Bureau of Statistics, 1892). The random sample was drawn from approximately 26,000 authors in W. Stewart Wallace, ed., *A Dictionary of North American Authors Deceased before 1950* (Toronto: Ryerson Press, 1951).

22. Relevant information was available for 111 authors. Geographical locations were based on where the author spent most of his life unless he wrote his book in a different location and the area strongly influenced his thought. For a discussion of the lack of Southern utopian works see Kenneth M. Roemer, "America as Utopia, 1888-1900: New Visions, Old Dreams," (Ph.D. diss., University of Pennsylvania, 1971), pp. 58-59.

23. Jay Martin, *Harvests of Change: American Literature, 1865-1914* (Englewood Cliffs, N.J.: Prentice-Hall, 1967), p. 225.

24. The occupational statistics were based on 99 authors for whom relevant information was available. Only about 17% of the utopian authors classified themselves as novelists or poets.

25. For Thomas see Glenn Negley and J. Max Patrick, eds., *The Quest for Utopia* (New York: Henry Schuman, 1952), p. 82. For Ramsey see Wallace, *Dictionary,* p. 371. For McDougall see "Walt McDougall is Found Dead," *The Evening Star,* 7 March 1938, p. A-2. For Peck see Wallace E. Davies, "A Collectivist Experiment Down East: Bradford Peck and the Cooperative Association of America," *New England Quarterly* 20 (December 1947): 471-91.

26. *Statistical Abstracts,* p. 266; William Miller, "American Historians and the Business Elite," *Journal of Economic History* 9 (November 1949): 207; and Seymour Lipset and Reinhard Bendix, *Social Mobility in Industrial Society* (Berkeley: University of California Press, 1967), p. 126.

27. Admittedly this percentage was based on only 62 authors. But even if *none* of the others went to college, the utopian authors would compare very favorably to the other groups mentioned.
28. *Dictionary of American Biography,* s.v. "Donnelly, Ignatius."
29. Review of *Looking Further Forward* by Richard C. Michaelis, *The Literary World,* 30 August 1890, p. 283; review of *San Salvador* by Mary A. Tinckner, *The Literary World,* 23 April 1892, p. 150.
30. Charles J. Rooney, Jr., "Utopian Literature as a Reflection of Social Forces in America, 1865-1917" (Ph.D. diss., George Washington University, 1968), pp. 53-57.
31. John L. Thomas, "Introduction" to *Looking Backward, 2000-1887,* pp. 1, 20-21. For a general discussion of these problems see Bruce Kuklick, "Myth and Symbol of American Studies," *American Quarterly* 24 (October 1972): 443-47; and R. Gordon Kelly, "Literature and Historical American Culture" (paper delivered at the Twenty-sixth Annual Meeting of the Rocky Mountain Modern Language Association, Tucson, Ariz., October 20, 1972), pp. 6-7.
32. Kelly, "Literature and Historical American Culture," pp. 2-4; Kuklick, "Myth and Symbol," p. 447.

Chapter 2

1. J. O. Bailey, *Pilgrims Through Space and Time: Trends and Patterns in Scientific and Utopian Fiction* (New York: Argus Books, 1947); Frederick Earl Pratter, "The Uses of Utopia: An Analysis of American Speculative Fiction 1880-1960" (Ph.D. diss., University of Iowa, 1973).
2. Ignatius Donnelly, *Caesar's Column,* ed. Walter B. Rideout (Cambridge: Belknap Press of Harvard University Press, 1960), p. 174; Richard C. Michaelis, *Looking Further Forward* (Chicago: Rand, McNally, 1890), p. 33; Edward Bellamy, "Postscript" to *Looking Backward,* p. 314; Edward Bellamy, *Equality* (New York: D. Appleton, 1897), pp. 310-13.
3. Bellamy, "Postscript" to *Looking Backward,* p. 314. See also the relevant bibliographies in Pratter, "Uses of Utopia," pp. 346-61.
4. Garry Wills, review of *Socialism* by Michael Harrington, *New York Times Book Review,* 30 April 1972, p. 1.
5. See titles by Roberts, Wheeler, and Sanders in the annotated bibliography.
6. William Dean Howells, *A Traveler from Altruria* (New York: Harper & Brothers, 1894), p. 270; Bellamy, *Equality,* pp. 321-22, 329.
7. See especially Ellene Ransom, "Utopus Discovers America or Critical Realism in American Utopian Fiction, 1798-1900" (Ph.D. diss., Vanderbilt University, 1946), p. 349.
8. Bellamy, *Equality,* p. 324; Albert A. Merrill, *The Great Awakening* (Boston: George Book Publishing Co., 1899), p. 53; George A. Sanders, *Reality* (Cleveland: Burrows Brothers, 1898), p. 9.
9. Josiah Strong, *The New Era, or, The Coming Kingdom* (New York: Baker & Taylor, 1893), p. v.; John Ransome Bridge as quoted in Thomas, "Introduction" to *Looking Backward,* p. 72.
10. Thomas Stewart Blair, *Human Progress* (New York: W. R. Jenkins, 1896), p.

316. See Thomas S. Kuhn, *The Structure of Scientific Revolutions* (Chicago: Phoenix Books of the University of Chicago Press, 1964).

11. Leon Howard, *Herman Melville; A Biography* (Berkeley and Los Angeles: University of California Press, 1967), p. 125. I am refering to Winthrop's "Model of Christian Charitie."

12. Sanders, *Reality,* pp. 160-61.

13. *Life in the Letters of William Dean Howells,* Vol. 2, ed. Mildred Howells (Garden City, N.Y.: Doubleday, Doran & Co., 1928), p. 242.

14. See Martin, *Harvests of Change,* pp. 202-39 and Alexander Saxton, *"Caesar's Column*: The Dialogue of Utopia and Catastrophe," *American Quarterly* 19, suppl. (Summer 1967): 224-38 for excellent alternatives to the standard interpretations.

15. Samuel Langhorne Clemens, *A Connecticut Yankee in King Arthur's Court,* ed. Hamlin Hill, Facsimile of 1st ed. (San Francisco: Chandler, 1963), p. 242.

16. David Ketterer, *New Worlds for Old; The Apocalyptic Imagination, Science Fiction, and American Literature* (Bloomington, Indiana: Indiana University Press, 1974), pp. 115-17.

17. Bellamy, *Looking Backward,* p. 101; Bellamy, *Equality,* p. 102; Bellamy, "Letter to the People's Party," *The New Nation,* 22 October 1892, p. 645.

18. See Mary S. Weinkauf, "Edenic Motifs in Utopian Fiction," *Extrapolation* 11 (December 1969): 15.

19. The typical examples of volcanic imagery quoted in these two paragraphs were taken from Donnelly, *Caesar's Column,* pp. 62, 70, 254, 296; Michaelis, *Looking Further Forward,* p. 93; [James M. Galloway]. *John Harvey* (Chicago: Charles H. Kerr, 1897), p. 387; Arthur Dudley Vinton, *Looking Further Backward* (Albany: Albany Book, 1890), p. 56; J. W. Roberts, *Looking Within* (New York: A. S. Barnes, 1893), p. 35; Alvarado M. Fuller, *A. D. 2000* (Chicago: Laird & Lee, 1890), pp. 169-98.

20. Martin, *Harvests of Change,* p. 213.

21. Ray Brosseau and Ralph K. Andrist, eds. *Looking Forward* (New York: American Heritage Press, 1970), pp. 92-93.

22. For example, see William Dean Howells, *Letters of an Altrurian Traveller,* in *The Altrurian Romances,* eds. Clara and Rudolf Kirk (Bloomington: Indiana University Press, 1968), p. 257; Thomas Lake Harris, *The New Republic* (Santa Rosa, Calif.: Fountaingrove Press, 1891), p. 18; Roberts, *Looking Within,* p. 234; Merrill, *The Great Awakening,* pp. 215, 308.

23. Another similar image used occasionally was the phoenix. See Merrill, *The Great Awakening,* p. 49; Donnelly, *Caesar's Column,* p. 290.

24. Here I've borrowed Ishmael's phrase from *Moby-Dick.*

25. See Charles S. Sanford, *The Quest for Paradise* (Urbana: University of Illinois Press, 1961), pp. 94-113.

26. Roger B. Salomon, *Twain and the Image of History* (New Haven: Yale University Press, 1961), p. 119.

27. Bellamy, *Looking Backward,* p. 102.

28. Bellamy, *Equality,* p. 323.

29. Ardrey Rene, *The Nationalist,* October 1890, p. 184.

30. Bellamy, *Looking Backward,* p. 123.

31. Harris, *The New Republic,* pp. 31, 59.

32. Ignatius Donnelly, *The Golden Bottle* (New York: D. D. Merrill, 1892), p. 156.

33. Bellamy, *Looking Backward,* p. 281.
34. Bellamy, *Looking Backward,* p. 281, 31; Bellamy, *Equality,* pp. 251-52; Harris, *The New Republic,* p. 5.
35. Richard Gerber, *Utopian Fantasy: A Study of English Utopian Fiction since the End of the Nineteenth Century,* 2nd ed. (New York: McGraw-Hill, 1973), pp. 8-9. McGraw-Hill has given me permission to make this long quote.
36. Merrill, *The Great Awakening,* p. 280.
37. Bellamy, *Looking Backward,* p. 230; [William Simpson], *The Man from Mars* (San Francisco: Bacon, 1891), p. 134; Howells, *Traveler from Altruria,* p. 310; Chauncey Thomas, *The Crystal Button* (Boston: Houghton, Mifflin, 1891), pp. 254-55.
38. Even before the publication of *Looking Backward,* critics of socialism were quick to note this. See especially Anna Bowman Dodd, *The Republic of the Future* (New York: Cassell & Cassell, 1887).
39. Blair, *Human Progress,* p. 168.
40. See Hart, *The Popular Book,* pp. 180-200.
41. Quoted from Joseph Wood Krutch, *The Modern Temper* in Salomon, *Twain and History,* p. 19.
42. See also Kenneth M. Roemer, "The Yankee(s) in Noahville," *American Literature* 45 (November 1973): 434-37.
43. Allen Guttman, "Mark Twain's *Connecticut Yankee*: Affirmation of the Vernacular Tradition?" *New England Quarterly* 33 (June 1960): 235; Hill, "Introduction" to *A Connecticut Yankee,* p. xviii.
44. Twain, *A Connecticut Yankee,* pp. 338, 292, 220, 120.
45. Henry Nash Smith, *Mark Twain's Fable of Progress* (New Brunswick, N.J.: Rutgers University Press, 1964), p. 65.
46. Salomon, *Twain and History,* pp. 105, 103; Smith, *Twain's Fable of Progress,* pp. 36-65. See also Roger B. Salomon, "Time and the Realists" in Cushing Strout, ed., *Intellectual History in America,* 2 vols. (New York: Harper & Row, 1968), 2: 47-59.
47. Elizabeth Hardwick, "Militant Nudes," *The New York Review of Books,* 7 January 1971, p. 3.
48. Saxton, "*Caesar's Column*: The Dialogue of Utopia and Catastrophe," p. 231; Frederic Cople Jaher, *Doubters and Dissenters* (London: Free Press of Glenco, 1964), p. 15.
49. This phrase is borrowed from the title of Buckminster Fuller's book, *Utopia or Oblivion: The Prospects for the Human Race* (New York: Bantam Books, 1969).

Chapter 3

1. As quoted in Arthur E. Morgan, *Nowhere Was Somewhere* (Chapel Hill: University of North Carolina Press, 1946), p. 177.
2. Quoted from B. F. Skinner, *Walden Two* in Robert Plank, "The Geography of Utopia: Psychological Factors Shaping the 'Ideal' Location," *Extrapolation* 6 (May 1965): 40.
3. Gerber, *Utopian Fantasy,* p. 95.
4. [Warren S. Rehm], *The Practical City. A Future City Romance* (Lancaster, Pa.: Lancaster County Magazine, 1898), p. 9.

5. See Salisbury, Mendes, Tinckner, Craig, Beale, Granville, Kinnear, and Frederic in the annotated bibliography. Salisbury and Mendes gave important secondary roles to America; Granville's hero used American industrial techniques in Australia; and Kinnear's American and British crusaders defeat the Antichrist at Armageddon.

6. Howells, *Traveler from Altruria*, p. 281.

7. Gerber, *Utopian Fantasy*, pp. 3-4. See also David Ketterer, *New Worlds for Old* (Garden City: Doubleday, Anchor Books, 1974), p. 101.

8. William Gilpin, *The Cosmopolitan Railway Compacting and Fusing Together All the World's Continents* (San Francisco: History Co., 1890), pp. 167, 230-31, 124.

9. Bellamy, *The New Nation*, 22 October 1892, p. 645.

10. Edward Bellamy, "Principles and Purposes of Nationalism," *The Nationalist*, April 1890, pp. 174-80.

11. *The Nationalist*, October 1889, pp. 204-14.

12. [William Simpson], *The Man from Mars* (San Francisco: Bacon, 1891), p. 73.

13. See Mary S. Weinkauf, "Edenic Motifs in Utopian Fiction," *Extrapolation* 11 (December 1969): 15-22.

14. They did, however, use Edenic imagery in generalities concerning the past and future of all America.

15. See Donald C. Burt, "Utopia and the Agrarian Tradition in America, 1865-1900" (Ph. D. diss., University of New Mexico, 1973).

16. Harold V. Rhodes, *Utopia in American Political Thought* (Tucson: University of Arizona Press, 1967), p. 17. See Gilpin, Astor, Miller, Houston, Lease, and Galloway in the annotated bibliography.

17. *Dictionary of American Biography*, s.v. "Gilpin, William."

18. Gilpin, *The Cosmopolitan Railway*, pp. 293, 172, 121, 122. See also Henry Nash Smith, *Virgin Land* (New York: Vintage Press, 1950), pp. 38-46.

19. The quotes in this paragraph were taken from Mary Elizabeth Lease, *The Problem of Civilization Solved* (Chicago: Laird & Lee, 1895), p. 235; John Jacob Astor, *A Journey to Other Worlds* (New York: D. Appleton, 1894), p. 262. See also Charles Willing Beale, *The Secret of the Earth* (London and New York: F. Tennyson Neely, 1899), pp. 190*ff*.

20. Gilpin, *The Cosmopolitan Railway*, p. iv.

21. [James Galloway], *John Harvey: A Tale of the Twentieth Century* (Chicago: Charles H. Kerr, 1897), pp. 13, 87, 299.

22. Milan C. Edson, *Solaris Farm; A Story of the Twentieth Century* (Washington, D.C.: Author, 1900), pp. 198-211.

23. Davenport, *"Uncle Sam's" Cabins. A Story of American Life Looking Forward a Century* (New York: Mascot, 1895), p. 299.

24. Donnelly, Reynolds, Salisbury, Merrill, Pomeroy, Mendes, Kinnear, and Davenport (*Anglo-Saxons, Onward!*, not *"Uncle Sam's" Cabins*).

25. The quotes in this paragraph were taken from Earnest Fitzpatrick, *The Marshal Duke of Denver* (Chicago: Donohue & Henneberry, 1895), p. 15; Henry B. Salisbury, *The Birth of Freedom*, 3rd ed. (New York: Humbolt, 1894), p. 90; William C. Pomeroy, *The Lords of Misrule. A Tale of Gods and Men* (Chicago: Laird & Lee, 1894), p. 278; Donnelly, *Caesar's Column*, pp. 260, 70.

26. Twain, *A Connecticut Yankee*, p. 85.

27. As quoted in Justin Kaplan, *Mr. Clemens and Mark Twain* (New York: Pocket Books, 1968), p. 346.

28. Twain, *A Connecticut Yankee,* pp. 512, 564, 570.
29. King Camp Gillette, *The Human Drift* (Boston: New Era, 1894), p. 87.
30. Albert Chavannes, *The Future Commonwealth* (New York: True Nationalist, 1892), pp. 4, 113; William H. Bishop, *The Garden of Eden, U.S.A.* (Chicago: Charles H. Kerr, 1895), p. 49; Corwin Phelps, *An Ideal Republic* (Chicago: W. L. Raynolds, 1896), p. 180; [Charles W. Caryl], *New Era* (Denver: New Era Union, 1897), p. 120; Albert Merrill, *The Great Awakening* (Boston: George Book Publishing Co., 1899), p. 48.
31. Bishop, *The Garden of Eden,* p. 55; Chavannes, *The Future Commonwealth,* p. 111.
32. Review of *What is Communism?* by Alcander Longley, *The Nationalist,* January 1891, pp. 428-29; Edward Bellamy, "Concerning the Founding of Nationalist Colonies," *The New Nation,* 23 September 1893, p. 434.
33. Adelia E. Orpen, *Perfection City* (New York: D. Appleton, 1897), p. 110.
34. Castello N. Holford, *Aristopia* (Boston: Arena, 1895), pp. 86, 125; [F. H. Clarke], *The Co-opolitan* (Chicago: Charles H. Kerr, 1898), pp. 28, 50; Charles Bellamy, *An Experiment in Marriage* (Albany: Albany Book, 1889), pp. 172, 205.
35. *The Nationalist,* March-April 1891, pp. 570-71.
36. Leo Marx, *The Machine in the Garden: Technology and the Pastoral Idea in America* (New York: Galaxy Books of Oxford University Press, 1961), pp. 280-81, 71.
37. Charles Bellamy, *An Experiment in Marriage,* p. 40.
38. Richard C. Michaelis, *Looking Further Forward* (Chicago: Rand, McNally, 1890), p. vii.

Chapter 4

1. Emile de Laveleye, "Two New Utopias," *Eclectic Magazine,* April 1890, p. 445.
2. Archibald McCowan [Luke A. Hedd], *Philip Meyer's Scheme. A Story of Trades Unionism.* (New York: J. S. Ogilvie, 1892), p. 135.
3. Joaquin Miller, *The Building of the City Beautiful* (Cambridge & Chicago: Stone & Kimball, 1893), p. 6.
4. See R. W. B. Lewis, *The American Adam: Innocence, Tragedy and Tradition in the Nineteenth Century* (Phoenix Books of the University of Chicago Press, 1967); Irving G. Wyllie, *The Self-Made Man in America: the Myth of Rags to Riches* (New York: Free Press, 1966).
5. Most of these authors were responding to Bellamy. For example, see Roberts, Michaelis, Vinton, and Wheeler in the annotated bibliography.
6. Gerber, *Utopian Fantasy,* p. 46.
7. Henry Athey and A. Herbert Bowers, *With Gyves of Gold* (New York: G. W. Dillingham, 1898), p. 115.
8. Bellamy, *Looking Backward,* p. 280; Bellamy, *Equality,* pp. 115-16, 385.
9. See Sylvia Bowman, *The Year 2000: A Critical Biography of Edward Bellamy* (New York: Bookman, 1958), pp. 23-24.
10. Bellamy, *Looking Backward,* pp. 141-43.

11. Ibid., pp. 309-10; William Dean Howells, "Edward Bellamy," *Atlantic,* August 1898, p. 254.
12. See also Edward Bellamy, "The Old Folks' Party," *The Blindman's World and Other Stories* (Boston: Houghton, Mifflin, 1898).
13. Bellamy, *Looking Backward,* p. 281.
14. Hence my list of heroes is quite different from Pratter's. See "Uses of Utopia," pp. 41-51.
15. Castello N. Holford, *Aristopia* (Boston: Arena, 1895), p. 7. Holford conformed to the general utopian theory of history but he set his story during the colonial period.
16. Review of *An American Emperor* (an English utopian work) by Louis Tracy, *The Literary World,* 16 October 1897, p. 358.
17. Lewis, *American Adam,* p. 85.
18. As quoted in Lokke, "American Utopian Anti-Novel, p. 131.
19. William Von Swartwout, *Olumbia: or Utopia Made Practical* (New York & London: New Columbia University Press, 1893), p. 29.
20. [Alcanoan O. Grigsby], *Nequa; or, Problem of the Ages* (Topeka: Equity, 1900), p. 133.
21. See Frederick A. Bushee, "Communistic Societies in the United States," *Political Science Quarterly* 20 (December 1905): 625-60.
22. One of the most common episodes in the utopian works is the enthusiastically received speech scene. The utopian authors were evidently would-be or frustrated orators.
23. Chauncey Thomas, *The Crystal Button, or, Adventures of Paul Prognosis in the Forty-Ninth Century* (Boston: Houghton, Mifflin, 1891), pp. 144-67.
24. James M. Galloway, *John Harvey: A Tale of the Twentieth Century* (Chicago: Charles H. Kerr, 1897), pp. 106 *ff.,* 151 *ff.,* 178 *ff.,* 341-51, 406.
25. Donnelly, *Caesar's Column,* p. 289.
26. F. U. Adams, *President John Smith* (Chicago: Charles H. Kerr, 1897), p. 153.
27. Twain, *A Connecticut Yankee,* p. 563.
28. [Samuel Crocker], *That Island* (Oklahoma City: C. E. Streeter, 1892), p. 53. This specific hero was one of the aristocrats.
29. Bellamy, *Equality,* 179.
30. See fn. 1, John S. Patterson, "Alliance and Antipathy: Ignatius Donnelly's Ambivalent Vision in *Doctor Huguet,*" *American Quarterly* 22 (Winter 1970): 824.
31. See Strong, Colburn, Waterloo, Gilpin, and Lease in the annotated bibliography. Gilpin actually used the word "whitewashed."
32. Frona Eunice Wait Colburn, *Yermah the Dorado, The Story of a Lost Race,* 2nd ed. (New York: Alice Harriman, 1913), p. 433.
33. Bellamy, *Equality,* p. 313.
34. Donnelly, *Caesar's Column,* p. 97; Benjamin Rush Davenport, *Anglo-Saxon's Onward!: A Romance of the Future* (Cleveland: Hubbell, 1898), p. 104. See also a futuristic war story, Oto Mundo, *The Recovered Continent; A Tale of the Chinese Invasion* (1898).
35. Patterson, "Alliance and Antipathy," pp. 824-25.
36. Walter B. Rideout, "Introduction" to *Caesar's Column,* pp. xviii-xix. The other popular novels were *Looking Backward, In His Steps,* and *A Connecticut Yankee.*
37. James G. Clark, review of *An Ideal Republic* by Corwin Phelps, *Arena,* August 1896, pp. 514-15.

38. Actually all criminals were sterilized in *Ionia;* but, before their extinction, the Jews were the worst criminals, hence they were sterilized most often. Harold Frederic's generally favorable portrayal of Jews in *Gloria Mundi* (1898) also helps to offset Craig's anti-Semitism.

39. Mortimer Dormer Leggett, *A Dream of a Modest Prophet* (Philadelphia: Lippincott, 1890), pp. 22, 28.

40. See Mendes, Lubin, Schindler, Chavannes, Dail, Daniel, and Schwahn in the annotated bibliography.

41. William Gilpin, *The Cosmopolitan Railway Compacting and Fusing Together All the World's Continents* (San Francisco: History Co., 1890), p. 153.

42. Walter McDougall, *The Hidden City* (New York: Cassell, 1891), p. 303.

43. Orpen, *Perfection City*, pp. 100, 206, 210.

44. Grigsby, *Nequa*, pp. 364-65.

45. Willing servants quote: Fayette Stratton Giles, *Shadows Before, or, A Century Onward* (New York: Humbolt, 1894), p. 107. [Edward A. Caswell], *Toil and Self* (Chicago and New York: Rand, McNally, 1900), p. 64-65. See also Russell and Fiske in the annotated bibliography.

46. Hugh M. Gloster, "Introduction" to Sutton E. Griggs, *Imperium in Imperio* (New York: Arno Press, 1969), p. ii.

47. Ibid., pp. 32, 61, 62, 133, 207, 245, 191, 264.

48. David Lubin, *Let There Be Light* (New York and London: Putnam's, 1900), p. 41.

49. Leggett, *A Dream of a Modest Prophet*, p. 115.

50. Ibid., p. 98.

51. Bellamy, *Looking Backward*, pp. 282-84.

52. S. Byron Welcome, *From Earth's Centre* (Chicago: Charles H. Kerr, 1894), p. 75.

53. Thomas Lake Harris, *The New Republic* (Santa Rosa, Calif.: Fountaingrove Press, 1891), p. 49.

54. Laurence Gronlund, *Our Destiny, The Nationalist,* July 1890, p. 305. For an excellent study of Bellamy's concept of the social self see Thomas, "Introduction" to *Looking Backward,* pp. 1-89.

55. As quoted in Edmund Reiss, "Afterword," *A Connecticut Yankee* (New York: Signet, 1963), p. 324.

56. Twain, *A Connecticut Yankee,* p. 540.

57. Leggett, *A Dream of a Modest Prophet*, p. 101.

58. See Paul Haedicke, *The Equalities of Para-Para* (Chicago: Schuldt-Gathmann, 1895), pp. 20-59, 127; J. W. Roberts, *Looking Within* (New York: A. S. Barnes, 1893), pp. 239, 244-47; Oliver Wendell Holmes, "Over the Teacups, III," *Atlantic,* February 1890, p. 241.

59. John Uri Lloyd, *Etidorhpa* (Cincinnati: John Uri Lloyd, 1895), pp. 276, 115, 113, 115, 241-45, 276, 296. Some utopian bibliographies include Francis H. Williams's *Âtman* (New York: Cassell, 1891), which describes a discovery that allows matching souls with bodies. But the book is mainly a fictional biography with little utopian content.

Chapter 5

1. As quoted in Gerber, *Utopian Fantasy,* p. 100. Wells meant this advice for

science-fiction writers as well as utopian authors. See also ibid., p. 84 and Bailey, *Pilgrims Through Space and Time,* p. 203.

2. For example see Sylvester Baxter, "Why the Name Nationalist," *The Nationalist,* July 1889, p. 82.

3. Henry Olerich, *A Cityless and Countryless World: An Outline of Practical Co-operative Individualism* (Holstein, Iowa: Gilmore & Olerich, 1893), pp. 8-9.

4. Charles J. Rooney, Jr., "Utopian Literature as a Reflection of Social Forces in America, 1865-1917" (Ph.D. diss., George Washington University, 1968), especially the tables on pages 53-57. Rooney's sample is not the same as mine, but similar trends can be traced in both samples.

5. Bellamy, *Equality,* p. 7; Bellamy, *Looking Backward,* p. 122.

6. Robert L. Shurter, "The Utopian Novel in America, 1865-1900" (Ph.D. diss., Case Western Reserve, 1936), p. 1.

7. Joseph Schiffman, "Edward Bellamy and the Social Gospel," Cushing Strout, ed., *Intellectual History in America,* 2 vols. (New York: Harper & Row, 1968), 2: 27; Thomas, "Introduction" to *Looking Backward,* p. 50.

8. Bellamy, *Equality,* p. 343; Thomas Lake Harris, *Brotherhood of the New Life. Its Fact, Law, Method and Purpose* (London: E. W. Allen, 1891), p. 12; Laurence Gronlund, *Our Destiny. The Influence of Nationalism on Morals and Religion, The Nationalist,* September 1890, pp. 142, 143.

9. Bellamy, *Equality,* pp. 265-67.

10. Charles L. Sanford, *The Quest for Paradise; Europe in the American Moral Imagination* (Urbana: University of Illinois Press, 1961), p. 185.

11. Howells, *Traveler from Altruria,* pp. 16, 60.

12. For detailed examinations of these criticisms see Flory, Ransom, Shurter, and especially Rooney in the secondary sources bibliography.

13. Thomas Lake Harris, *The New Republic: A Discourse of the Prospects, Dangers, Duties and Safeties of the Times* (Santa Rosa, Calif.: Fountaingrove Press, 1891), pp. 49, 59.

14. Bellamy, *Looking Backward,* pp. 221-22. See also David Bleich, "Eros and Bellamy," *American Quarterly* 16 (Fall 1964): 445-59.

15. Howells, *Traveler from Altruria,* pp. 278-79, 283-84, 262, 280. See also Tinckner and Frederic in the annotated bibliography.

16. See Charles Willing Beale, *The Secret of the Earth* (1899) in the annotated bibliography.

17. See Chavannes, Dail, Schwahn, Michels, and Giles in the annotated bibliography.

18. As quoted by Thomas in "Introduction" to *Looking Backward,* p. 6.

19. Donnelly, *Caesar's Column,* p. 186.

20. Ibid., pp. 179-89.

21. [William Simpson], *The Man from Mars* (San Francisco: Bacon, 1891), pp. 38-41.

22. Bellamy, *Looking Backward,* p. 272.

23. Mortimer D. Leggett, *A Dream of a Modest Prophet* (Philadelphia: Lippincott, 1890), p. 207.

24. Beverley O. Kinnear, *Impending Judgments on the Earth; or "Who May Abide the Day of His Coming"* (New York: James Huggins, 1892), p. 7. Italics mine.

25. Chauncey Thomas, *The Crystal Button* (Boston: Houghton, Mifflin, 1891), pp. 158-59.

26. Bellamy, *Equality,* pp. 259-61; Cyrus Cole, *The Auroraphone* (Chicago: Charles H. Kerr, 1890), p. 92; Simpson, *The Man from Mars,* pp. 39-41; Leggett, *A Dream of a Modest Prophet,* pp. 11, 116-17, 86, 43-51, 204. Because of his fear of the power of any unified church, Twain was the only author who wanted more denominational separation.

27. Amos K. Fiske, *Beyond the Bourn* (New York: Fords, Howard & Hulbert, 1891), p. 77.

28. Simpson, *The Man from Mars,* p. 52.

29. Leggett, *A Dream of a Modest Prophet,* p. 71; Cole, *The Auroraphone,* pp. 91-126; Lubin, *Let There Be Light* (New York and London: Putnam's, 1900), pp. 239-42.

Chapter 6

1. [Henry Francis Allen], *A Strange Voyage* (St. Louis: Monitor, 1891), p. 225.

2. W. T. Harris, "Edward Bellamy's Vision," *Forum,* October 1889, p. 205; review of *Equality* by Edward Bellamy, *The Literary World,* 7 August 1897, p. 252.

3. A few authors, especially Milan C. Edson, did emphasize the role of cars, but before Edgar Chambless's *Roadtown* (New York: Roadtown Press, 1910), there weren't really any auto utopian works.

4. Barry Love, a former graduate student in the History and Sociology of Science Department at the University of Pennsylvania, began a dissertation on technology in utopian literature but withdrew it.

5. Chauncey Thomas, *The Crystal Button* (Boston: Houghton, Mifflin, 1891), p. 170.

6. Henry Matthews Williams, "The Mission of Machinery," *Arena,* 19 (February 1898), 207.

7. Bellamy, *Equality,* p. 43.

8. Ibid., p. 314.

9. [William Stanley Child], *The Legal Revolution of 1902* (Chicago: Charles H. Kerr, 1898), p. 323.

10. F. U. Adams, *President John Smith* (Chicago: Charles H. Kerr, 1897), p. 164.

11. Bailey, *Pilgrims Through Space and Time,* p. 98.

12. A. James Stupple, "Utopian Humanism in America, 1888-1900" (Ph.D. diss., Northwestern University, 1971), pp. 15*ff.,* 187-88.

13. The following is a revised version of Kenneth M. Roemer, "1984 in 1894: Harben's *Land of the Changing Sun," Mississippi Quarterly* 26 (Winter 1972-73): 29-42.

14. Gerber, *Utopian Fantasy,* p. 56.

15. Will[iam] N. Harben, *The Land of the Changing Sun* (New York: Merriam, 1894), pp. 54, 111, 123-30, 173-76, 29, 33, 76, 93, 104, 24, 121, 44, 49, 69, 47, 157, 214-31.

16. Bellamy, *Equality,* p. 271.

17. For example see Joseph Jones, "Utopia as Dirge," *American Quarterly* 2 (Fall 1950): 214-26.

18. Milan C. Edson, *Solaris Farm: A Story of the Twentieth Century* (Washington, D.C.: Author, 1900), pp. 227-28; Solomon Schindler, *Young West: A Sequel to Looking Backward,* 2nd ed. (Boston: Arena, 1894), pp. 30-33; [Warren S.

Rehm], *The Practical City. A Future City Romance, or, A Study in Environment* (Lancaster, Pa.: Lancaster County Magazine, 1898), p. 15.

19. Seymour Lipset and Reinhard Bendix, *Social Mobility in Industrial Society* (Berkeley: University of California Press, 1967), p. 126. See also William Miller, "American Historians and the Business Elite," *Journal of Economic History* 9 (November 1949): 207.

20. Bellamy, *Looking Backward*, pp. 236-38.

21. Ibid., p. 283.

22. See especially Mortimer Dormer Leggett, *A Dream of a Modest Prophet* (Philadelphia: Lippincott, 1890), pp. 93-106; Laurence Gronlund, *Our Destiny. The Influence of Nationalism on Morality and Religion, The Nationalist*, May 1890, p. 39.

23. Addison Peale Russell, *Sub-Coelum: A Sky-Built Human World* (New York: Houghton, Mifflin, 1893), p. 112.

24. See Albert Chavannes, *The Future Commonwealth, or, What Samuel Balcom Saw in Socioland* (New York: True Nationalist, 1892), p. 89.

25. See David J. Pivar, *Purity Crusade; Sexual Morality and Social Control, 1868-1900* (Westport, Conn.: Greenwood Press, 1973), pp. 79-83.

26. Edson, *Solaris Farm*, pp. 227-28, 286-98, 327-46. Edson admitted that he was influenced by the psychologist Elmer Gates.

27. See Leggett, *A Dream of a Modest Prophet*, pp. 100-01, 123, 153-55; Bellamy, *Looking Backward*, p. 239.

28. Schindler, *Young West*, pp. 38-42.

29. Bellamy, *Looking Backward*, p. 239.

30. Fayette Stratton Giles, *Shadows Before or A Century Onward* (New York: Humbolt, 1894), p. 62.

31. Rehm, *Practical City*, p. 15. See also [Mary E. Lane]. *Mizora: A Prophecy* (New York: Dillingham, 1889), p. 36; *The Beginning: A Romance of Chicago as It Might Be* (Chicago: Charles H. Kerr, 1893), p. 32; Schindler, *Young West*, pp. 70-73, 121-36.

32. Schindler, *Young West*, pp. 70-73, 121-28.

33. Edson, *Solaris Farm*, pp. 164, 171, 176. The following section is a revised version of Kenneth M. Roemer, "Sex Roles, Utopia and Change: The Family in Late Nineteenth-Century Utopian Literature," *American Studies* 13 (Fall 1972), pp. 33-48.

34. Bellamy, "How I came to Write 'Looking Backward,'" *The Nationalist*, May 1889, p. 3.

35. Barbara C. Quissell, "The Sentimental and Utopian Novels of Nineteenth Century America: Romance and Social Issues" (Ph.D. diss., University of Utah, 1973). See especially Chapter 4.

36. Austyn Granville, *The Fallen Race* (New York and Chicago: F. T. Neely, 1892), pp. 133, 137, 138.

37. See Stupple, "Utopian Humanism in America," pp. 74-78.

38. See Sondra R. Herman, "Loving Courtship or the Marriage Market: The Ideal and Its Critics, 1871-1911," *American Quarterly* 25 (May 1973): 236.

39. Richard C. Michaelis, *Looking Further Forward* (Chicago & New York: Rand, McNally, 1890), pp. 78-80; J. W. Roberts, *Looking Within* (New York: A. S. Barnes, 1893), p. 6; Henry Athey and A. Herbert Bowers, *With Gyves of Gold* (New York: Dillingham, 1898), p. 107; David Hilton Wheeler, *Our Industrial*

Utopia and Its Unhappy Citizens (Chicago: A. C. McClurg, 1895), pp. 52, 195; Eva Wilder (Brodhead) McGlasson, *Diana's Livery* (New York: Harper, 1891), pp. 215-16, 220.

40. William E. Bridges, "Warm Hearth, Cold World: Social Perspectives on the Household Poets," *American Quarterly* 21 (Winter 1969): 769.

41. Michaelis, *Looking Further Forward,* pp. 78-80.

42. Bellamy, *Looking Backward,* p. 266; Edward Bellamy, "Woman in the Year 2000," *Ladies' Home Journal,* February 1891, p. 3; Howells, *A Traveler from Altruria,* pp. 37, 39.

43. Besides the authors listed in fn. 39, see Niswonger, Orpen, Sanders, Vinton, Satterlee, Bradshaw, Bartlett, and Chambers in the annotated bibliography.

44. Herman, "Loving Courtship," 241-44.

45. Thomas Lake Harris, *The New Republic* (Santa Rosa, Calif.: Fountaingrove Press, 1891), p. 31.

46. William H. Bishop, *The Garden of Eden, U.S.A. A Very Possible Story* (Chicago: Charles H. Kerr, 1895), pp. 157-58, 176; Bellamy, *Equality,* p. 141.

47. See Pivar, *Purity Crusade.*

48. See [Alice Ilgenfritz Jones and Ella Merchant], *Unveiling a Parallel* (Boston: Arena, 1893), p. 173. See also Harris, *The New Republic,* p. 70. Even he felt that it was a debased moral climate that encouraged Vassar girls to want to be whores. For an analysis of nineteenth-century female sex drives see Carl N. Degler's "What Ought To Be and What Was." *American Historical Review* 79 (December 1974): 1467-90.

49. Crawford S. Griffin, *Nationalism* (Boston: C. S. Griffin, 1889), p. 59; Solomon Schindler, "Is Marriage a Failure?," *The Nationalist,* June 1889, pp. 47-51.

50. William V. Shannon, "A Radical, Direct, Simple, Utopian Alternative To Day-Care Centers," *The New York Times Magazine,* 30 April 1972, pp. 13, 71, 76, 78, 82, 85.

51. See Janice Law Trecker, "Sex, Science and Education," *American Quarterly* 26 (October 1974): 352-66.

52. Rehm, *The Practical City,* p. 15.

53. Bellamy, *Looking Backward,* pp. 168, 188; Bishop, *The Garden of Eden, U.S.A.,* pp. 125-27.

54. Ronald G. Walters, ed., *Primers for Prudery; Sexual Advice to Victorian America* (Englewood Cliffs, N.J.: Prentice-Hall, 1974), p. 143.

55. Bellamy, *Equality,* pp. 410, 269-70.

56. Allen, *A Strange Voyage,* p. 99.

57. Schindler, "Marriage," p. 51.

58. Gronlund, *Our Destiny,* pp. 306-07.

59. Bellamy, *Looking Backward,* pp. 155, 262-66; Bellamy, *Equality,* p. 43. In *Equality* women are more "occupationally liberated" than in *Looking Backward.*

60. Bellamy, *Looking Backward,* p. 266. Bellamy did modify his position in "Woman in the Year 2000," p. 3.

61. [John McCoy], *A Prophetic Romance, Mars to Earth* (Boston: Arena, 1896), pp. 245-49.

62. James Cowan, *Daybreak, A Romance of an Old World* (New York: George H. Richmond, 1896), pp. 245-49. The fact that the catastrophe was in part stemmed by the efforts of a female journalist suggests that utopian women are still liberated from the kitchen.

63. Nicholas P. Gilman, "The Way to Utopia," *Unitarian Review*, July 1890, p. 60; "Two Utopias," *The Literary World*, 1 February 1890, p. 41.

64. Charles E. Rosenberg, "Sexuality, Class and Role in 19th-Century America," *American Quarterly* 25 (May 1973): 135, 139.

65. Henry Olerich, *A Cityless and Countryless World. An Outline of Practical Co-operative Individualism* (Holstein, Iowa: Gilmore & Olerich, 1893), pp. 65-66, 265-73. For a very different view of sexual intercourse see Dail and Howard in the annotated bibliography.

66. William L. O'Neill, *The Woman Movement: Feminism in the United States and England* (London: George Allen and Unwin, 1969), p. 26.

67. Donald Meyer, *The Positive Thinkers* (Garden City, N.Y.: Doubleday, 1965); Edward C. Kirkland, *Dream and Thought in the Business Community, 1860-1900* (Ithaca, N.Y.: Cornell University Press, 1956).

68. Walters, *Primers for Prudery*, p. 158.

Chapter 7

1. Charles J. Rooney, Jr., "Utopian Literature as a Reflection of Social Forces in America, 1865-1917" (Ph.D. diss., George Washington University, 1968), pp. 53-55; Margaret Thal-Larsen, "Political and Economic Ideas in American Utopian Fiction, 1868-1914" (Ph.D. diss., University of California, Berkeley, 1941), pp. 44-183, 199, 200, 205.

2. James Cowan, *Daybreak, A Romance of an Old World* (New York: George H. Richmond, 1896), p. 56.

3. Bellamy, *Equality*, p. 21.

4. For example see Harold V. Rhodes, *Utopia in American Political Thought* (Tucson: University of Arizona Press, 1967), pp. 42-44; Jean Pfaelzer, "Utopian Fiction in America 1880-1900: The Impact of Political Theory on Literary Forms" (paper delivered at the Eighty-ninth Annual Meeting of the Modern Language Association of America, New York, December 27, 1974), pp. 7-8.

5. Bellamy, *Equality*, p. 20.

6. F. U. Adams, *President John Smith* (Chicago: Charles H. Kerr, 1897), p. 199; Chauncey Thomas, *The Crystal Button* (Boston: Houghton, Mifflin, 1891), p. 257.

7. Amos K. Fiske, *Beyond the Bourn* (New York: Fords, Howard & Hulbert, 1891), p. 121.

8. Bellamy, *Looking Backward*, pp. 229-30.

9. Henry Olerich, *A Cityless and Countryless World: An Outline of Practical Co-operative Individualism* (Holstine, Iowa: Gilmore & Olerich, 1893), pp. 245-46.

10. Fayette Stratton Giles, *Shadows Before, or, A Century Onward* (New York: Humbolt, 1894), p. 138.

11. *The Works of Chaucer*, ed. F. N. Robinson (Boston: Houghton Mifflin, 1961), p. 28.

12. See especially Harben, Thomas, Galloway, and Allen in the annotated bibliography.

13. Cyrus Cole, *The Auroraphone* (Chicago: Charles H. Kerr, 1890), pp. 226*ff.*

14. For example, see Edward Bellamy, "How I Came to Write 'Looking Backward,'" *The Nationalist*, May 1894, pp. 1-4.

15. [Henry Francis Allen], *A Strange Voyage* (St. Louis: Monitor, 1891), p. 272; Ludwig Geissler, *Looking Beyond* (New Orleans: L. Graham & Son, 1891), p. 99.
16. Allen, *A Strange Voyage*, pp. 129, 165-66; Geissler, *Looking Beyond*, pp. 95-97.
17. Bellamy, *Equality*, pp. 207-10; [James M. Galloway], *John Harvey; A Tale of the Twentieth Century* (Chicago: Charles H. Kerr, 1897), p. 406.
18. Bellamy, *Looking Backward*, p. 254.
19. William Dean Howells, *Letters of an Altrurian Traveller* in *The Altrurian Romances*, eds. Clara and Rudolph Kirk (Bloomington: Indiana University Press, 1968), p. 216.
20. Galloway, *John Harvey*, p. 133.
21. Albert Chavannes, *In Brighter Climes, or Life in Socioland* (Knoxville: Chavannes, 1895), p. i; B. O. Flower, "The Highest Function of the Novel," *Arena*, April 1890, p. 630.
22. Alvarado M. Fuller, *A.D. 2000* (Chicago: Laird & Lee, 1890), p. 9.
23. Howells, *Traveler from Altruria*, pp. 207-08.
24. Laurence Gronlund, *Our Destiny, The Nationalist*, September 1891, p. 141.
25. Lokke, "American Utopian Anti-Novel," p. 142.
26. Bellamy, *Looking Backward*, p. 184.
27. Bellamy, *Equality*, p. 378.
28. For examples see Kinnear, Salisbury, Tinckner, Mendes, Schindler, and Blair in the annotated bibliography.
29. Edward Bellamy, "Concerning the Founding of Nationalist Colonies," *The New Nation*, 23 September 1893, p. 434.
30. Ignatius Donnelly, *The Golden Bottle* (New York and St. Paul: Merrill, 1892), pp. 213; George A. Sanders, *Reality* (Cleveland: Burrows Brothers, 1898), p. 160.
31. Donnelly, *The Golden Bottle*, pp. 202-63.
32. Josiah Strong, *The New Era, or, The Coming Kingdom* (New York: Baker & Taylor, 1893), p. 80.
33. William Gilpin, *The Cosmopolitan Railway Compacting and Fusing Together All the World's Continents* (San Francisco: History Co., 1890), p. 59.
34. Isaac Morrison Swift, *A League of Justice* (Boston: Commonwealth Society, 1893), pp. 25-26; Bellamy, *Looking Backward*, p. 228.
35. [M. Louise Moore], *Al-Modad* (Shell Bank, Cameron Parish, La.: M. L. Moore & Beauchamp, 1892), p. 54.
36. Adams, *President John Smith*, pp. 25-26.
37. Henry O. Morris, *Waiting for the Signal. A Novel* (Chicago: Schulte, 1897), pp. 106-14.
38. W. W. Satterlee, *Looking Backward and What I Saw*, Introd., Arthur O. Lewis, Jr. (New York: Arno Press, 1971), p. 30; David Hilton Wheeler, *Our Industrial Utopia and Its Unhappy Citizens* (Chicago: A. C. McClurg, 1895), p. 17.
39. John Uri Lloyd, *Etidorhpa* (Cincinnati: J. U. Lloyd, 1895), p. 23. For an interesting solution to the liquor question see Crawford S. Griffin, *Nationalism* (Boston: C. S. Griffin, 1899), p. 77. In Griffin's utopia, poverty, frustrated ambitions, lovers' and family quarrels, and other inducements for drinking had disappeared. Moreover, the government supplied liquor for free to anyone who wanted it; hence liquor was neither a status symbol nor a forbidden fruit.
40. The exceptions were S. Byron Welcome's utopians who loved silk top hats and some of the lavishly dressed peoples in Charles W. Beale's utopia.

41. Bellamy, *Equality,* pp. 391, 57-61, 49. Compare this to Bellamy, *Looking Backward,* p. 117.

42. William H. Bishop, *The Garden of Eden, U.S.A.* (Chicago: Charles H. Kerr, 1895), pp. 271-75.

43. [John McCoy], *A Prophetic Romance, Mars to Earth* (Boston: Arena, 1896), pp. 163-64.

44. Bailey, *Pilgrims Through Space and Time,* p. 222.

45. See especially Moore, *Al-Modad,* pp. 81-114.

46. Fayette Stratton Giles, *The Industrial Army* (New York: Baker & Taylor, 1896), pp. 170-73; Bellamy, *Looking Backward,* p. 202.

47. Charles M. Sheldon, *In His Steps* (Chicago: Advance, 1897), pp. 27-40, 81-82, 129-30, 154-56; Fuller, *A.D. 2000,* p. 240; Allen, *A Strange Voyage,* p. 103; Solomon Schindler, "Dr. Leete's Letter to Julian West," *The Nationalist,* September 1890, p. 83.

48. Bellamy, *Looking Backward,* pp. 163-66; Bellamy, *Equality,* pp. 247, 255-57.

49. J. W. Roberts, *Looking Within* (New York: A. S. Barnes, 1893), pp. 163, 211, 212; Wheeler, *Our Industrial Utopia,* pp. 292, 313.

50. David J. Pivar, *Purity Crusade: Sexual Morality and Social Control, 1868-1900* (Westport, Conn.: Greenwood Press, 1973), p. 233.

51. Bradford Peck, *The World a Department Store* (Lewiston, Me. and Boston: B. Peck, 1900), p. 109; Bellamy, *Equality,* pp. 146-53; Robert C. Adams, "Co-operative Amusements," *The Nationalist,* March-April 1891, pp. 56-64.

Chapter 8

1. This chapter is a revised version of Kenneth M. Roemer, "The Heavenly City of the Late 19th-Century Utopians," *Journal of the American Studies Association of Texas* 4 (1973): 5-17.

2. See Roy Lubove, "The Roots of Urban Planning," *The Urbanization of America: An Historical Anthology,* ed. Allen M. Wakstein (Boston: Houghton Mifflin, 1970), pp. 315-24.

3. William Dean Howells, *Letters of an Altrurian Traveller* in *The Altrurian Romances,* eds. Clara and Rudolph Kirk (Bloomington: Indiana University Press, 1968), p. 202; [John Brisbane Walker], *A Brief History of Altruria, Cosmopolitan,* November 1895, p. 88.

4. Charles M. Sheldon, *In His Steps; "What Would Jesus Do?"* (Chicago: Advance, 1897), p. 196.

5. *The Beginning* (Chicago: Charles H. Kerr, 1893), pp. 101-13; Henry Athey and A. Herbert Bowers, *With Gyves of Gold* (New York: Dillingham, 1898), p. 241; Oliver Bell Bunce, "The City Beautiful," *The Story of Happinolande and Other Tales* (New York: Appleton, 1889), pp. 98-140; Henry Olerich, *A Cityless and Countryless World* (Holstein, Iowa: Gilmore & Olerich, 1893), pp. 32, 99; Bellamy, *Looking Backward,* p. 112; Howells, *Letters of an Altrurian Traveller,* pp. 238, 282; Joaquin Miller, *The Destruction of Gotham* (New York and London: Funk & Wagnalls, 1886), p. 22.

6. Joaquin Miller, *The Building of the City Beautiful* (Cambridge and Chicago: Stone & Kimball, 1893), p. 177.

7. Bellamy, *Looking Backward*, p. 123.
8. For a thorough analysis of the compromises the utopian authors made between agrarian and urban values see Donald C. Burt, "Utopia and the Agrarian Tradition in America, 1865-1900" (Ph.D. diss., University of New Mexico, 1973).
9. Miller, *City Beautiful*, pp. 32-33.
10. Howells, *Letters of an Altrurian Traveller*, pp. 199, 202.
11. For example, see Titus K. Smith, *Altruria* (New York: Altruria, 1895), p. 37; [William Stanley Child], *The Legal Revolution of 1902* (Chicago: Charles H. Kerr, 1898), 260; [Albert Waldo Howard], *The Milltillionaire* (Boston: n.p., [1895]). p. 7.
12. See especially Sam B. Warner, Jr., *Streetcar Suburbs* (New York: Atheneum, 1970), pp. 11-14. See also Burt, "Utopia and the Agrarian Tradition," Chapters 3 and 4, especially pp. 38-47, 72; Bailey, *Pilgrims Through Space and Time*, p. 229.
13. For example, see Smith, *Altruria*, p. 35; Olerich, *A Cityless and Countryless World*, p. 32.
14. Howells, *Traveler from Altruria*, p. 181.
15. Fayette S. Giles, *Shadows Before, or, A Century Onward* (New York: Humbolt, 1894), p. 37.
16. Howells especially longed for the brotherhood of a small community: in Altruria "a man is born and lives and dies among his own kindred, and the sweet sense of neighborhood, of brotherhood, which blessed the golden age of the first Christian republic [Christ and his followers] is ours again" (*Traveler from Altruria*, pp. 280-86). For an interesting discussion of Howells's village utopia see Quissell, "Sentimental and Utopian Novels," pp. 234-67.
17. Howells, *Traveler from Altruria*, pp. 283, 285; D. L. Stump, *From World to World* (Asbury, Mo.: World to World, 1896), pp. 31-32, 107.
18. For example, see William H. Bishop, *The Garden of Eden, U.S.A.* (Chicago: Charles H. Kerr, 1895), pp. 119-27; Thomas and Anna Fitch, *Better Days* (San Francisco: Better Days, 1891), p. 195; Henry B. Salisbury, *The Birth of Freedom*, 3rd ed. (New York: Humbolt, 1894), pp. 133, 137, 139; [William Simpson], *The Man from Mars* (San Francisco: Bacon, 1891), p. 145.
19. Smith, *Altruria*, p. 31.
20. Chauncey Thomas, *The Crystal Button* (Boston: Houghton, Mifflin, 1891), pp. 77-87.
21. King Camp Gillette, *The Human Drift* (Boston: New Era, 1894), pp. 94-107.
22. Crawford S. Griffin, *Nationalism* (Boston: C. S. Griffin, 1889), p. 47.
23. Bellamy, *Equality*, p. 296. This ideal landscape is very similar to the "middle landscape" analyzed throughout Leo Marx, *The Machine in the Garden: Technology and the Pastoral Ideal in America* (New York: Galaxy Books of Oxford University Press, 1961).
24. "Letter to Howard Pyle, 29 October 1893," *Life in Letters of William Dean Howells*, 2 vols., ed. Mildred Howells (Garden City: Doubleday, Doran & Co., 1928), 2:40. Howells was actually quoting D. P. Burnham's mother, but he agreed with her.
25. Howells, *Letters of an Altrurian Traveller*, pp. 198-219.
26. Bellamy, *Looking Backward*, p. 254.
27. Howells, *Traveler from Altruria*, p. 281.
28. Athey and Bowers, *With Gyves of Gold*, p. 236.

29. Clark Edmund Persinger, *Letters from New America* (Chicago: Charles H. Kerr, 1900), pp. 11-15; Simpson, *The Man from Mars,* p. 103.

30. Charles W. Caryl, *New Era* (Denver: New Era Union, 1897), pp. 100-21.

31. Olerich, *A Cityless and Countryless World,* p. 103.

32. William Irwin Thompson, *At the Edge of History* (New York and Evanston: Harper & Row, 1971), p. 10.

33. See Thomas Pynchon, *The Crying of Lot 49* (Philadelphia: J. B. Lippincott, 1966).

Chapter 9

1. Edward Bellamy, "Letter to the People's Party," *The New Nation,* 22 October 1892, p. 645.

2. "Toward a Psychological History of Utopias," Frank E. Manuel, ed., *Utopias and Utopian Thought* (Boston: Beacon Press, 1967), p. 70.

3. Laurence Gronlund, *Our Destiny, The Nationalist,* April 1890, p. 21.

4. Bellamy, *Equality,* p. 322.

5. Ibid., p. 336.

6. As quoted in Gerber, *Utopian Fantasy,* p. 130.

7. Charles W. Caryl, *New Era* (Denver: New Era Union, 1897), pp. 180-83, 186.

8. As quoted in Thomas, "Introduction" to *Looking Backward,* p. 66.

Index

Utopian writings, American: as an index to American attitudes, xii-xiii, 86, 172–78; causes, 4–7; decline, 7–8, 178; definitions, xiii, 9, 33; functions, xii, 6, 54, 85, 161, 176–80; influence, 2–3, 174–75; literary sources, 6–7; popularity, 2–3, 6, 12–13. *See also* Catastrophic predictions; Early American; Modern American

Vinton, Arthur Dudley, 23, 72, 190
Virgin land: as related to American history, 44, 173–74; four versions, 46–54; imagery, 44, 54–55
Volcanic imagery, 22–24, 178
Von Swartwout, William H., 21, 64, 91, 136, 196

Walker, John Brisben, 199
Walker, Samuel, 49, 192
Waterloo, Stanley, 22, 48, 71, 114, 205
Welcome, S. Byron, 77, 91, 136, 198
Wells, H. G., 84, 112, 177
Wheeler, David Hilton, 93, 94, 147, 150, 200
Wilson, Grosvenor, 208
Windsor, William, 66, 120, 131, 148, 202–03
Winthrop, John, 1, 4, 7, 20, 24, 51, 75, 153
Woman's role in society, 85, 122–23, 125–26, 128–30, 132–33, 142, 154, 174. *See also* Family life
Woods, Katharine Pearson, 96, 188
Worley, Frederick U., 91, 190
Wright, W. H., 208

Kenneth M. Roemer received his B.A. from Harvard and his Ph.D. in American Civilization from the University of Pennsylvania. Presently he is Managing Editor of *American Literary Realism,* Assistant Dean of the Graduate School, and Associate Professor of English at the University of Texas at Arlington. He has published in a variety of journals including *American Literature, American Studies,* and *College English.*